D0213206

The Rude Hand of Innovation

Religion in America Series

Harry S. Stout, General Editor

A Perfect Babel of Confusion
Dutch Religion and English Culture in the Middle Colonies
Randall Balmer

The Presbyterian Controversy
Fundamentalists, Modernists, and Moderates
Bradley J. Longfield

Mormons and the Bible
The Place of the Latter-day Saints in American Religion
Philip L. Barlow

The Rude Hand of Innovation
Religion and Social Order in Albany, New York 1652–1836
David G. Hackett

Seasons of Grace
Colonial New England's Revival Tradition in Its British Context
Michael J. Crawford

The Muslims of America
edited by Yvonne Yazbeck Haddad

The Frank S. and Elizabeth D. Brewer Prize Essay
of the American Society of Church History

The Rude Hand of Innovation

Religion and Social Order
in Albany, New York   1652–1836

DAVID G. HACKETT

New York   Oxford
OXFORD UNIVERSITY PRESS
1991

Oxford University Press

Oxford New York Toronto
Delhi Bombay Calcutta Madras Karachi
Petaling Jaya Singapore Hong Kong Tokyo
Nairobi Dar es Salaam Cape Town
Melbourne Auckland

and associated companies in
Berlin Ibadan

Copyright © 1991 by David G. Hackett

Published by Oxford University Press, Inc.
200 Madison Avenue, New York, NY 10016

Oxford is a registered trademark of Oxford University Press

All rights reserved. No part of this publication may be reproduced,
stored in a retrieval system, or transmitted, in any form or by any means,
electronic, mechanical, photocopying, recording or otherwise,
without the prior permission of the publisher.

Library of Congress Cataloging-in-Publication Data
Hackett, David G.
The rude hand of innovation : religion and social order
in Albany, New York, 1652–1836 / David G. Hackett.
p. cm. — (Religion in America series)
Includes bibliographical references and index.
ISBN 0-19-506513-1
1. Albany (N.Y.)—Social conditions.
2. Albany (N.Y.)—Religion.
3. Social change.
4. Albany (N.Y.)—Ethnic relations.
5. New York (State)—History—Colonial period, ca. 1600–1775.
6. New York (State)—History—1775–1865.
I. Title. II. Series: Religion in America series (Oxford University Press)
HN80.A33H33 1991 306'.09747'43—dc20 90-42496

9 8 7 6 5 4 3 2 1

Printed in the United States of America
on acid-free paper

*For my mother and father
Caroline and Roger Hackett*

Acknowledgments

This inquiry began nine years ago with the question, "What is the relationship between religion and social order?" I found my first answers in the sociology of religion through the theoretical writings of Emile Durkheim, Max Weber, and their contemporary followers. As I became familiar with concepts such as "modernization," "secularization," and "civil religion," however, I questioned their empirical validity. Needing to ground theory in data, I turned to American religious history. Here I learned of America's Puritan origins, eminent theologians, and the myriad influences of religion on the shape and substance of American culture. Intellectual history, though, limited my historical understanding to the thought of leading clergymen and denominations, while telling me little about the religious experience of church members and even less about the "unchurched." Next I read my way into social history. Studies of geographic mobility, the family, racial and ethnic groups, and the human adjustments to industrialization held my interest. But I found that few social historians paid attention to the role of religion in social life. Each of these disciplines advanced my understanding, yet left unanswered my original question. And so I began my research into the religious and social history of one of America's oldest colonial settlements with a puzzle and for seven years I tried to solve it.

I am delighted to have the opportunity to thank those people who helped me find the historical information on which this study is based. When I arrived in Albany I was fortunate to meet Stefan Bielinski, Director of the "Colonial Albany Social History Project," sponsored by the Division of Research and Collections at the New York State Museum. His research goal of documenting the lives of Albany's pre-1800 inhabitants through all available social sources meant that much of the social data for my early chapters was already collected in one room. Steve generously shared this information, later read and offered comments on a draft of the first two chapters, and remained a valuable resource as my work evolved. Joseph Meany, senior historian in the Division of Research and Collections, shared with me his thorough knowledge of the military occupation of Albany by the British during the French and Indian War. James Corsaro and the staff of the Manuscript and Special Collections division of the New York State Library were unfailingly helpful in assisting my search for a host of early Albany public documents and church records. I am also grateful to the staffs of the New York State Archives, the Albany Institute of History and Art, and the Sienna College Library; and to local church historians, especially Orvilla Yost at First Presbyterian. As my research took me outside of Albany I was assisted by staff members at the New York Public Library, New York Historical Society, and the Presbyterian Historical Society. Keith Arbour of the American Antiquarian Society was particularly helpful in my search for old Albany newspapers, sermons, and ephemera. In addition, I want to thank the reference staff at Green Mountain College in Poultney, Vermont, where the Methodist's Troy Conference Archives can be found, and the staff at the Colgate-Rochester Divinity School's American Baptist Archives. I am indebted also to Mary, Peter, Margaret, and Beth Gray who welcomed me into their home during my Albany research visits.

A number of historians and sociologists have helped me to interpret this historical material. Early on, Jonathan Prude alerted me to the problems inherent in theoretical notions of modernization and guided me to the writings of social historians whose writings were relevant to my Albany research. At different times, Paul E. Johnson, Patricia Bonomi, Ned Landsman, and Daniel Walker Howe commented on portions of the manuscript. The veteran New York historian David Ellis saved me from several embarrassments by putting the final draft under careful scrutiny. At a critical stage, Randall Balmer offered several helpful suggestions for revision. My colleagues at the University of Florida, Samuel Hill, Patout Burns, Bertram Wyatt-Brown, Darrett Rutman, and David Leverenz were always available for my questions and helpful in their responses. Among sociologists, N. Jay Demerath, Rodney Stark, and Wade Clark Roof offered comments and encouragement at different stages. I am grateful, too, to a number of younger historical sociologists within the Society for the Scientific Study of Religion, especially Roger Finke, George Thomas, Kevin Christiano, and Howard Schneiderman for our continuing discussions of each other's work. Finally, I want to thank Emory University, the Scholarships Foundation, and the Society for the Scientific Study of Religion for financial support.

Some of the ideas expressed in this book were first formulated in shorter essays. Portions of Chapters 2 and 5 on the social origins of nationalism first appeared in *The Journal of Social History* (Vol. 21, June, 1988). The historical relationship between the sociology of religion and American religious history was explored in *The Journal for the Scientific Study of Religion* (Vol. 27, December, 1988) and is briefly discussed here at the beginning of Appendix A. The relationship between culture and social order in American history was considered in my chapter in David Bromley, ed., *Religion and Social Order: New Developments in Theory and Research* (Greenwich: J.A.I. Press, 1991). Portions of this essay appear in different form in Chapters 1 and 2, and Appendix A. I wish to thank these journals and J.A.I. Press for permission to use this material.

I owe my greatest scholarly debt to E. Brooks Holifield and Steven M. Tipton who have been with this book from its beginnings as a dissertation prospectus through to the final draft. By taking my often confused questions seriously, Brooks Holifield shared with me his infectious delight in the mysteries of American religious history. At the same time, he regularly, and painstakingly, helped me to express my thoughts more clearly. Steve Tipton lead me to an array of possible theoretical approaches for solving my Albany puzzle and trusted me to find my own way. As my mentor, dissertation director, and now colleague in the field, Steve has been responsive to my personal trials and intellectual quandaries, providing thoughtful and steady guidance to my development as a scholar. I am grateful, too, to John A. Coleman, S.J., and Robert J. Egan, S.J., my first teachers in religious studies, who pointed me in the general direction of this work.

Many people helped in the preparation of the manuscript. Nancy Savage edited all of it several times. Julianne Means prepared the index. Lisa Fletcher, Linda Johnson, Ann Sumler, Karen Besch, and Lisa Watts all helped in typing and copying, while amiably enduring the drone of the office printer. Cynthia Read, my editor at Oxford University Press, provided the title and with Stanley George and colleagues carried the manuscript smoothly through to publication. Finally, I want to thank the American Society of Church History for selecting this manuscript for the Frank S. and Elizabeth D. Brewer Prize, which included a generous subvention for publication.

This book is for all the members of my family who have always given me love and support: my grandmother Gladys Gray, Anne and Dan, Brian and Debra, Katie, Ellen, and Meg. Most of all it is for my parents, Caroline and Roger Hackett.

Contents

Tables, *xiii*
Maps, *xv*

Introduction, *3*

Chapter *1*
Religion and Social Order in Colonial Albany, *9*

The World of the Albany Dutch, *11*
English Authority and Dutch Culture, *22*
The British Occupation, *32*

Chapter *2*
From Albany Townspeople to Americans:
The Social Origins of Nationalism, *37*

Economy, *40*
Politics, *44*
Methodists, *46*
Calvinists, *48*
The Social Origins of Nationalism, *49*

Chapter *3*
The Yankee Invasion, *57*

Religious Life in the 1790's, *58*
Presbyterians, *61*
A Yankee Town, *69*

Chapter 4
The Twilight of Calvinism,   77

Social Changes, 78
Calvinism in the Early Nineteenth Century, 82
The Methodist Ideology, 90
The Mechanics' Ideology, 95
Methodists and Mechanics, 98

Chapter 5
The Changing Meaning of Nationalism
in the Early Nineteenth Century,   101

Social Changes, 102
Patriotic Productivity, 106
Workingmen, 111
Temperance: Moral Revision and Cultural Change, 119

Chapter 6
The Emergence of the New Society,   123

Fourth Presbyterian Church, 126
The Social Background of Evangelicals, 135
Workingmen and Evangelicals, 144

Conclusion,   153

Appendix A A Note on Method, 159
Appendix B Social Differences Between
the Workingmen and Their Rivals, 165
Notes, 175
References, 215
Index, 231

Tables

2.1   1756 Loudoun inventory of occupations, 41

2.2   Polarization of wealth, 1709–1767, 43

6.1   Albany church growth, 1828–1836, 125

6.2   Established and evangelical church growth, 1828–1836, 125

6.3   Evangelical and established long-term male church members, 136

6.4   Occupations of Baptist and Methodist long-term male church members, 136

6.5   Occupations of evangelical and established male church members in 1830, 137

6.6   Expanding male occupations and evangelical church membership in 1830, 138

6.7   Occupations of male Baptist, Methodist, and Fourth Presbyterian church members in 1830, 138

6.8   Occupations of evangelical church leaders, 139

6.9   Occupations of Baptist, Methodist, and Fourth Presbyterian church leaders in 1830, 139

6.10 Specific occupations of Baptist, Methodist, and Fourth Presbyterian church leaders in 1830, 140

6.11 Women and church membership at Second Presbyterian and Fourth Presbyterian churches in 1831, 142

6.12 Church membership and political activism, 145

6.13 Political activity and denominational membership, 145

6.14 Political party and denominational membership, 146

6.15 Occupations of Workingmen and Regency supporters in the established churches, 146

B.1 Political activity and community commitment, 166

B.2 Support among long-term residents for the Regency and Workingman political parties, 167

B.3 Long-term residents who were Workingman Party supporters in 1830 and had previous political experience, 167

B.4 Occupations and wealth in 1830, 168

B.5 Occupations, wealth, and political affiliation in 1830, 169

B.6 Occupational group and political affiliation in 1830, 170

B.7 Growth of the twenty-six largest occupations, 1817–1830, 170

B.8 Expanding occupations and political activism in 1830, 172

B.9 Expanding occupations and party membership in 1830, 173

Maps and Illustrations

1. *Early 17th-century map of New Netherlands,*   8

2. *1695 Miller map,*   14

3. *View of Albany in 1715,*   22

4. *James Eights watercolor,*   36

5. *Plan of the city in 1794,*   56

6. *First Presbyterian Church engraving,*   62

7. *View of Albany in 1818,*   76

8. *Street scene in 1819,*   100

9. *Map of Albany neighborhoods in 1830,*   105

10. *Engraving of the entrance to the Erie Canal,*   112

11. *Street scene in the 1830's,*   122

The Rude Hand of Innovation

Introduction

In 1790, the Albany Common Council passed a law that required all house-holders to saw off their gutters.[1] Ever since the Dutch beginnings of this frontier outpost, the townspeople followed their ancestors' practice of extending their gutters out over the street and away from the dirt foundations of their homes. Like their gabled roofs and ornamented chimneys, these water spouts were one element in a living Dutch cultural tradition that for more than seven generations gave meaning and order to the townspeoples' lives. Measured against early eighteenth-century standards, however, Albany's Dutch culture had deteriorated badly. Where once before, and in recent memory, the Dutch church had stood proudly in the middle of the intersection of the town's two main streets, commanding the allegiance of most of the people; now the church was overrun by Yankee wagons moving down State Street and on into western New York. New ideas and practices accompanied this onslaught of New Englanders who, by 1800, more than doubled the size of the town. The decision to saw off the town's gutters was one element in the Yankee effort to bring about "improvements." By shortening the gutters and paving the streets, these newcomers argued that passersby would no longer be "doused" by rainwater and their wagons "fairly mired" in the town's streets. "Stimulated by motives of public spirit," as one Yankee saw it, these New Englanders were also establishing "manufactories of every kind," starting an academy, and building new churches.[2] Most long-term Albanians reacted with dismay to the Yankee invasion. "The rude hand of innovation," as one remarked, "was felt as an injury or resented as an insult." A town that once

3

before was "antique, clean, and quiet" now was beset by a "restless, levelling, innovative spirit."[3]

*   *   *

This book is about the transformation of religious and social life in Albany, New York, from the town's beginning in 1652 to the end of its revival period in 1836. I will attempt to explain what happens when the inner connection unravels between the way a people understand their world and the social institutions that nourish their faith by ordering how they live in the world. To do this I adopt a broader concept of religion as a cultural system and argue that culture influenced social order differently in different historical periods. For most of Albany's colonial period, culture influenced social order by providing limited possibilities for change. Following the Revolution, the townspeople embarked on a long search for social and cultural definition. During this period, overt political and religious ideologies emerged to influence social behavior directly. The social circumstances in which they emerged, however, determined which ideologies flourished and which ones faded away.

Social scientists frequently have considered the religious and social transformation of traditional societies as a process of modernization. Between the founding of this Dutch community in the 1650's to the emergence of the new society in the 1830's, Albany did undergo changes characteristic of a bipolar movement from "traditional" to "modern" life. Extended family networks, the traditional basis for social stability, were disrupted by large waves of European and New England immigrants with fewer kin and weaker local roots. The Dutch monopoly of the fur trade gave way to a competitive commercial economy that emphasized technical innovation and increased productivity. Patriarchal political rule by leading merchants, who were also elders of their church, was replaced by popular politics administered by professional politicians. Finally, Calvinism gave way to evangelical congregations with diminished influence over society as a whole.

Modernization, however, assumes too much about the rapidity and direction of these developments. In particular, theories of modernization often conceive change in terms of zero-sum equation. In this abstract, theoretical process, an organic, communal, religious, and personal society becomes more individualistic, market-oriented, secular, and impersonal. Critics of this approach frequently cite its ideological assumptions, which tend to slant interpretive outcomes toward the implied superiority of modern American society. Others question the ability of elaborate deductive models, often based on secondary sources, to tell us something new about the actual human experience of social transformation in changing societies.[4] I will not debate the relative merits of modernization theory for sociological approaches to history. Instead, I suggest that, at least in terms of Albany,[5] the theory is too restrictive. There never was a simple and straightforward movement from a traditional to a modern way of life in Albany. The religious beliefs and social institutions of the Dutch townspeople did not passively fall away before larger processes of social change.

The alternative theoretical approach employed in this study begins with an understanding of religion as a cultural system.[6] Instead of following the lead of intellectual historians, who frequently rely on literary sources such as the sermons of leading clergymen or the proceedings of church meetings, I argue that religious beliefs and moral ideas are not limited to the public thoughts of ministers nor to certain kinds of religious activities, social relationships, or institutions. They are part of every person's daily life. To see religion this broadly is to expand the admissible symbolic vehicles of meaning to include formal cultural practices such as religious rituals and civil ceremonies, informal practices such as customs and language, and the artifacts of material culture such as dress and architecture. By reconstructing the symbolic content and conceptual coherence of human experience, religion can be seen not as an intrusion from outside but as emerging from a broader symbolic framework tied to all aspects of the individual's life in society.

Culture influences social order differently, however, in diverse historical periods.[7] During most of Albany's comparatively stable colonial period, the townspeople made sense of their lives by drawing on a disparate assortment of Dutch and British cultural elements. Here, culture is not understood to be a coherent system of meaning that directly influences social behavior. It is more like a group of often contending symbols, stories, and rituals that people choose from in various combinations in order to make their world meaningful. Moreover, out of the available symbolic meanings enduring patterns of thought and behavior are created and assumed to be inherent in the natural structure of the world. In colonial Albany these were the religious beliefs of Calvinism and the social institutions of the Dutch community. Culture influenced social order in colonial Albany, therefore, by providing a limited range of Dutch and British possibilities for what might happen.

In contrast to cultural action during most of the colonial period, just before the Revolution the town's inhabitants began a prolonged period of social transformation during which overt political and religious ideologies emerged to influence social behavior directly. Ideologies here are new ways of thinking and acting that arise in response to social change and a lack of adequate cultural resources to make sense of that change.[8] Ideologies offer meaning to people living within a problematic social reality. As explicit meaning systems, they have a more immediate impact on social behavior than the more implicit and diverse cultural patterns of more stable periods. Moreover, these movements are always in competition with other ideologies and with the received cultural patterns of earlier, more stable periods, which may themselves become ideologies. Following the Revolution, Albany was a contested cultural arena where republican, Calvinist, evangelical, mechanic, and other ideologies complemented and contradicted one another while directly influencing social behavior. Throughout Albany's period of social transformation, therefore, explicit ideologies directly influenced social action. The actual social situation in which these ideologies appeared, however, decided which ones survived.

As a study of one of America's oldest colonial settlements, this book follows the lead of social historians who, in recent years, have sought answers to their questions through a thorough knowledge of single towns. I chose Albany because of its location in the still largely understudied Middle Colonies, the town's lengthy history of social and cultural change, and its rich historical resources. My research relies on sources used by both intellectual and social historians. Knowledge of Albany's religious history and ideological movements comes primarily from church records, sermons, the publications of voluntary societies, newspapers, and public documents. For social information I have particularly relied on local tax, census, and occupational lists, wills, and government records. The book ends in 1836 at the end of the town's great revival period, just prior to the economic panic of 1837 and the beginning of a new phase of large-scale Catholic immigration, industrialization, and decline of government intervention in economic policy.[9] Like all local studies, this book risks describing an atypical town. Colonial Albany was an overwhelmingly Dutch trading town rooted in the religious culture of Calvinism. Outweighing the risk of describing a unique society, however, is the opportunity of staying with this one community as it absorbed British people and customs into its way of life and then was transformed by the Revolution, Yankee immigration, new ideologies, and the initial spurt of a capitalist economy. Through this approach, regionally confined yet detailed in its analysis of human actions and beliefs, I have tried to offer a new interpretation of the relationship between religion and social order for at least some early Americans during the colonial and revolutionary periods of American history.

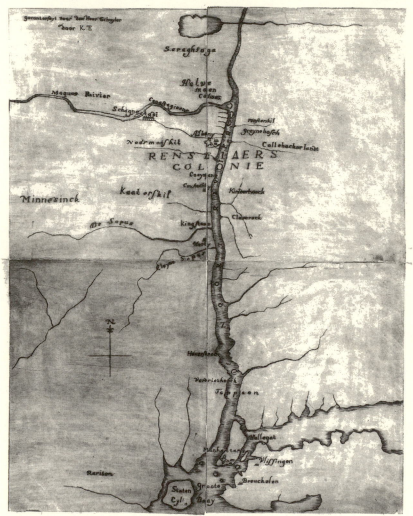

Figure 1. Dutch map of the Hudson River from New York to "Saraghtoga." A facsimile of a seventeenth-century map made by L. G. van Loon. (The Albany Institute of History and Art, McKinney Library Map Collection.)

Chapter 1

Religion and Social Order in Colonial Albany

In 1609, Henry Hudson went up the river that bears his name in search of a northwest passage to the Far East. Hudson's explorations on behalf of the Netherlands took place two years after the English settlement of Jamestown, Virginia, and eleven years before the arrival of the Pilgrims at Plymouth Rock. His journey ended at the river's headwaters, not far from the present Albany, New York, where he found Indians willing to barter their beaver furs. The Dutch trading village that grew up in this vicinity shared with all other early European settlements the trials of accommodation to the New World. Unlike many other towns, however, the Albany Dutch lived within their seventeenth-century world well into the eighteenth century. When the British gained control over New Netherland in 1664, a prolonged period of Anglo-Dutch accommodation shaped the local dynamics of cultural change.

Like the inhabitants of all of America's early European towns, the people of Albany were involved in both horizontal and vertical social processes.[1] The first years of settlement were marked by disorder as a changing collection of strangers sought to establish themselves in relation to each other and the fur trade. This was followed by the emergence of the horizontal dimension of community life, a time of comparative stability when dense family networks provided the basis for common life and activity. Although the local leaders were traders, rather than the farmers of New England's towns or the landed aristocrats of Virginia, they displayed a similar patriarchal control over economic, political, and religious life.[2] At the same time that the townspeople turned inward toward themselves,

9

they were also involved in extra-local relationships that brought them into provincial affairs. Negotiating for control over the northern fur trade, importing finished goods to trade for beaver furs, and appealing for protection from Indian attack all involved associations beyond the local community. These vertical relationships often conflicted with the horizontal dimension of community life. As Darrett Rutman states, "the homogeneous and personal community . . . tended (and tends) toward conservatism and resistance in the face of changes pressed by heterogeneous and impersonal associations pursuing particular goals."[3] Even though Albany differed from other colonial towns in the degree of interpenetration between the horizontal and vertical dimensions of its social life, it shared with all of these settlements an involvement in both local and extra-local social processes.

Unlike most colonial towns, the people of Albany maintained their communal way of life until the eve of the American Revolution. In contrast to Boston's merchant leaders in 1700, whom Bernard Bailyn has described as a heterogeneous group at odds with the Puritan establishment and politically divided by economic interests,[4] Albany's merchant families were leaders of both the Common Council and the Reformed Church and held a monopoly over the fur trade. And unlike the colonial coastal cities, prior to the 1760's Albany was not characterized by a rapid rate of geographic mobility, wide distribution of wealth, growth of poverty, occupational specialization, or the rise of professionalism.[5] Moreover, compared to inhabitants of New England's towns, Albany's Dutch did not experience a substantial erosion of their communal ideal.[6] There was no prolonged period of religious decline, nor was there a First Great Awakening. In fact, during the same period that religious pluralism developed in New England, the weekly pilgrimage of Dutch families to the church at the center of town remained the most consistent and continuous aspect of community living.

Certainly colonial Albany changed. Yet the pattern of cultural change was not a unilateral erosion of the Dutch communal ideal.[7] Instead, cultural change in Albany resulted from the interplay between the provincial authority of the British and the local autonomy of the Dutch community. The British attempted to impose their culture on the Dutch through their own forms of government, legal system, trade regulations, and religious worship. The Dutch limited these incursions into their way of life but, at the same time, the two cultures intermingled. Former British soldiers settled in town, took Dutch wives, and joined the Dutch church. Dutch attitudes toward who should rule the town and how property should be divided were retained within British legal forms. Local Dutch leaders acted as mediators between the provincial British and local Dutch, using their knowledge of British affairs to preserve the autonomy of the local community while advancing their financial interests. In sum, Albany's townspeople created their world from the available British and Dutch cultural resources. By 1750, English language, dress, and customs had been adopted by a few of the town's most successful merchants, and nearly one-quarter of the inhabitants were of British descent. Still, it would take an invasion by the British Army, resisted by both the Dutch church and the Common Council, before changes in the fundamental political, economic, and religious patterns of the Dutch would become possible.

The World of the Albany Dutch

For most of the forty years of Dutch rule in New Netherland (1624–1664), the primitive trading post that became the village of Albany endured in isolation, surrounded by a dangerous wilderness. The first European immigrants to the area were soldiers, traders, and families sent by the Dutch West India Company to establish the fur trade.[8] In 1624, these settlers built a trading post at the head of the navigable waters of the Hudson River and named their settlement Fort Orange. Two years later the threat of Indian attack led all but sixteen men to abandon their stockade and shelters and retreat to Manhattan. A meager crew apparently maintained trade at Fort Orange until the 1630's, when a change in West India Company policy toward increased settlement and away from the sole interest in the fur trade led to the next wave of immigration. During the 1630's and 1640's several hundred settlers were sent to the lands surrounding Fort Orange by Kiliaen Van Rensselaer, an Amsterdam diamond merchant and director of the West India Company, who hoped to turn his newly purchased manor into an agricultural colony.[9] In 1646, the Jesuit missionary Isaac Jogues described the little outpost in this way.

> There are two things in this settlement . . . first a miserable little fort called Fort Orange, built of logs. . . . Secondly, a colony sent here by this Rensselaers . . . composed of about a hundred persons, who reside in some twenty-five or thirty houses built along the river. . . . There is little land fit for tillage, being hemmed in by hills, which are poor soil. . . . [however] Trade is free for all; this gives the Indians all things cheap, each of the Hollanders outbidding his neighbor, and being satisfied provided he can gain some little profit.[10]

The attraction of Rensselaer's settlers to the easy profits of the fur trade led to jurisdictional bickering between the West India Company's traders at Fort Orange and Van Rensselaer's agent. In 1652 the company successfully ended these disputes by granting complete control over the fur trade on the northern frontier to the newly established, autonomous village of Beverwyck (literally Beaver village),[11] just north of Fort Orange.

Beverwyck began as a rowdy and sometimes violent trading post of clashing nationalities and people in motion. According to one local historian, during the 1650's the little village attracted a variety of adventurers, including:

> Flemings, Scandanavians, Frenchmen, Portuguese, Croats, Irishmen, Englishmen, Scotsmen, Germans, Spaniards, Blacks from Africa and the West Indies, Indians and people of mixed blood, all of whom lived together in varying relationships. A small group of officials represented the forces of law and order and the most literate section of the population. At the other extreme was an equally small but obstreperous company of troublemakers, drawn together by a mutual aversion to authority. Occupying a not entirely enviable position in the middle were the burghers, tradesmen, tavern keepers, mechanics, artisans, Indian traders, and slaves.[12]

In 1657 the Dutch minister described the town as existing by trade alone. The population grew when trade was brisk and fell off when beavers were scarce. In an outpost of at least two hundred people and thirty homes, taprooms, "taverns and villainous houses" were common.[13] The local court minutes report frequent bloody fights and knifings.[14] The number of such violent encounters among relative strangers decreased, however, as newcomers found their niche in the local economy, married, and settled into the growing network of family and friendship ties that became the foundation of the local social order.

The stable core of Albany's colonial population was provided by young Dutch families who emigrated from scattered cities and towns in the Netherlands during the last seven years of Dutch rule (1657–1664). As Oliver Rink has argued, the changing character of immigration to New Netherland, away from rootless European adventurers and toward young Dutch families, reflected a campaign by the West India Company to provide the colony with the people it had long needed. Prior to the 1650's, immigrants to New Netherlands were primarily restless young men and foreigners whose fringe involvement in Holland's economy as soldiers, sailors, and laborers made them susceptible to promises of a better life overseas. During the 1650's, young Dutch families replaced single men on the lists of passengers sent to the colony from the Netherlands. This change can perhaps be traced to propaganda campaigns conducted throughout the Netherlands by the West India Company to attract settlers to the New World. Young families also may have been seeking to escape the limited horizons of their hometowns. Whatever their motivation, between 1657 and 1664 family heads with ordinary farming and artisan skills brought their wives and young children from communities all over the Netherlands to the New World.[15] Following the imposition of British rule in 1664, this boom in Dutch migration came to an end. Out of this ordinary slice of Dutch social life the people of Albany created their social order.

Like all of America's early European settlers, the Albany Dutch relied on a way of life brought with them from their native land that they adapted to the frontier. To create their society, all colonists fell back on the beliefs and practices instilled in them in childhood by elders, custom, the church, and civil authorities. In Albany this social education was reinforced by the widespread use of the Dutch language. Unlike both the peasant agricultural communities built by New England's Puritans and the country manors that the English carved out of Virginia, the town that the Albany Dutch created for themselves, as late as 1754, resembled a Netherlands trading village.

Nestled amid tall pines, 150 miles inland, and with the Hudson River as its lifeline, seventeenth-century Albany looked like a runaway medieval village perched on the northern periphery of the colonial world. A 1695 map reveals a compact seven-sided hamlet surrounded by a three-quarter mile palisade wall. The wall was a defensive measure commonly employed by English and Dutch towns, as was the fort that stood on the west side and the blockhouses whose gates gave access to major streets. The village and its surrounding countryside were sharply distinguished, and most townspeople, following the custom of medieval townsfolk, kept livestock that the town's herdsman drove each day to a common pasture outside the walls.[16]

Within the walls, the Dutch recreated a low-country townscape. As Donna Merwick persuasively argues, seventeenth-century Albany's land use and architecture mirrored a Dutch sense of scale.[17] Plot frontages were narrow like European townlots. Dutch stone and brick dwellings dominated each site, with houses placed so close together that homeowners included clauses in their deeds that protected their property from damages caused by a neighbor's downspout. By comparison, Boston's first settlers declared that "each settler would have his house and garden; beyond it would be the fields which the generality would cultivate."[18] Since Boston

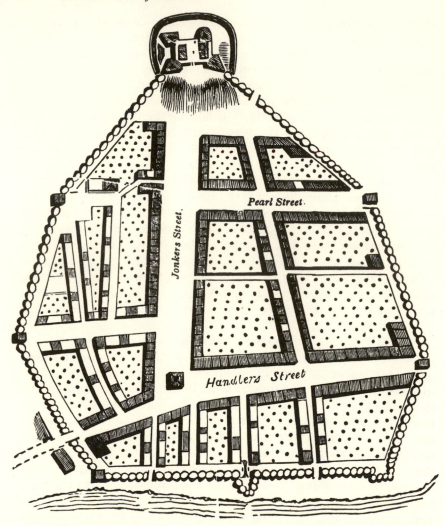

Figure 2. 1695 Miller map of the City of Albany. (The Albany Institute of History and Art, McKinney Library Map Collection.)

was founded as a farming community, land disputes were the source of its earliest tensions. The Dutch, however, placed their wealth in movable property or in commercial networks. Hence, their earliest disputes were over trade. Instead of building their houses on spacious lots and competing for the largest and most productive pieces of farmland, Albany's traders built their houses close together and competed for houselots nearest the gates in order to be the first to trade with Indian customers.

Certainly seventeenth-century Albany merchants could have become like Virginia's English nobility and demonstrated higher social status with landscaped country manors. English merchants characteristically withdrew their fortunes from trade when they made enough money to purchase an estate and introduce their children into the country gentry. A few eighteenth-century Albany merchants did imitate the life of the English nobility. However, for Albany's seventeenth-century Dutch burghers, the town was the center of civilized life. Here the townsman identified his wealth with an extended family network that remained in the city for generations, building political and social power. He did not measure his worth by the accumulation of landholdings but by the acquisition of credit and commercial connections that he handed over to his children. Hence the roster of merchant families in Dutch cities and in Albany remained stable for generations.[19]

Closely interwoven family networks embodied colonial Albany's social order. Prior to the beginning of the French and Indian War in 1754, people of Dutch descent accounted for more than two-thirds of the inhabitants.[20] The 1697 census included more than 150 family names from whom nearly all of Albany's eighteenth-century Dutch inhabitants were descended.[21] Although Albany's original settlers established satellite communities in the upper Hudson and Mohawk river valleys, the home community continued to grow. Between 1697 and 1757 the town's population more than doubled from 724 to about 1800; most of the growth was internal, through the multiplication of Dutch families.[22] The common pattern was for the children of the first immigrants to grow up, marry their neighbors, and raise large families. Albany's colonial mothers who lived to the end of their childbearing years usually gave birth to eight children.[23] By the beginning of the eighteenth century, growing subsections of the town were bound together by blood ties. The Schuyler clan, for example, lived in nine separate households. The growth and intermarriage of these large families, their proximity of residence, and ongoing business relationships provided the basis for community stability. These kinship relations were reinforced by the stipulations of Dutch family wills that commonly bound children to the care of their parents and children to each other in mutual support and continuation of the family enterprise.[24]

Like European townspeople, Albany's families divided themselves into two kinship networks. As early as 1657, "great burghers" and "small burghers" were legally distinguished. Great burghers paid fifty guilders for the liberty of holding office; small burghers paid twenty guilders for the privilege of doing business in Beverwyck.[25] The recognition of these two classes continued the guild system of the Old World, where all had to submit themselves to regulation by the town corporation. These distinctions were retained under English rule in the fees required of merchants and artisans in order to be admitted to civic privileges.[26] The hierarchical relations between these family networks extended through the economic, political, and religious spheres of their life. A 1709 tax list, for example, identifies 181 household heads who together paid 3,831 British pounds in taxes on their real and personal estates. Thirty-six Albany families paid about half of these expenses. These were primarily merchant families with names like Schuyler, Bleecker, and Van Rensselaer.[27] According to Alice Kenney's survey of the 250 men who served on the Common Council between 1686 and the Revolution, most of the town's political leaders came from these same closely intermarried merchant families.[28] Moreover, the fathers, brothers, sons, uncles, and cousins of these families dominated the office of elder in the Dutch Reformed Church.[29]

Although they played a less prominent role in community activities, a second network of artisan families was tied to the town's merchant leaders by overlapping obligations of neighborhood, covenant, and contract.[30] Divided by wealth, merchant and artisan families still did not live apart. The 1709 tax list indicates that affluent and less affluent were evenly distributed throughout the town's three wards. Families, too, were spread out in nuclear units. Neighborly duties were reinforced by religious bonds. Nearly all of the members of the Dutch community were also members of the Dutch church. There, merchant-elders were responsible for the spiritual well-being of their artisan-laity. In turn, the laity were bound through their obedience to God to follow the direction of their church leaders.[31] Similar covenantal relationships were apparent in apprenticeship contracts between artisans and parents. In these agreements, which every Albany artisan had to fulfill in order to practice his occupation in the city, one of the community's master craftsmen took responsibility for teaching a child a trade and also for his room, board, and religious instruction. In turn, the child's parents promised his service and obedience for a period of time.[32]

Albany's Dutch Reformed Church supplied the moral ties that bound the community's hierarchical social order. The location of the church, in the middle of the intersection of the town's two main streets, was a powerful reminder of the centrality of religion in social life. A 1683 list of communicants included nearly every member of the community.[33] Church and town records demonstrate that throughout the colonial period church members kept the vital statistics for the town, married and buried nearly all of the inhabitants, and cared for the poor.[34] As late as 1773, in fact, when the province of New York extended its laws "for the relief of the poor" to Albany, the act stipulated that nothing in it should be construed to "diminish the rights and privileges" of the Albany Dutch church.[35] Attendance at public worship was the most enduring collective social action of the colonial Dutch community. During these divine services, the town's constables walked the streets carrying staves and under instruction to eliminate all working, playing, and drinking.[36] The community came to the church for special services of prayer and fasting when external force threatened the life of the town.[37] And it was here that the sacred rituals of the Dutch Reformed liturgy represented and affirmed the community's collective identity.[38]

The Dutch community's most fundamental religious ideas derived from the Heidelberg catechism. Sunday services followed the prescribed liturgy of the Reformed church of the Netherlands. This consisted of a sermon based on the catechism, framed by congregational psalm singing and recitation of their creed. To control the content of sermons, the Netherland's church divided the catechism into 52 sections and instructed that a different section form the content of the sermon for each successive Sunday of the year.[39] The minister used this same catechism to teach Christian principles to the community's children. Two of Albany's colonial ministers wrote and published catechisms for children.[40] Parents were urged to use this fundamental book of Christian principles in the instruction of their children. Estate inventories of Albany's Dutch householders reveal the presence of the catechism and the Bible, and little other reading material, in their homes.[41] Since the manner of religious instruction was memorization, the religious ideas expressed in the Heidelberg catechism were deeply impressed on the minds of Dutch Albanians.[42]

The Heidelberg catechism taught that only three things are necessary to know in life: our misery, our deliverance because of God's mercy, and the gratitude we owe God for our redemption. Our misery is due to the defiance of God by Adam. As a result of Adam's original sin, we are "wholly incapable of doing any good and inclined to all wickedness." Moreover, God is "terribly disappointed" with our behavior and will punish us with an eternal punishment to both body and soul. No effort of our own can make restitution for our sins; in fact, "daily we increase our debt." God, however, out of His mercy, sent His only Son Jesus to offer his suffering for our sins. Out of obedience to his Father, Jesus suffered, died, and was buried and then rose to sit at the Father's right hand. From there he, with the Father, sends the Holy Ghost to save God's people from their sins. An obedience similar to that of Jesus is required of us, God's people.[43]

According to this catechism, the only way we can escape our terrible punishment entailed by Adam's defiance of God is through a "true faith" in the salvation offered to us through the suffering of Jesus for our sins. "True faith," however,

> . . . is not only a certain knowledge, whereby I hold for truth all that God has revealed to us in his word, but also an assured confidence which the Holy Ghost works by the gospel into my heart; that not only to others, but to me also, remission of sin, everlasting righteousness, and salvation, are freely given by God, merely of grace only for the sake of Christ's merit.[44]

We cannot be certain of our salvation until we experience this "assured confidence." Until then we can be certain only of our eternal damnation.

At least the Albanians who served as leaders of the church presumably experienced the "assured confidence" of the Holy Ghost. In their ordination to the office of elder or deacon they vowed that they "felt in their heart" called by God to "this holy office."[45] Two elders and two deacons were elected each year and served two-year terms. These officials, with the minister, were equal members of the church's "Consistory."[46] At the end of their stewardship, these men joined the "Great Consistory," which functioned as an advisory body. This assembly of more than forty older men was composed of members of merchant families. The new deacons and elders were almost always the brothers, cousins, sons, nephews, and grandsons of Great Consistory members.[47] Their "election" came through nomination by the current Consistory and the approval of the congregation through the ritual of ordination. "As watchmen over the house and city of God," they were responsible to God for the moral behavior of the congregation. In turn, the members of the congregation were bound by their baptism to obey God.[48]

The value of this hierarchical social organization to the Dutch congregation was physically displayed in the arrangement of church seats and the rules for their ownership. The seventy-nine men who were the magnates of the city sat together on raised benches along the walls of the main floor.[49] This may have been a defensive measure adopted prior to the construction of the stockade in the late seventeenth century. Other Dutch churches in New York observed similar arrangements.[50] These men are said to have smoked their pipes and worn their cocked-hats throughout the service, sitting below windows embellished with their families' coats of arms, most if not all of which were assumed in the New World and created on the spot.[51] In turn, those among them who governed the church as elders or deacons sat to the right and left of the pulpit, facing the congregation. If they were Common Council members, they sat in the pew reserved for the corporation. In the early eighteenth century, each burgher's social position overlooking and encircling the congregation was made permanent by burial beneath his seat.[52]

Like an extended family, the rest of the worshipers were seated according to generation and gender. Groups of older women, women with young children, young women, and young girls sat together on long benches within the circle of patriarchs. Other men, young men, and boys sat on the south and west sides of the gallery.[53] The remaining east side of the gallery was reserved for African slaves whose particular seats were not identified in church records. The separation of men and women reflected the prevailing custom in the Netherlands and probably had its post-Reformation origin in Zwingli's separation of the sexes in his church liturgy. Elements of the liturgies of Zwingli, Calvin, and Melanchthon can be found in the established Reformed liturgy of the Netherlands.[54] Both the circle of older men and the separation by generation and gender may have had earlier origins.

Once church seats were purchased and assigned, rules of heredity, not of wealth or status, governed the location of men and women by generations. In Dutch Albany, an ambitious burgher would strive to make a fortune not so much that he might sit among the elders himself but so that his son or daughter would marry into an affluent merchant family and his grandson might sit there. When seats in the enlarged church of 1715 were first sold, status distinctions were established among the gentlemen seated around the main floor. The first numbered, and most desirable, pews were located "behind the church elders and deacons," apparently along the front wall of the sanctuary. Shortly after 1715 these were assigned to the leading male members of the most prominent merchant families. After this initial purchase and assignment of seats, heredity dictated subsequent ownership. In 1719 these rules were stated for the men as follows:

> . . . whenever any of these seats is vacated by death, it shall descend to the eldest son of the last occupant living in the county;[55] and in default of sons, to a son-in-law; and in default of sons-in-law, to an own brother; always descending successively to own sons, or if there be no sons or they shall be

absent then to sons-in-law; then to own brothers; the first occupant paying
thirty shillings for his seat, and his successor fifteen shillings for transferring
the same . . . in default of a successor . . . seats shall revert to the church.[56]

Ownership of each woman's seat was regulated by similar rules of ma-
trilineal descent. Because of these rules, prominent merchants in 1715 were
able to maintain their positions of honor as a hereditary right. Their sons
would inherit their fathers' seats on the main floor, and, from there, would
invariably succeed their fathers as church elders. Upward mobility was
certainly possible, but largely through intermarriage and over several generations. As members of the Dutch church, nearly all of the town's people
submitted themselves to the leadership of this hereditary hierarchy of
merchant-elders who, in turn, committed themselves to oversee the congregations's spiritual welfare in obedience to God.

This sacred bond between elders and congregation was similar to the
civil bond between Common Council members and citizens. Usually the
elders of the church were related to the officers of the Common Council
officers and most, at some point, served on the Common Council. The
overlapping of sacred and secular obligations can be seen in the required
oath of office for Common Council members that stipulated that the
officer perform his duty in obedience to God.[57] In turn, inhabitants who
came before the Common Council or the Mayor's Court addressed their
superiors as "your worshipful" mayor or alderman. As the authority in
both religious and civil government, members of merchant families con-
vened the meetings of the Common Council and the Consistory of the
Dutch Reformed Church. Their dual role as civil and church authorities
raises the question of how this relationship between secular and sacred
authority was understood.

Albany's church-state relations were similar to those proposed by John
Calvin. Calvin believed that government by a council of elders, whose
members criticized and supported each other, was better than a single,
uncontrolled ruler. Popular suffrage, with only the old and wise eligible
for office, was viewed as superior to the people governing themselves.
Calvin's ideal was the council of Judges that, with Moses, had governed
Israel. Then, the people selected seventy of the oldest and wisest men to
"bear the burden" of the state along with Moses (Numbers 11:16–17). The
people were to choose their leaders, but the choice was restricted by the
quality of the candidates. They had to be old and respected "elders of the
people."[58] The Dutch church's Great Consistory emulated the Hebrew
patriarchs. And, through their families, these same leaders protected the

privileges of the community for the benefit of all. In this sense, freedom for Calvin and the Albany Dutch was intended not for the individual's self-interest but for that of the entire community.[59]

Political inequality was also understood by Calvin and by Albanians as ordained by God. Calvin held that rulers enjoy no special privileges, only greater responsibility, because of their higher station. In turn, subjects suffer no deprivation or oppression because of their lower station.[60] In Albany, the merchants paid the majority of the town's expenses and held the major civic offices. Through the authority granted them as members of the Common Council, they wrote the city's laws, appointed the local constables and themselves to enforce them, sat in judgment in both city and county courts on the guilt or innocence of lawbreakers, and determined punishment. They also raised the money to support the town by assessing taxes on the inhabitants and appointing a tax collector.[61] Prior to 1760 there is little evidence that Albany's townsmen were unhappy with this arrangement or were unwilling to serve in the minor civic offices to which they were appointed. Apparently they perceived their subordinate position as natural and harmonious with the whole social pattern.

What, then, was Calvin's concept of the relationship between the Christian church and civil authority? Calvin conceived of all human beings as a single organism; all share a common nature bestowed by God. Humanity is not, however, identical with Christendom. Only the "elect" belong to the "true and invisible" church, and they are chosen only by God's grace. To the visible church belong only those who confess God and Christ, are baptized, receive the sacraments, and listen to the proclamation of the Word (as the Heidelberg catechism affirms). Humanity, therefore, is divided into Christendom, on the one hand, and infidels, on the other. Eschatologically, God will reunite humanity into a single organic whole under the single head of Christ, but that time is not yet. Neither the ecclesiastical nor the civil authority may hope thus to reunite humanity under its direction; nevertheless, God rules the whole world and not just that segment called Christendom. Therefore He employs both church and civil rulers to carry out his rule. Through the church He cares for humanity's spiritual salvation; through the civil order He cares for their worldly welfare.[62] Since God employs both orders in this complementary fashion, they must have the closest imaginable connection and cooperation. Merchant kinship provided that close relationship in Albany. Together the members of extended merchant families ruled both the world and the church. Although the ambitions of individuals, families, and rising generations often worked against the interests of the community, we will see that

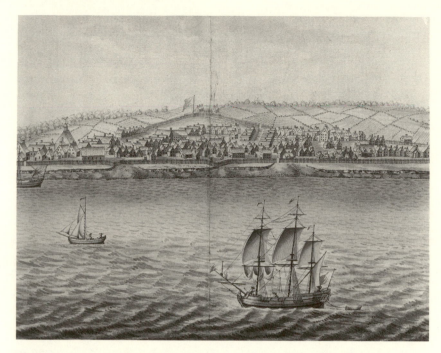

Figure 3. View of Albany around 1715. A wash drawing done in 1763 by Thomas Davies. (Collection of the Albany Institute of History and Art.)

whenever the community's survival was at stake the townspeople united to protect their common interests.

English Authority and Dutch Culture

The English presence in Albany began in 1664, when British soldiers took control of Beverwyck as part of the British conquest of New Netherland. Since the town records for the 1660's have disappeared, it is difficult to assess the immediate effect of this English takeover on the Dutch community. Apparently only formal changes occurred. A garrison of British soldiers was installed at the fort. Local magistrates were confirmed in office, and previous judicial decisions were permitted to stand.[63] Beverwyck was renamed Albany, one of the many titles of the Duke of York, later King James II, but the magistrates made no attempt to use the English language even for formal proceedings.

By the 1690's the expansion of French power in North America became a primary concern. As the British consolidated their defenses on the northern frontier, imperial policy was reshaped to reflect the interests of the English rather than the prerogatives of the Dutch. During the three colonial wars that followed—King William's War (1690–1698), Queen Anne's War (1702–1712), and the French and Indian War (1754–1760)—Albany was a staging area for British military expeditions against the French. As British subjects, Albany's Dutch inhabitants were expected to support the imperial war effort. The town fathers, however, assumed that their primary responsibility was the physical safety and economic well-being of the Dutch community. These local sentiments were strongly reinforced by the French and Indian massacre of sixty inhabitants of nearby Schenectady during the winter of 1690 and the failure of a poorly organized and underequipped English and colonial retaliatory attack on Montreal the following summer. After 1690, as the town's leaders became increasingly reluctant to risk their community's survival by engaging in punitive actions against the French, Albany gained a reputation throughout the province as a place where English patriotism was regularly sacrificed to Dutch self-interest.[64] From the local perspective, however, the Dutch were only doing what they had to do in order to protect their way of life.

The Inclusion of Outsiders

In her study of Anglo-Dutch conflict in the Albany of the 1670's, Donna Merwick illuminated the process by which former soldiers were absorbed into the life of the town.[65] Most of the thirty-odd British soldiers, traders, and adventurers in Albany at that time lived in and around the fort. Living side by side with them were twenty-seven Dutch artisans and traders. Merwick demonstrates that most altercations between Englishmen and townsmen took place in this ethnically mixed enclave. She shows that these men drank together at the same taverns, hired one another's services, and shared business alliances. Conflict between these two ethnic groups therefore represented "the dark counterpoint of their personal and business relationships."[66] As time passed, a number of these Englishmen, with little to return to in their native land, entered into Dutch society.[67] During the early eighteenth century, the number of ex-soldiers in the community gradually increased. In 1697, 7 percent of the town's household heads had English names. This figure reached 13 percent by 1720 and, by 1756, nearly 25 percent of the heads of Albany's households were of English descent.[68]

Since nearly all of these British inhabitants had been soldiers, they often served the town as firemasters, constables, and in the local militia. Moreover, they represented loyalty and responsibility to British authorities and therefore were frequently given political appointments as sheriffs and county clerks. In fact, between 1720 and 1760, eight of the thirteen sheriffs and five of the six county clerks appointed by the governor were of British descent.[69] Although favored by British authorities and limited in upward mobility by the Dutch, most of these British householders crossed into the Dutch community through marriage, holding minor civic offices, and joining the Dutch church.

The Yates family exemplified this process. Joseph Yates was part of the small invasion force that demanded the surrender of New Amsterdam on behalf of the Duke of York in August 1664. By the 1680's Yates had moved up the Hudson River to Albany, where he sought entrance into the Dutch community by learning the Dutch language, adjusting the spelling of his name to the more Dutch-sounding "Yetts," and marrying into an ordinary Dutch family.[70] By 1692 he had become a blacksmith and supplier of wood for the garrison at the fort. Along the way he was recognized as a freeholder of the town and served in the local militia. Joseph's eldest son Christoffel (1684–1754) extended the Yates inroads into the Dutch community by marrying the niece of Assemblyman Peter Winne; he was appointed captain in the local militia and was elected firemaster and high constable in the second ward. When Joseph Yetts died in 1730, his offspring and their families were living in Albany and Schenectady. The men worked as artisans and farmers while serving in minor city offices. Prior to the 1760's no Yates family member attained the wealth of Albany's leading merchants, served on the Common Council, or was elected to the eldership of the Dutch church, but they continued to intermarry with Dutch families, baptize their children in the Dutch church, and bear the civic responsibilities shared by every community member.[71]

The Retention of Dutch Cultural Practices Within English Legal Forms

At the same time that British people were absorbed into the Dutch community, Dutch practices were retained within English legal forms. The English imposed their will on Albany primarily through political appointments and legal action backed by military force. In 1686 Governor Thomas Dongan presented the town with a new city charter that replaced the

Dutch magistrate system with a Common Council. This English form of government consisted of a mayor and recorder, annually appointed by the governor, and six aldermen and six assistants from the city's three newly created wards, elected annually by male property holders.[72] Englishmen or Scots took over the positions of sheriff and court secretary. Members of the local militia and soldiers enforced city ordinances.[73]

As the structure of local government was altered to fit the English model, an English legal system was introduced that changed public life. In 1675, the office of court secretary was permanently altered by the appointment of newcomer Robert Livingston to a position traditionally filled by a burgher who guided court cases with the benefit of his familiarity with the community's legal precedents.[74] In 1691 the Judicial Act dissolved the Roman-Dutch law based on local precedent and replaced it with a legal system that derived its procedures from English common law. Official records were now to be written in English. Prior to 1705 a few jury trials occurred, and court records occasionally identified a Dutch attorney. It is doubtful, however, that any local Dutchman had sufficient knowledge of English procedures to implement the common law. Instead, significant changes occurred after John Collins, an officer at the fort and a lawyer, arrived at the Mayor's Court.[75] In 1705, Collins successfully requested that the court establish rules for the formal, written submission of declarations and pleas prior to trial. His own declarations demonstrated the English form of indictment, including specific descriptions of the accused, the offense, use of Latin, and formulaic phrases. These were imitated by local practitioners. By 1720 the writ of habeas corpus in defense of personal liberty was introduced.[76] In addition, the imperial system of law made it possible to appeal court decisions beyond the jurisdiction of local authorities.[77] As time passed, Albany's merchants saw the need to acquaint themselves with the intricacies of the common law and written procedures or depend on professional English counsel.

Despite the power of political appointments and the acquiescence of the townspeople to the precedents of the common law, it would be wrong to conclude that the Dutch were at least politically integrated by the British into their empire. Albany's inhabitants found ways to resist the British alteration of public life. The practice of popularly electing political leaders, in particular, was never developed in Dutch towns. The "Liberties of Englishmen," defined by the Magna Carta and fought for by seventeenth-century English parliaments, were outside the Dutch frame of reference. More understandable to the Dutch was the Calvinist idea of "election," whereby the godly "elect" ruled the unregenerate. While they may have been elected rather than appointed by their merchant fathers, brothers, cousins, and uncles, Common Council members continued a tradition of aristocratic rule by great burgher families begun in medieval Netherland towns. Moreover, they continued to act like Dutch burghers.[78] Even though what became known as the Dongan Charter imposed a foreign system of government on Albany, it also extended the town's privileges. In exchange for a 300 pound fee, the town's leaders were able to secure from Governor Dongan a provision in that charter that expanded the city's lands and required that all fur trade was to be carried on "within the walls" of the city—thereby securing the town's monopoly of the fur trade on the British northern frontier.[79] Similar to this retention of Dutch practices within an English form of government were the actions of local Dutch representatives to the New York Assembly. They did not react strongly to many of the curtailments of individual liberty that caused the English colonists to revolt, but they tenaciously resisted incursions into their communally held privileges. Indeed, the only issue in which local representatives to the New York Assembly were prominent, and ultimately successful, was the British governor's 1721 effort to tax out of existence their illicit trade with Canada.[80]

The advance of British authority was similarly restrained by the retention of Dutch inheritance practices within English wills. After 1691 the procedures and content of Albany wills were changed to fit the British model. Formerly, Albany's householders made their wills orally, in the privacy of their homes. These were recorded by a notary public and followed the Dutch merchant custom of dividing the assets equally among all the children. After 1691 all wills were written in English, submitted to the local court as a matter of public record, and required the practice of primogeniture. This latter provision, employed by the English to prevent the fragmentation of landholdings by giving the family estates to the eldest son, made little sense to Dutch merchants, whose commercial ventures required movable wealth. The equal division of their assets among their children was intended to bind their children to each other in mutual support and continuation of the family enterprise. Holding to this practice despite British rules of primogeniture, most Albany wills show that only token gifts were given to the eldest son. For example, in 1709 Abraham Schuyler willed five pounds to his eldest son David "for his birthright," yet he also instructed that his substantial estate "be equally divided among my children, share and share alike."[81]

Dutch economic patterns were particularly resilient in the face of imperial policy. The English conquest was, in fact, a boon to local trade. The English goods that came to be used for barter proved far superior to those traded by the French, so that much of the trade formerly carried on with the French was diverted to Albany. Since local traders also offered up to four times the price paid by the French for furs, even the French trappers began to deliver their furs to Albany. During the 1670's and 1680's, this trade swelled to the point that more than half of the total quantity of beaver annually produced in Canada passed through Albany.[82] Although trading with Canada ran directly against the Navigation Acts, which required that all provincial trade be conduced within the British Empire, the British did little to prevent it.

Indeed, by the late 1680's, Albany's traders were having it their way. Without leaving town, they received furs from French Canada and the Great Lakes region. Their control over local government prevented competition from unlicensed traders and fixed prices for furs. Moreover, their New York City importers and English contacts, who supplied barter goods to trade for the Indians' furs, were certainly willing to use their influence on provincial authorities to assure that the illegal Canada trade might continue. Albany's merchants were well aware that their trade with Canada violated the Navigation Acts, but they also knew that it would be difficult for the English officials to protest, since it was French rather than British mercantilism that suffered.[83] Despite this success of the town's leaders in turning imperial economic policy into local profits, some of the townspeople resented the advantages gained by those merchants who were most willing to accommodate imperial authority. These tensions provide an avenue for assessing the role of the town's leaders in mediating between British authority and the interests of the local community.

Dutch Leaders as Cultural Mediators

Peter Schuyler and Robert Livingston led the community's effort to secure a monopoly over the fur trade. Schuyler was the son of Philip Schuyler, an immigrant from Amsterdam who, on arriving in Beverwyck in 1650, married the daughter of Brant Van Slichtenhorst, Van Rensselaer's agent in charge of Rensselaerwyck, and soon thereafter became an "Indian Commissioner," regulating and participating in the fur trade. Peter married the daughter of his father's partner; when she died, he married the daughter of Van Rensselaer. In 1686 Peter Schuyler was twenty-nine years old. Already he was a substantial fur trader, a deacon in the Dutch church, knew some English through studies with a British schoolmaster sent to Albany in 1664, and had inherited his father's and father-in-law's contacts in provincial affairs.[84] Robert Livingston was raised in Rotterdam,the son of an expatriate Scottish Presbyterian minister. Arriving in Albany in 1675, Livingston married Schuyler's sister, the widow of a Van Rensselaer, joined the Dutch church, and established himself as a merchant. Although he was a Scot, he had lived in Rotterdam for nine years, spoke Dutch, knew the Dutch commercial methods, and understood Dutch customs. In 1686, Robert Livingston was only thirty-two years old, yet he had parlayed his advantageous marriage and knowledge of Dutch and English cultures into a successful business of importing British goods through imperial contacts; he had also been appointed by the governor to the local offices of town clerk and secretary to the commissioners for Indian affairs.[85]

When Peter Schuyler and Robert Livingston brought the city charter, with its provision for local control over the entire fur trade, from Governor Dongan's residence in New York City to Albany in 1686, these ambitious young burghers were well received. After their arrival, the charter "was published with all ye joy and acclamations imaginable; and ye said two gentm received ye thanks of ye magistrates and burgesses for their diligence and care in obtaining ye same."[86] The governor appointed Schuyler mayor and Livingston town clerk. They may have been the only burghers in town who understood how the new system worked. Trouble arose, however, when older competitors in the fur trade found they were placed under the power of these new city officers by the provisions of the charter. These differences took on ethnic overtones in 1689, when James II, the pro-Catholic, pro-French king of England abdicated his throne in favor of his Protestant daughter Mary and her husband William III.

When news of this "Glorious Revolution" reached the New World, Jacob Leisler, a New York City Dutch church elder and militia captain, seized control of the provincial government and turned against the merchant and landed families who had worked with the royal government and come to dominate provincial trade. Leisler attacked these families as "papists" for their support of James II and announced that his rebellion was "for the glory of the protestante interest." His principal New York City supporters were a dozen years older and did not possess the affluence and political influence of the Dutch Anglicizers.[87] Several Albany fur traders, including Johannes Cuyler, Johannes Wendell, and Jochim Staats, were related to Leisler's supporters and became leaders of a local pro-Leisler faction that opposed the Schuyler group and its instrument, the city charter. These men also were somewhat less affluent and influential leaders than the Schuyler partisans, and they were a number of years older.[88]

When Leisler gained control of the provincial government in New York City, Schuyler and his associates avoided legal submission by abandoning the city charter and creating an extralegal government called the Convention. They denied being "traitors" and "papists" and at once proclaimed William and Mary as their sovereign. Only forty "Principall Men of the Towne," however, signed an affirmation of loyalty to this group. Shortly afterward, in November 1689, "Near a hundred persons, most youthes, and them that were no freeholders," chose Jochim Staats as captain of a contingent of men sent by Leisler to Albany under the charge of his son-in-law, Jacob Milbourne. While in Albany Milbourne encouraged the "Common People" to overthrow the Convention and "free themselfs from ye Yoke of arbitrary Power and Government under which they had Lyen so long."[89] The brunt of his attack, and indeed the whole thrust of the rebellion in Albany, was directed toward Anglicizers who supported the "Popish" government of James II and gained for themselves the "arbitrary power" of the city charter. Milbourne reasoned that since James II was a "papist" and therefore an "illegal" monarch, everything granted by him, especially Albany's city charter, was "null and void." The Convention responded by denouncing Milbourne for urging the people to "undertake some Desperate Design and breake there Covenant with us kept so many years Inviolable." If things "were Carried on as Milbourne would have (them) all Authority would be turned Upside Doune."[90]

This confrontation was short lived. On the night of February 8, 1690, Frenchmen and Indians massacred sixty inhabitants of Schenectady. Townspeople from both Schenectady and Albany fled downriver to safety in New York. The population of Albany city and county, which has been 2016 in 1689, dropped to 1476.[91] Those who remained united in the town's defense. That summer hostile Indians killed and scalped isolated farmers. The attacks became so severe that by August it was reported that Albany was "full of disorder, the people ready to desert it; about 150 farms deserted and destroyed by the French and late disorders."[92] In the fall of 1690 William and Mary sent a military expedition to assert their control over the government of New York. In May 1691 the new governor hanged Leisler and Milbourne. During the next eight years, a tenacious core of burghers and farmers led by Peter Schuyler joined with three companies of Redcoats to protect the city from the constant threat of French and Indian attack.

One effect of Leisler's rebellion in Albany was to reveal ethnic Dutch hostility toward the English.[93] It was expressed in anger toward those who cultivated English contacts. The city charter was a triumph for all in the community, but it gave particular privileges to the charter officers who were to regulate the fur trade. These younger men had gone outside the Dutch community to the English to gain leadership and power within the community. During Leisler's rebellion, this ethnic resentment was particularly directed toward Albany's Dutch minister, Dominie Dellius who, like other Reformed ministers in the colony, aligned himself with the Anglicizing merchants and against the less affluent Dutch. The limited English influence in Albany spared the local church the reign of violence that followed the hangings of Leisler and Milbourne in New York City. Nonetheless, the persecution directed toward Dominie Dellius was sufficient to force his departure from the city for six months. On returning to Albany, Dellius found a congregation now more "peaceable" than before and certainly less contentious than the more "opinionated" people of New York City. Yet he worried about the breakdown of discipline among his people.

Considering the situation of the colony as a whole, Dellius prophesied the emergence of a new religious movement composed of farmers and artisans, independent of church authority, and emphasizing personal piety. Writing to the Classis of Amsterdam, he warned that

> . . . soon some marvelous kind of theology will develop here; ministers will be self-created, and the last will be the first, and the first will be last. Rev. Gentlmen it grieves us that . . . our church and its ordinations have become a matter of ridicule.[94]

Randall Balmer has shown that this prophecy was soon to prove true as the Dutch pietist movement emerged from popular ethnic discontent.[95] There is little evidence, however, for the emergence of this religious movement in Albany. Instead, the townspeople turned their immediate attention to the community's survival and, over time, the families who had touched off what became an ethnic rebellion intermarried.

Perhaps the most enduring result of Leisler's rebellion in Albany was the acknowledgment by the entire community that their local interests were of greater value than individual economic advantage. The Leislerian leaders gave up trying to overthrow the Dongan Charter and now sought to attain their aims within its framework. The Schuyler partisans, concurrently, recognized they could not run the community without paying attention to the desires of the rest of the townspeople. Johannes Schuyler, Peter Schuyler's younger brother, married Elizabeth Staats Wendell in 1695. Elizabeth Wendell was the widow of a prominent Leislerian and a sister to three other Leisler leaders. Several marriages between younger members of families of the two previously warring families ensued. Although they were still commercial rivals, by 1717 the two groups of fur traders had intermarried into a single network that held eleven of the twelve seats on the Common Council.[96] Peter Schuyler's cultivation of imperial authority for personal gain was resented by many of the townspeople, but they recognized the role he played in securing benefits for all the community through the fur monopoly provisions of the city charter.

During the early eighteenth century, Schuyler remained prominent in provincial affairs and in all vital efforts to preserve the autonomy of the local community. His high standing among the British was affirmed through his appointment as mayor, his seat in the Provincial Assembly, and his service as interim governor during a change in administrations. Schuyler's service to the British authorities as Indian commissioner is said to have resulted in the offer of a knighthood by Queen Anne. At the same time, Schuyler's appearance at the court of Queen Anne, where he presented several Mohawk chieftains to the imperial family, was aimed at dramatizing the need for British action against the threat of French assault on Albany.[97] Throughout Queen Anne's War, he was leader of all efforts to defend the community against Indian attacks.

In 1715, Schuyler and his followers denounced the planned construction of an Anglican church in the town on the grounds that such construction violated the "rights and privileges of this city."[98] Additionally nettlesome was the location of the church at a more lordly elevation on State Street "above" the Dutch church.[99] Acting on their convictions, the local court arrested the masons who had begun the work, and the town clerk was ordered to hire a New York lawyer to "find a proper court where this work may be stope."[100] When it seemed that they were going to lose their case, the Common Council went so far as to make an unsuccessful offer to the governor of another piece of land for the church. Evidence of lingering Dutch resentment toward this forceful imposition of a "foreign" church on the town can be found as late as the 1790's, when the English congregation's effort to remove their original church to another location met with prolonged antagonism from the Dutch members of the Common Council.[101]

The British Occupation (1754–1760)

As late as the 1740's, Albany continued to be seen by outsiders as a pecu-liarly Dutch provincial town. According to Swedish naturalist Peter Kalm, who passed through Albany in 1749, "The inhabitants of Albany and its environs are almost all Dutchmen. They speak Dutch, have Dutch preachers, and the divine service is performed in that language. Their manners are likewise quite Dutch."[102] Kalm noticed the Dutch houses with gable ends to the street, and he went inside to find fireplaces deco-rated with Dutch tiles and Dutch cupboard beds. The local diet empha-sized salad, bread, and dairy products, not the beer and beef of the En-glish. Local customs requiring face-to-face contact with the inhabitants brought complaints from Peter Kalm and the British doctor, Alexander Hamilton, who visited the city in 1744. Hamilton groused about being introduced "into about 20 or 30 houses where I went thro' the farce of kissing most of the women, a manner of salutation which is ex-pected . . . from strangers coming there."[103] Similarly, Kalm protested the local custom of sitting outside one's house on pleasant evenings—"this is rather troublesome because a gentleman has to keep his hat in constant motion, unless he shock the politeness of the inhabitants."[104] Hamilton added that he grew "quite tired of this place where there was no variety of choise, either of company or conversation."[105] And he concluded that the people were

> . . . att best rustick and unpolished . . . [they have] little desire for conversa-tion and society, their whole thoughts being turned upon profit and gain which necessarily makes them live retired and frugall. At least this is the common character of the Dutch every where.[106]

In spite of a half century of English and Dutch cultural interaction, at least in the eyes of outsiders, Albany remained a uniquely Dutch provincial town.

Fundamental changes began to occur in 1754. Skirmishes between Brit-ish and French forces over control of northern New York had made Al-bany the last physically secure community on the northern frontier. Refu-gees fled to the security of the town's fortified walls, increasing the population from 1800 to more than 3000.[107] They took shelter in every house, built shacks in the town's back gardens, and created a shantytown outside the north gate.[108] When, in 1755, the French built a large stone fortress at Ticonderoga to the north, the British needed a large profes-sional army to attack this citadel. To prepare for this campaign, they assembled several thousand redcoats and provincial auxiliaries around Albany during the spring and summer of 1755. That winter, provincial troops were dismissed to their homes, but British troops were quartered forcibly in every available shelter. As many as 1400 officers and soldiers were moved into the already doubly occupied Dutch homes. During the winter of 1756, Albany's tightly circumscribed world was composed of seventy-five acres filled with 355 households and a teeming population of more than 4000 natives, refugees, and soldiers.[109] Spring and summer brought many more British and provincial troops. Perhaps as many as thirty thousand soldiers occupied or passed through the city in the next several years. In 1760 the army marched triumphantly northward, leaving behind a city forever changed by its presence.

Albany's political and religious leaders resisted the British occupation. For all of the town's Dutch inhabitants this sustained British intrusion meant invasions of their private world and a constant assault on their way of life. The Common Council members particularly resented the arrival of British merchants, who made their livelihood from supplying the army. They registered their antagonism toward these interlopers by selective enforcement of the city's laws and unequal taxation.[110] In 1756, for example, the Council began enforcing an act outlawing the sale of rum to the Indians. William Corey, a recent English arrival, complained to William Johnson, an English trader who lived among the Mohawks, that "they picked out the Strangers from one end of Albany to the other with much discretion and Judgt. but the persons that might readily be suspected of the right breed they passed over." Two English merchants were convicted and fined fifty pounds, while a Dutchman, who admitted he had violated the act, was set free.[111] Tax rates were determined by public assessors. They evaluated each man's worth and determined the portion of the tax they should pay. By raising the assessment of British merchants, the assessor could impose on them an undue portion of the tax burden. John Macomb, an Irish merchant who settled in Albany in 1757, complained to a local military officer:

> To confirm the general dislike the Dutch have to the Europeans here, in aplotting the contingent money for the Citty of Albany, they have acted the most partially anyone could imagine. . . . Ever since I came here we have been charged above double our proportion of all public charges. . . . Upon my applying to the chief magistrates I was told that I must pay whatever sum the taxers charged me with, and that it was not in my power to have any redress made me from any person whatever.[112]

These legal actions, taken by the Common Council to insure continued Dutch control over local trade, were supported by the moral outrage of the community's religious leaders.

Theodorus Frelinghuysen, Jr., led the Dutch church's attack on the moral behavior of the British troops. Frelinghuysen was the eldest son of the Dutch minister who had helped begin the Great Awakening in New Jersey. Like his father, Frelinghuysen was concerned with practical piety.[113] In 1757 the young minister focused his efforts on the decadent influence of British fads and fashions on the young people in his congregation. Mrs. Anne Grant, a daughter of a British officer, described the situation.

> A regiment came to town abut this time [1757], the superior officers of which were younger, more gay, and less amenable to good counsel than those who used to command the troops, which had formerly been placed on this station. . . . Several had families and those began to mingle more frequently with the inhabitants: who were as yet too simple to detect the surreptitious tone of lax morals and second hand manners, which prevailed among many of those who had but very lately climbed up to the stations they held, . . .[114]

The gradual assimilation of English manners among the young "alarmed and aggrieved" the Albany minister.

> . . . and what, alas, could Frelinghuysen do but preach! This he did earnestly, and even angrily, but in vain. Many were exasperated but none reclaimed. The good dominie, however, and those who shared his sorrows and resentments, the elder and wiser heads of families, indeed a great majority of the primitive inhabitants, were steadfast against innovation.[115]

Despite the efforts of the minister and the parents in the community, the Anglomania continued to spread.

> A sect arose among the young people, who seemed resolved to assume a lighter style of dress and manners, and to borrow their taste in those respects from their new friends. Under the auspices of [The colonel of the regiment] balls, began to be concerted, and a degree of flutter and frivolity to take place—[and soon] the very ultimate of degeneracy, in the opinion of these simple, good people was approaching; for now . . . preparations [were] . . . made for acting a play. The play . . . was acted in a barn and pretty well attended . . . the novices . . . laughed very heartily at seeing the gay young ensigns . . . with painted cheeks and colored eyebrows, sailing about in female habiliments . . . the fame of their exhibition went abroad, and opinions were formed of them in no way favorable to the actors or the audience.[116]

Mrs. Grant goes on to tell how upset the older Albanians were with the manners and entertainment of the young British officers who "were themselves a lie," and therefore, deeply threatened the "truth" of Dutch life.[117] Despite the moral outrage of the Dutch church and the legal maneuvers of the Common Council, after the French and Indian War the world of the Dutch was forever changed.

Figure 4. *The Rich Man's Dwelling*. A watercolor on paper by James Eights. (Collection of the Albany Institute of History and Art. Bequest of Ledyard Cogswell, Jr.)

Chapter 2

From Albany Townspeople to Americans: The Social Origins of Nationalism

For some time, American historians have attempted to explain the emergence of a new devotion to the nation during and after the Revolution. The recent scholarship of intellectual historians has explored the political and religious aspects of this nascent nationalism. On the one hand, Bernard Bailyn's examination of political pamphlets has demonstrated that colonial political leaders worked over several decades to adapt British Whig political culture to the colonies so that individual liberty and property became central tenets of the emerging cause.[1] On the other hand, Nathan Hatch's analysis of the political content of sermons has shown how New England's ministers extended the canopy of religious meaning so that republican ideas became sacred.[2] Edmund Morgan has called the resulting nationalism "the strongest force binding Americans of the Revolutionary generation together."[3] This conviction is particularly strong among historians who emphasize the consensus achieved by the rebelling colonists, yet it is also shared by those who stress conflict among the colonists. Gordon Wood's analysis of political debates between 1776 and 1787 underscored this conflict within consensus approach by demonstrating that Americans used a shared language and a common conceptual framework to debate very real political differences.[4]

Several attempts have been made to consider these differences in the light of social history. For example, Eric Foner's study of Tom Paine placed its subject in relation to the crowds and mechanics of Philadelphia. Foner demonstrated the ways in which Paine's vivid cries for "liberty" and "revolution" spoke to and for people who sought individual rights in a future egalitarian society.[5] In contrast, Rowland Berthoff and John Murrin have linked similar Revolutionary rhetoric to the conservative interests of a ruling elite who controlled a hierarchical social structure well into the nineteenth century. Berthoff and Murrin's belief that Revolutionary ideology "powerfully stimulated a nostalgic attachment to seventeenth century simplicity"[6] suggests that at least in some places appeals for "liberty" and "revolution" signaled a desire to restore an older communal ideal. Taken together, these studies indicate that, while the national ideology of the Revolutionary generation was widely shared, particular communities and even subgroups within those communities understood its tenets differently.[7]

One explanation for the different reasons advanced by Revolutionary-era Americans for supporting the new nation is the different experiences of social change undergone by the inhabitants of late eighteenth-century cities and towns. A number of investigators have suggested that trends such as population growth, commercialization, and social differentiation, experienced first in the seaboard cities, upset the equilibrium of an older system of social relations and turned these urban centers into crucibles of revolutionary agitation.[8] It was in these cities, Gary Nash has argued, that "almost all the alterations associated with the advent of capitalist society happened first . . . and radiated outwards to the smaller towns, villages, and farms of the hinterland."[9] These commercial centers may have predicted the future, yet only one in twenty colonists lived in them in 1775.[10] On the eve of the Revolution most Americans lived in villages and towns where religion was as significant as politics or the economy in shaping the life and values of the new nation. This was particularly true, as Patricia Bonomi has posited, in northern towns that had a "settled character and compactness."[11] In these communities an older communal way of life prevailed. We know a great deal about the encompassing role of religious life in the villages and towns of the early colonial period.[12] We are coming to know more about the emergence of revolutionary agitation among workingmen in the larger cities.[13] What we do not know is the social origins of the new devotion to the nation which emerged in those towns that still clung to their older communal ideal in the face of mounting social changes before and after the Revolution. A portrayal of Albany in the late eighteenth century may help us discover how many new Americans understood their new commitment to the nation.

*   *   *

Following the French and Indian War, the comparative peace and stability of colonial Albany's Dutch society was disrupted by rapid social changes. During the 1760's, European immigration and subsequent economic development transformed the town from an isolated trading post into a bustling regional shipment center. Wealthy "gentlemen" and landless poor emerged around the local townsmen, creating new economic and social chasms. These changes affected the town's political structure and prevailing theological doctrines. New political leaders who relied on popular support challenged the merchant-elders who wielded power based on social rank. Theological doctrines emphasizing free will and universal salvation challenged the idea of predestination and leadership by the "elect." These economic, political, and theological challenges to the old order were growing when cut short and temporarily postponed by the urgent need for all the townspeople to join forces to combat a common enemy.

The eve of the Revolution brought together a coalition of Dutch, Scotch-Irish, and English leaders called on by their fellow townsmen to assert their traditional leadership. By 1760 Albany's Dutch leaders knew of British economic and legal practices, spoke English, and dressed in the English manner. As mediators between the local community and the British authorities, they remained bound to the old moral order of family, church, and town while possessing extra-local ties that brought them into continual contact with strangers. With the imminent threat of British invasion, these Dutch leaders joined with leaders from the growing Scotch-Irish and English communities to form the local Committee of Correspondence. As the threat of British invasion engulfed the town, these leaders shifted the basis for local political unity from Dutch ethnicity to American citizenship. Following the Revolution, a similarly heterogeneous federation of community leaders sanctified this new union through Fourth of July rituals in which they enacted and articulated the new civil faith. A common identity as Christians supplanted Dutch church membership as the moral foundation for community order. Despite these new, broad, political and religious ties, differences persisted. Still, the new ideological unity did link the townspeople to each other and to other colonial communities who, together, formed a nation. Similarly, while the new devotion to the nation did not check the social trends that were creating tensions in the community, it did provide the town's diverse inhabitants with a common language and rituals for debating their differences.

Economy

After the French and Indian War, Albany's economy changed. Indians were pushed further away from the town, allowing for an increase in regional settlement. Between 1749 and 1771 the population of the county quadrupled from 10,634 to 42,706.[14] From 1756 to 1779, the town's population increased by only 66 percent, from 1800 to 3000.[15] Most of the area's new settlers were born in Europe and had few vocational skills. Two 1762 muster rolls of men called to the militia from the city and county of Albany indicate that two-thirds of these new soldiers were born in Ireland (29 percent), Germany (14 percent), England and Wales (13 percent), or Scotland (3 percent), with less than one-third coming from the Middle Colonies (13 percent), New England (9 percent), or the Albany area (9 percent).[16] Most of these immigrants settled in the county, although many with artisan skills found their niche in the town, where they added to the size and skills of Albany's community of artisans.

By 1756, Albany's skilled tradesmen were growing in number, and differentiation was taking place within the merchant and artisan occupations. As recently as 1742, the town's residents were about equally divided between merchants and artisans. In 1756, however, a British inventory of the town's householders and their occupations indicates that merchants accounted for about 36 percent of the work force and artisans for 54 percent (See Table 2.1).[17] This change in the relative sizes of the merchant and artisan groups was accompanied by differentiation within each occupation. Those who formerly were identified as merchants now were further described[18] as general merchants, Indian traders, and shippers, as well as tavernkeepers and small shopkeepers. Artisans were also subdivided within their trades, for example, builders were divided into carpenters, masons, and bricklayers. New craftsmen such as brasiers, glaziers, and gunsmiths were now present in addition to the longstanding blacksmiths and silversmiths.[19]

The place of the town's British minority within the local work force suggests that the framework for the city as an urban center was transplanted from England. In 1756, nearly one-third of Albany's 325 household heads and almost one-half of the town's artisans were of British descent. They were the primary workers in longstanding crafts, such as butchers, tailors, and blacksmiths. They also added new skills as brasiers, saddlers, and wigmakers. The Dutch remained in control of merchant life, accounting for nearly two-thirds of those listed as merchants, yet this was less than the near monopoly they had formerly enjoyed. Also, all of the city's innkeepers, tavernkeepers, and dram shop owners were of British ancestry.

Table 2.1. 1756 Loudoun Inventory of Occupations

250 Occupations	107 (43%) British	143 (57%) Dutch
I. Professionals 8 (3%)	3 (38%) British	5 (63%) Dutch
Doctor	0	1
Lawyer	1	1
Schoolmaster	1	1
Clergyman	1	1
Mayor	0	1
II. Merchants 91 (36%)	35 (38%) British	56 (62%) Dutch
Merchant	13	35
Shipper	2	13
Indian trader	3	7
Innkeeper	4	0
Tavernkeeper	2	0
Dram shop	5	0
Shopkeeper	1	0
Apothecary	0	1
Retailor of liquor	3	0
Sutler	1	0
Tobacconist	1	0
III. Artisans 134 (54%)	60 (45%) British	74 (55%) Dutch
Shoemaker	6	16
Carpenter	8	11
Cooper	5	6
Baker	3	6
Tailor	5	2
Weaver	5	2
Blacksmith	4	2
Gunsmith	1	4
Smith	0	4
Brewer	2	3
Mason	1	3
Silversmith	2	1
Hatter	3	0
Waggoner	0	3
Butcher	2	0
Barber	2	0
Britchesmaker	2	0
Turner	0	2
Brasier	2	0
Saddler	1	0
Mariner	0	2
Glasier	0	1
Mantuamaker	1	0
Wigmaker	1	0
Sawmaker	1	0
Hoopmaker	1	0
Bricklayer	1	0
Pilot	0	1
Sloopman	1	0

(continued)

Table 2.1. (*Continued*)

250 Occupations	107 (43%) British	143 (57%) Dutch
Sexton	0	1
Wampum maker	0	1
Wheelmaker	0	1
IV. Unskilled 17 (7%)	8 (47%) British	9 (53%) Dutch
Farmer	2	7
Laborer	1	0
Carter	0	1
Carman	3	0
Crier	0	1
Soldier	1	0
Watterman	1	0

This is significant because it was in this British environment that most of the socializing of Dutch and British inhabitants took place. Finally, a British lawyer, schoolmaster, and a clergyman joined with a Dutch lawyer, schoolmaster, clergyman, and doctor to constitute a budding professional class. Taken together, the town's social centers, important trades, and professions were now in the British domain, while the Dutch no longer held a monopoly over merchant affairs.[20]

Changes were also evident within the Dutch merchant community. By the 1760's a new generation of general merchant families had taken the place of the old fur trading elite in directing the interests of the community. Leendert Gansevoort and his contemporaries, Sybrant Van Schaick and Jacob C. Ten Eyck, were prominent community leaders in the 1760's. Their families began their rise to power in the 1730's. The Gansevoorts broke into the ranks of the merchant elite by catering to the needs of a continuing population expansion that led to the settlement of county farms. The farmers sold their flour and grains and bought their materials in the diversifying Albany marketplace. Some of these new merchants, like Sybrant Van Schaick, were scions of fur trading families and therefore already among the elite. Others, like Jacob C. Ten Eyck, the son of an artisan, were non-elite by birth. Unlike those families who were most involved with the fur monopoly and ran the Common Council, the Gansevoorts, Van Schaicks and Ten Eycks were among the first general merchants who would ride to prominence on the rising tide of regional settlement. The names of their family members first appeared among the

Common Council aldermen in the 1730's and 1740's.[21] At the same time, these same names began to appear among the patriarchs on the first floor of the Dutch church.[22] Together they formed a group whose economic, political, and religious influence was expanding during the 1760's while that of the fur trading families was receding.[23]

By 1767 divisions were developing between the community's rich and poor, Dutch and British, that placed unprecedented demands on this new generation of Dutch leaders. When a tax list from that year is compared with a similar list from 1709, two conclusions are apparent (See Table 2.2). First, a smaller number of the community's wealthiest citizens accounted for a larger percentage of the town's wealth. In 1709, 20 percent of the taxpayers accounted for nearly 50 percent of the wealth. In contrast, in 1767 only 10 percent of the citizens held about half of the wealth. Second, a larger number of the community's poorest citizens held a smaller percentage of the wealth. In 1709, almost half of the taxpayers held 15 percent of the wealth. In 1767, more than 75 percent of the taxpayers held less than 33 percent of the wealth.[24] Contributing to this polarization of rich and poor was the comparatively large number of less affluent British immigrants. British immigrants now accounted for 36 percent of the town's population but only 28 percent of the community's wealth. The 10 wealthiest citizens were all Dutch merchants, while a majority of the city's poor were British.[25] These divisions placed growing pressure on the town's political system.

Table 2.2 Polarization of Wealth, 1709–1767

Distribution of Wealth in 1709

Tax group (total: 3831 pounds)	*Number (181)*	*Work force, %*	*Wealth, %*
Upper (over 30 pounds)	36	20	49
Middle (15–29 pounds)	57	32	36
Lower (1–14 pounds)	88	49	15

Distribution of Wealth in 1767

Tax group (total: 6661 pounds)	*Number (563)*	*Tax payers, %*	*Wealth, %*
Upper (over 30 pounds)	55	10	48
Middle (15–29 pounds)	70	12	20
Lower (1–14 pounds)	438	78	32

Politics

During the 1760's, population growth, commercialization, and social differentiation led to increased demands on the sources of political power. By 1766 the Common Council met twice as often as it did in 1750 to discuss the sale of new lots, problems of fire and health hazards, the purchase of oil lamps to protect and direct evening activities, and the paving and cleaning of crowded city streets. Continuing commercialization made time and efficiency more important. The Common Council responded by placing a clock high in one of the town's steeples and building three docks for the easier shipment of cargo at the port. Social differentiation also was a cause for political activity. The Council noted an increase in delinquent rents for city lots and a new demand for poor relief.[26] These new signs of poverty were countered with new signs of wealth. The richest inhabitants built new, English-style houses, and several lived along the main East-West thoroughfare, called by the Dutch "Jonkheer" or "Gentleman's Walk."[27] The growth of Albany's population threatened to outpace the capacity of its political institutions.

This was more than simply a growth in population and a polarization of wealth. It was also a matter of increasing numbers of English and Scotch-Irish immigrants becoming dependent on the wealth of that small minority of their countrymen who were successful, the long dominant Dutch families, or the Common Council to maintain their lives. It was therefore a matter of deeply divided interests as some offered while others sought housing, money, and employment. This "foreign" minority's growing dependence, separate interests, and disproportionately high representation among the town's poor, in a predominantly Dutch town where the long-term inhabitants maintained a monopoly over the local sources of power, were the ingredients of political conflict.[28] It is not surprising, therefore, that Albany's politics changed along with its population and economy. Wealthy Dutch merchants, who were also leaders in their church, still dominated the Common Council. But now they were joined by a few recent non-Dutch immigrants and descendants of British soldiers formerly stationed at the fort.[29] Rather than relying on the traditional requirements of social rank and wealth as prerequisites of political leadership, these insurgents turned to the support of a popular following.

Abraham Yates, a former sheriff and grandson of a British soldier who settled in the town, was the leader of these rebels.[30] Yates was typical of that generation of Albany townspeople who were descended from former soldiers who came to the town at the end of the previous century. Like his father and grandfather, Yates married a local Dutch woman and changed his name to the more Dutch-sounding "Yetts." He also held a seat in the Dutch church, though in the balcony, and at some distance from the patriarchs' seats of power encircling the first floor.[31] Like every other local resident of British military background, Abraham Yates was unable to penetrate the Dutch control of local trade and therefore sought advancement through law and politics. Appointed sheriff in October 1754, he joined forces with the town's long-term inhabitants in opposing the British occupation. Yates' political rise was stymied in 1758 when several Dutch merchants had him fired for fear that his zealous enforcement of community ordinances would cause the British army to retaliate by exposing the merchants' illegal trade with Canada. After the war, he changed his name back to Yates, supported the Anglican church, and mounted a campaign for political office based on the support of the people. His new approach to politics may well have been motivated by what he read in the tracts of the early eighteenth-century radical Whigs while working in a local lawyer's office, his experiences of British military abuse during their occupation of the city,[32] or his resentment toward the ruling Dutch families for using their influence to force him from his office as sheriff. Together, these influences contributed to his view of local politics as a practical struggle for those of the "common sort" to secure for themselves the economic and political opportunities denied by the "aristocrats."

During the early 1760's, Yates was affiliated with members of the New York City Livingston family, who had begun to appeal to ordinary voters as well as to elite families. The Livingstons' home base was no longer in the city of Albany. Instead, since the 1720's, they lived in the English style at their manor in the upper Hudson Valley. William Livingston was one of the few New Yorkers of his generation who attended Yale College. There he observed the New England town meeting system in which ordinary voters expressed their opinions and voted on issues. Individuals won election to town offices on the basis of their positions on these issues as well as their wealth and family relationships.[33] Livingston employed this system to appeal to the large proportion of New England voters who had settled in New York City and Long Island. Starting with a New York Assembly faction of a few important families who employed the English system of patronage to attach supporters to themselves, the Livingstons' placed this faction atop a base of independent voters whom they expected to vote on issues in the New England manner. A new kind of professional politician was then depended on to hold both ends of the party together. He was a member of the party either through family relationship or patronage. At the same time, he could articulate the specific issues that would win the votes of ordinary people.[34]

Initially, the Livingstons' new system made little sense in Dutch Albany, where elections were a small part of the Dutch political tradition and voting on issues was completely foreign to their system of governance. Abraham Yates was the first to introduce the new techniques into Albany elections. Although unsuccessful in his 1761 bid for an assembly seat, Yates won election to the Common Council in 1763 and continued to be re-elected for the next ten years. His supporters were drawn from his own extensive family, including long-term Albany Englishmen, non-elite Dutch kinsmen, and newly arrived immigrants. Yates referred to his "party" as early as the 1761 election, but the first evidence for its existence was in the Common Council election of 1772, when two of Yates' nephews were elected to join their uncle on the Common Council.[35]

The point is that, immediately prior to the Revolution, Abraham Yates and his followers were beginning to see their political circumstances from a different perspective than that of the Dutch. Largely of less affluent origin, with few opportunities for economic or political advancement, they saw local politics as a practical struggle to secure for themselves the economic and political opportunities denied them by the ruling Dutch families. Following the Revolution, Yates became New York's most influential and articulate Anti-Federalist.[36] His argument against the Federal Constitution contained repeated attacks on British imperialism and Dutch aristocracy. Against these evil forces Yates employed a host of Biblical analogies, suggesting a malevolent lust for power, and punctuated his argument with references to Montesquieu, Franklin, Adams, and other Enlightenment thinkers. This was intended to portray the Federalist's Constitution as but one more sad example of aristocracy's effort "to get the Power out of the Hands of the People."[37] For Abraham Yates and his Albany followers, fighting for American liberty would mean fighting for freedom from both British imperialism and Dutch aristocracy.

Methodists

At the same time that Abraham Yates and his followers were developing a new political ideology, a new evangelical theology was being preached in Albany that similarly diverged from the Dutch perspective by emphasizing human ability and universal salvation. In the fall of 1766, an enthusiastic convert to Methodism, the one-eyed British soldier Captain Thomas

Webb, returned to Albany from England. In July 1765 Webb had been appointed Albany's barrack master. Shortly after assuming his post his wife died. "Seeking solace from his grief and some readjustment to his life,"[38] Webb was given leave to return home to Bristol, England. There he came under the influence of a Moravian preacher whose words consoled him while "peace and joy through believing filled his heart."[39] Webb was subsequently introduced to the Methodist society at Wesley Chapel in Bristol and was invited to tell the story of his conversion. When John Wesley, the Methodist founder, heard of his conversion, Webb was granted the status of a local preacher.

On his return to Albany, Captain Webb apparently lost little time in taking up the work of the Lord that was now the motivating force of his life. Methodist historians tell us that he told the story of his conversion to soldiers and friends in his private residence and "in the public streets."[40]

> It was a strange thing for a military officer, arrayed in the habiliments of his office, with his sword by his side, or lying on the table before him, to assume the place of an ambassador of the Lord Jesus Christ. The people went to hear him out of curiosity, but were not unfrequently wounded by the sword of the spirit which he wielded with great power. He presented the truths of the gospel in a new light, and made Christ appear more inviting and attractive than he had hitherto appeared. Some gladly opened their hearts to the Saviour he exhibited and were happy in his love.[41]

There were no evangelical preachers in the Albany area at this time, nor were there Methodist preachers in New York State. Nevertheless, Captain Webb was an "instant success,"[42] converting several of the new British residents as well as a few slaves.[43] His Methodist activity was commended by his commander, General Gage. During the captain's 6-year stay in Albany, General Gage relieved him from many of his routine tasks so that he could preach in New York City and throughout the region.

Like all the early Methodist preachers, Thomas Webb offered hope to a people in transition. His audiences of recent immigrants were people largely of British stock and meager means, who desired greater individual freedom yet were still rooted in communal values. Accommodating both the past and the future, evangelists like Thomas Webb appealed to the Calvinist insistence on human depravity and a new emphasis on personal autonomy, free will, and good works. Unlike the Reformed faith, which offered no hope to those not chosen by God, the Methodists offered some reassurance. They held that even though you are a sinner and there is nothing in you that merits the goodness of God, God is ready to welcome all of you as His children, if you seek to attain His grace and live a life of holiness that will allow you to enter into His kingdom.[44] Like political innovations, however, these changes in the religious life of the town would be interrupted by the Revolution. The record of evangelical religion in Albany breaks with Webb's departure in 1771, to begin again with the founding of the first local Methodist society in 1792. Nevertheless, it is evident that, just prior to the Revolution, political and religious divisions were emerging in the town.

Calvinists

The members of the Dutch church may have regarded these new developments as signs of a growing evil that threatened the existence of their traditional world. Despite the changes the community was undergoing in its economic, social, and political life, throughout the 1760's and on into the 1780's the religious life of the Dutch continued. Richard Pointer has argued against the widely held assumption that religious life in New York was mostly suspended during the war. Many churches were closed and church property damaged, but Pointer has found that some churches continued to function.[45] This was particularly true in Albany, where the Anglican church was closed and the fledgling Presbyterian and Methodist congregations suspended operation, yet the regular rhythm of Sunday services at the Dutch church persisted. After the crisis over English manners during the British occupation, the Dutch community called Eilardus Westerlo from the University of Groningen. Westerlo apparently healed the schism between young and old within the congregation so effectively that the Common Council awarded him the freedom of the city a year after his arrival.[46] Even though English language and manners gradually spread throughout the community, it was more than twenty years before an English-speaking minister was called to the church to assist the Dutch minister.[47] This indicates that the Dutch language continued to be easily understood by the congregation and that the Dutch townspeople were accustomed to using it in their houses. Westerlo's nickname, "Pope," given to him derisively by British outsiders, suggests their perception of the control he maintained over his congregation. At least until the 1780's, the Albany Dutch remained a coherent and dominant group within the expanding local population.

As the Dutch watched their good, simple, consensual world give way to an evil, complex, and diverse society, confused by conflicting interests, they may have seized the Revolution as an opportunity to revolt against the persistent intrusions of an aggressive British overlord.[48] Traditional Dutch society could account for revolt but not revolution. Like Leisler's rebellion in the 1690's, traditional revolts consisted of mob violence touched off by infringement on communally held privileges. In this earlier rebellion, the townspeople turned their anger on those among them who were developing English contacts and customs. Similarly, the Albany Dutch might have viewed the Revolution as a revolt, now of the entire Dutch community against the forced occupation of the town by the British military and the subsequent wave of European immigrants. Throughout the Revolutionary War, Dominie Westerlo regularly gathered the community's Dutch leaders and their families into the large stone church that continued to stand in the middle of the intersection of the town's two main streets.[49] The pew records show that during the 1760's and 1770's nearly all of the town's Dutch merchants and Common Council members held seats in the church.[50] Here they continued to spend every Sunday morning and afternoon attending two divine services and listening to the eternal message of the Heidelberg catechism. This unvarying Sunday ritual evoked and reinforced their common memory of an idyllic and holy past. As old habits of thought and action became less applicable to new circumstances, the Dutch may have welcomed the Revolution as an opportunity to restore traditional order to their town. Moreover, the departure of British merchants during the Revolution gave them reason to believe they had succeeded.[51] Perhaps for reasons of revolt then, rather than of revolution, Albany's Dutch merchant leaders joined leaders from the town's British and Scotch-Irish ethnic groups to confront their common imperial enemy.[52]

The Social Origins of Nationalism

The specter of the American Revolution first appeared on the local scene in 1766. In January of that year, Albany's representatives to New York's general assembly returned to report a new British tax on newsprint that required a stamp as evidence that the tax was paid. The reaction to this Stamp Act was immediate and violent. On the evening of January 4, a large crowd assembled at a local tavern, formed a court, and demanded that seven men suspected of applying for the post of stamp distributor be brought before them. These men, four British and three Dutch, were awakened from their beds and brought to the tavern. Four admitted applying for the post, three denied it, and all but one, Henry Van Schaick, swore an oath never to serve in the position. The following night a mob of nearly 400, calling themselves for the first time the "Sons of Liberty," marched on and destroyed the interior of Van Schaick's house. After this Van Schaick signed the oath, but then complained of his treatment to the local authorities. Nothing was done. In fact, so sympathetic were the town's leaders to the actions of this mob of Dutch and British townspeople that by the coming summer the British had stationed 200 to 300 troops at the fort to protect the rights of the citizens who remained loyal to the crown on this matter.[53]

Later that year, the participants in this mob action formed an extra-legal organization that they called the "Sons of Liberty." The names of the ninety-two signers of their constitution indicate that this first post-1750's communitywide organization spoke for both the Dutch and British inhabitants. Two-thirds of the signers were Dutch and the other one-third British, reflecting their proportions in the larger community. Many of the Dutch were related to current council members. Five were members of the council and 14 shared the surnames of current city leaders. Moreover, these Dutchmen were wealthier than the average inhabitant, and nearly two-thirds were merchants. In view of the involvement of affluent Dutch merchants well connected to the community's sources of power, it is little wonder that the mob had been able to force suspected British sympathizers to take an oath and, following the incident, receive no punishment from the community's leaders. The British members of the Sons of Liberty also represented their portion of the community. A mixture of both old and new city residents, they were only about one-third as wealthy as their Dutch counterparts, and 70 percent were artisans. Taken together, the Albany Sons of Liberty were also younger men, ranging in age from nineteen to forty-two, with thirty-one being the median. Many of them would serve in city government following the Revolution. Moreover, the constitution they signed underscored the transitional state of the community's social philosophy.[54]

The constitution of the local Sons of Liberty can be seen as both the response of a Dutch mob to the oppression of their overlord and the actions of a younger generation intent not on revolt but on revolution. On the one hand, as has been stated, the very idea of revolution was foreign to traditional Dutch townsmen. They regarded their traditional political system as the foundation for their communal independence. Therefore it would hardly have occurred to them that the people should have a right to alter or abolish it. From this perspective, the actions of the Sons of

Liberty were consistent with the occasional revolts in which traditional townspeople seized power long enough to bring to the attention of their overlord his particular infringement on their privileges. Seeking vindication of their communally held rights and privileges, the document's signers identify the "Stamp Act in particular" as "oppressive" while at the same time assuring the British government "That we have the highest esteem of his most sacred Majesty King George the Third, the Sovereign Protector of our Rights, and the successional by Law established, and will bear true Allegiance to him and his Royal House forever."[55] Like a traditional revolt, the Stamp Act incident alerted the overlord to stop this particular infringement on the community's privileges without directly challenging British control over the town.

On the other hand, this document also suggests that the Sons of Liberty had more than traditional intentions. The fact that the constitution was written at all is evidence that the protesters were already able to think beyond the outbursts of violence characteristic of a traditional mob and engage in long-term planning. The group's preference for majority rule for their organization, a concept wholly foreign to Dutch towns, indicates that they were willing to entertain political ideas that might result in revolutionary changes in the town's government. Their constitution's first article states:

> . . . we will choose from our Body a Committee of thirteen men who are hereby empowered to choose their President and Clerk, to continue as the Committee during good behavior, or till a majority of the Subscribers think proper to call for a new choice . . . we shall thereupon give public notice for a new Election, with all convenient speed.[56]

Although this was the plan of government for this mixed group of young British artisans and Dutch merchants and not for the community as a whole, it does reflect some of the new thinking of Abraham Yates and his followers, who were clamoring for an overhaul of government by the privileged few. The varied reasons that distinguished the thinking of the Sons of Liberty further suggest the different motives that likely characterized Albany's widespread support for the American Revolution.

*   *   *

The external threat of war forced the people of Albany to find a new basis for unity within a dividing community. As British-colonial tensions erupted into war, Albany's townspeople revealed the persistence of their traditional habits by turning once again to their patriarchs to guide them through this crisis. After the Battle of Lexington in April 1775, the townspeople were asked to elect a local Committee of Correspondence. This complied with a resolution of the Continental Congress recommending the appointment of committees of correspondence to protect the political welfare of the colonies. Given the opportunity to select their own representatives, the city's freeholders elected mostly church elders. Abraham Yates was elected, but he was joined by more than a dozen men who served at one time as leaders within their Dutch, Anglican,[57] and Presbyterian churches.[58] Each congregation maintained a distinction between merchants and artisans in their selection of religious leaders. This interethnic federation of merchant-elders acted as a mediator between the local community and the national war effort, collecting and forwarding supplies for the army, providing for refugees, attending political conventions, and enforcing local laws.[59] These duties inevitably involved extra-local relationships that were justified in terms of the national mobilization. The first communitywide recognition of this new nationalism came as a result of the effort to discover and send out of the county all inhabitants who were sympathetic to the British.

To identify these Tories, the Committee of Correspondence created an oath of allegiance that articulated a new basis for community membership. The few British merchants and Dutch sympathizers who refused to sign were shunned by the townspeople, then jailed, and finally banished. This oath changed the traditional basis of community membership from Dutch ethnicity and Dutch church membership to American citizenship and belief in God. Its critical passages included the following:

> PERSUADED that the salvation of the Rights and Liberties of America depends under God on the firm Union of its Inhabitants. . . . We the Freemen, Freeholders and Inhabitants of the City and County of Albany. . . . Do in the most Solemn Manner resolve never to become Slaves; and do associate under all the Ties of Religion, Honour, and Love to our Country.[60]

Every inhabitant was asked to reach beyond local and ethnic political and religious bonds to affirm their common national and religious ties.

Following the Revolution, new civil rituals sanctified the bonds of this new union. The primary carriers of Albany's new commitment to America were the members of the Common Council, who were also leaders of the community's Dutch (74 percent), Presbyterian (13 percent), and Anglican (13 percent) churches.[61] Despite their obvious differences in ethnicity and religious affiliation, most of these men served together on the Committee of Correspondence or in the local militia during the war. They were repeatedly elected to the Council by a similarly heterogeneous population who also held in common Albany's experience of the Revolution. As supporters of the nation, Albany's leaders came together as Americans and Christians, not as Albanians or members of particular churches. Together they believed in the "liberty of America" and the need to unite under the leadership of God.

Annual Fourth of July rituals enacted and affirmed the community's common American and Christian ties. These day-long rites combined the traditional military parade and dinner toasts to the king on his birthday with an interdenominational church service. On a typical Albany Fourth of July:

> The day was announced by a morning gun. At sunrise the bells commenced their loud peels, and continued for half an hour—the musicians at the same time paraded through the principal streets, performing several pieces of martial music. At 9:30 the citizens assembled at the City Hall—the military escort in front of Wendell's Tavern—and at 10:30 marched to the City Hall, and lined the way to the Dutch Church. The Procession then formed and moved to the church as follows: Sheriff, Marshall, Constables; Common Council; Governor and Cabinet; Judges—Supreme Court and Common Pleas; Clergy; Military Officers; Law Society; Citizens and Strangers.[62]

The church in which this liturgy took place varied from year to year. Usually more than one local clergyman presided, and a regular order of worship, including a reading of the Declaration of Independence followed by a sermon, was followed. The procession then marched through the principal streets and returned to City Hall. There a "Federal Salute" was fired by the military, three cheers were given "by the whole assemblage of citizens" as "the church bells continued to peel." That evening, in a custom formerly used to honor the king on his birthday, the governor invited the members of the Common Council and the "most respectable" citizens to a dinner during which 14 patriotic toasts were given. The highlight of these rites was the clergyman's sermon. On these solemn occasions, the town's religious leaders articulated the community's new faith in the nation.

In the first Fourth of July sermon published in Albany,[63] the Dutch minister John Barent Johnson drew an analogy between God's liberation of Israel and the role God played in America's struggle for independence.[64]

> As Jehovah not only broke the chains and secured the liberty of his ancient people, but also gave them a name among nations; so we can call to mind his

providential interference in those measures which led to the establishment of our Independence.[65]

America was the promised land for Albany's European settlers. God had led His people to establish a new nation. By this "wonderful interposition of the God of Battles, in our behalf," Johnson continued, a "purer" form of church participation became possible through the separation of church and state. No longer was Christianity's beauty to be "tarnished, and its purity polluted by an illegitimate connexion with the state."[66] God's liberation of America freed Americans as a people and as Christians. As Americans, they were free from British colonial rule; as Christians, they were free to worship according to the precepts of God and the dictates of their own conscience. To maintain this "two-fold liberty," Johnson warned, Albany's heterogeneous people had to come together as a "firm and united band of brothers . . . and inculcate the principle of UNION as the rock of our political salvation."[67] To do this they needed to "cultivate wisdom and practice religion," for this was the "best security and essential support of republican governments."[68] In conclusion, the Dutch minister declared that Americans now needed to carry out actively God's will on earth. During the two decades after the Revolution, the ministers of Albany's leading churches emphasized this pressing need for political unity that required the support of denominational worship and the active participation of Americans in carrying out the will of God.[69]

Johnson's sermon, and others like it, provided a religious context within which Albany's leaders could come to terms with their new political reality. On the local level, the struggle to secure American liberty had meant a struggle for a no longer homogeneous community to find a new basis for unity. In colonial Dutch Albany's Calvinist world view, God's will had entailed resistance to all efforts to change the community's traditional and homogeneous way of life. The town's political leaders had worked closely with their brother church elders to resist the imposition of "foreign" elements. The liberation of America, however, brought a reversal of these traditional values. As God had led Americans to independence so, too, had He led Albany's diverse inhabitants to embrace one another in civil unity. A common identity as Americans and Christians therefore replaced Dutch ethnicity and Dutch church membership as the moral foundation for community order. After the war, the traditional alliance between Common Council members and church elders continued. The community leaders, however, were no longer from the same ethnic background, nor did they worship at the same church.

Even more striking is the contrast between the attitudes of the earlier Dutch and these postwar leaders toward the establishment of new churches. Rather than resisting all efforts that further dissolved the community's Dutch homogeneity, the still largely Dutch Common Council members saw the establishment of new churches as the best way to promote the common religious bonds of an increasingly diverse population. Between 1780 and 1800 the Common Council willingly gave city land for the construction of new Presbyterian, Methodist, and Dutch church buildings.[70] Moreover, Common Council members and religious leaders were prominent in their financial support of denominations other than their own.[71] Unlike the town's colonial Dutch leaders, who resisted all threats to the homogeneity of their people and the monopoly of their single, established church, the advocates of Albany's new civil faith encouraged the political unity of ethnically diverse peoples and supported the establishment of new churches.

Out of these social circumstances Albany's new commitment to the nation was born. A once homogeneous community was overcome by a wave of new immigrants who precipitated a local political crisis. This crisis was temporarily resolved during the Revolutionary War and its aftermath when the basis of community membership was redefined to include people of different ethnic backgrounds and churches. After the Revolution, the responsibility for the welfare of the whole community passed from the church to the town. When the Dutch moved their house of worship away from the onslaught of Yankee wagons passing through the center of town on their way west, this also signaled the withdrawal of their care for every community member. By the end of the century, the traditionally Dutch responsibility for the community's poor was taken over by a subcommittee of the Common Council known as the Overseers of the Poor.[72] The town, now larger than and distinct from the Dutch community, became responsible for the welfare of the community as a whole. Thus, in lieu of the identification of the political sphere with a particular church, the new nationalism provided unity in Albany by incorporating traditional religious functions into a newly separated political sphere and by broadening the moral basis of unity to include multiple denominations. As late as 1820, this new Christian American identity had not supplanted the inhabitants' divergent Dutch, English, Scotch-Irish, and Yankee identities.[73] This ideology, however, did give the town's people a national identity that linked the town to other American communities. Finally, the new civil faith, while not arresting social trends that threatened to split the community, did provide the townspeople with a common theological and political language, rituals, and symbols within which to articulate their differences.

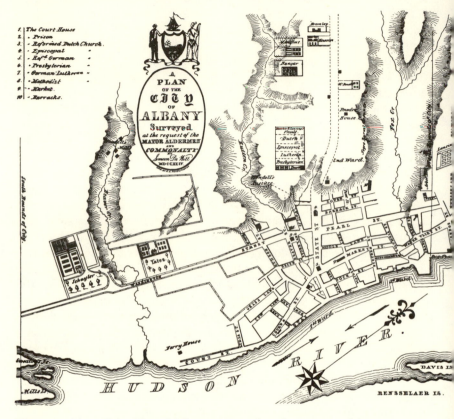

1. The Court House
2. Prison
3. Reformed Dutch Church
4. Episcopal
5. Ref.ᵈ German
6. Presbyterian
7. German Lutheran
8. Methodist
9. Market
10. Barracks

A PLAN OF THE CITY OF ALBANY Surveyed at the request of the MAYOR ALDERMEN AND COMMONALTY Simeon De Witt MDCCXCIV

Figure 5. Plan of the City of Albany, surveyed at the request of the mayor, aldermen, and commonality by Simeon DeWitt in 1794. (The Albany Institute of History and Art, McKinney Library Map Collection.)

Chapter 3

The Yankee Invasion

It was at the age of eighteen, and in the autumn of the year eighteen hundred, that I first set my foot within the precincts of the ancient and far-famed city of Albany. . . . I had then just launched my "light untimbered bark" upon the ocean of life; with no guide but Providence, and with no hand but my own to direct its course. Never shall I forget the deep feeling of loneliness that came over me when the receding headlands of my native bay disappeared in the distance, and I found myself, for the first time in my life, alone on the waters.[1]

After the Revolution, New Englanders migrated to the west of the Appalachians. Most of these immigrants did not find their mooring in Albany. Many had no intention of staying but merely passed through, at a rate as high as several hundred each day,[2] to the newly secure farmlands to the west. Between 1779 and 1799 the town lost two-thirds of its residents, but they were more than doubly replaced by an ever-changing stream of transients.[3] From 1790 to 1820 Albany's population increased nearly four-fold, from 3490 to 12,630.[4] By 1820, the Dutch accounted for no more than 5 percent of the inhabitants.[5] A new Yankee merchant and manufacturing elite rode to prosperity on this wave of western migration. Yankee shops and stores lined the main streets, warehouses dominated the riverfront, and factories rose on the outskirts of town. Prior to the Revolution, the Dutch lived within a tightly knit, relatively static society; after the Revolution, the town's Americans passed through a bewildering era of accelerating mobility and economic expansion.

By the end of the eighteenth century, the old way of life had deteriorated badly. The Dutch were asked to divide their allegiance between their church and the city as a whole. At the same time, they were encouraged to welcome ethnically different neighbors and passing strangers. Despite evangelization from the community's postwar leaders, the immediate effect of the new nationalism on the religious life of the Dutch was a decline in church attendance and growing indifference. The collective restraint of the Dutch merchants was similarly overwhelmed by the economic innovations of immigrant entrepreneurs. The continuing erosion of the communal meaning of liberty was tangibly manifest, moreover, in the emigration of one third of the Dutch townspeople, appeals for the return of runaway slaves, apprentices, and even merchants, and Anti-Federalist demands for individual rights. None of these issues were resolved during the 20 years following the Revolution; instead, a quest for social and cultural identity began and would continue at least until the 1830's.

The pervasive malaise in the lives of the Dutch contrasted with the tightly harnessed energies of the new Presbyterians. Following the war, those new immigrants who were able to join a church were twice as likely to establish themselves in the community. Throughout the last two decades of the eighteenth century, no more than half of Albany's inhabitants were members of congregations. Church members, however, accounted for more than two-thirds of the city residents who remained in the community.[6] Many of these new people who were able to remain in the community found solace for their loneliness in the Presbyterian church and an anchor for their enterprise in the dozens of new shops and stores that catered to their passing countrymen. Between 1785 and the mid-1790's, the members of Albany's Presbyterian church were largely Scotch-Irish immigrants.[7] Driven by anxiety over their salvation, as Max Weber argues, yet also concerned with their economic survival, these foreigners managed to establish themselves in the town rapidly. Then, with the flood of Yankee craftsmen and shopkeepers and the more hopeful theology of a Connecticut minister, the Presbyterian church emerged as the leading denomination in a decidedly Yankee town.

Religious Life in the 1790's

In contrast with the consensus view of American religious historians, who have consistently described the postwar era as one of spiritual decline, yet different too from Richard Pointer's recent depiction of postwar denominational life in New York as marked by an energetic response to the new religious situation, religious life in Albany during the 1790's was marked by both malaise and new energy.[8] Throughout the 1790's the Dutch church remained the wealthiest and most prestigious congregation, but it was crippled by internal disputes over the use of the English language and remained turned inward toward itself. The Episcopal church, in contrast, showed clear signs of reorganization and growth, yet suffered from a lingering ethnic prejudice. Class prejudice was evident in the attitude of the town's leaders toward the Methodist church, founded in 1792. It remained a small congregation of less affluent immigrants at least until 1810. In contrast, First Presbyterian attracted most of the new immigrants who joined churches in the 1790's and led in the development of a moderate Calvinist theology better able to adapt to the changing environment.

Only with great reluctance did Albany's Dutch church members sever their ecclesial and linguistic ties to their home country. In 1787, the Albany church was among the last five Dutch Reformed congregations to join the new ecclesiastically self-sufficient American governing body. Ever since the early eighteenth-century emergence among some of the Dutch clergy of a movement in support of native trained ministers and a substantial transfer of authority to the colonies, Albany's church elders had consistently voted against any attempt to weaken their religious bonds to the Netherlands. Dominie Westerlo did not speak English from the pulpit until 1780, and then only in a separate English language morning service that he followed with an afternoon service in Dutch.[9] Following Westerlo's resignation due to ill health in 1790 and continuing at least until 1805, bitter debates over the adoption of the English language pitted an influential minority of older members from the most prominent families against a rising generation.[10] During this period, church membership declined and several prominent Dutchmen became members of the new Episcopal and Presbyterian churches.[11] In contrast to the new ecumenical spirit of the town's civic leaders, the congregation gave only minimal support to a new, immigrant-inspired academy that responded to a newly perceived need for higher education. The church was also reluctant to support the community's poor, directing most if its alms to a newly formed "charity school" intended only for the poor members of their church. Finally, Dutch members of the Common Council manifested their continuing resentment toward the British by using legal maneuvers to harass the Episcopal congregation in their attempt to move their church building. In 1805 the Albany church signaled the waning importance of their Dutch heritage by calling a non-Dutch-speaking, Brown University-trained, Presbyterian minister to their pulpit. At least until the end of the eighteenth century, however, Albany's Dutch congregation remained divided by cultural and generational disputes and turned inward toward itself.[12]

St. Peter's Episcopal Church, although hampered by lingering Dutch prejudice, adapted more quickly to the new situation. Following the war, the Episcopal church in America moved rapidly to gain ecclesial independence from the Church of England and to identify itself with the new republic's political principles. The Episcopalians established a representative national body and, in 1785, this body altered the church liturgy to make it consistent with state constitutions, outlined plans to secure the consecration of bishops, and adopted a constitution proclaiming the freedom of their congregations from all foreign authority. In 1787 The Reverend Thomas Ellison became the rector at St. Peter's and found in his small congregation of 30 communicants a number of influential men who had served as community leaders during the war. In 1790 the congregation adopted the new liturgy and prayer book of the American Episcopal Church.[13] The statistics for 1787 to 1792 show that the church was growing rapidly, there were 219 baptisms and 50 marriages.[14] The Reverend Ellison was also an early proponent of education, tutoring several pupils for college, including James Fennimore Cooper, and leading his congregation's efforts to establish an academy. Despite these signs of growth and reorganization, Ellison also reported that "the prejudice of the generality of people (was) running very high against our Church." This prejudice was manifest in the resistance, particularly on the part of the Dutch members of the Common Council, to the vestry's desire to move the church building to a location where it could expand. Ellison noted that the Common Council had willingly granted city land without charge to the Dutch, Presbyterian, and Methodist churches and made promises to the Catholics, yet did not make a comparable offer to the Episcopalians, leaving them to pay for their new land.[15] These anti-English sentiments seem to have diminished by the early 1800's, as the growing congregation continued to welcome influential community members into its communion.[16]

Class rather than ethnic prejudice hampered the development of Methodism in Albany. In 1792, Albany's first Methodist Society was founded. By 1811 it remained a small congregation of less than one hundred journeymen, shopkeepers and laborers.[17] Despite the city fathers' public actions of support for the Methodists by providing them with free public land for their church, rarely did the names of their ministers appear alongside the names of the Dutch, Episcopal and Presbyterian ministers among the leaders of the first ecumenical organizations. The two instances when this did occur, in 1795 when a list of trustees was proposed for Union

College[18] and in 1813 when a similar list was proposed for the Albany Academy,[19] seem to have been efforts to demonstrate ecumenism to the state legislature rather than to share power with the Methodists. The names of Methodist ministers do not appear elsewhere in the proceedings of these institutions. The new church also was internally troubled by a series of financial "embarrassments" surrounding the construction of their church and support of their ministers, as well as reversals in their membership due to migration and the widely diverging effectiveness of itinerant preachers.[20] Not until at least the second decade of the nineteenth century would Methodism secure a solid foothold in Albany. In contrast, after the Revolution, Albany's Presbyterian church grew rapidly in wealth and numbers to become the most influential church in town.

Presbyterians

For most of this century, Max Weber's *The Protestant Ethic and the Spirit of Capitalism* has provided the point of departure for debates over the relationship between religion and the rise of capitalism.[21] The outcome of these discussions depends on the relative importance of cultural as opposed to economic factors in social change. Weber's point of view resisted economic reductionism and argued for the independent significance of religious ideas. Briefly, Weber held that there was an "elective affinity" between Calvin's doctrine of predestination and rational capitalism. This doctrine, which states that people can do nothing to assure their salvation, resulted in feelings of "inner loneliness." Believers in predestination, Weber argued, dealt with their anxiety by devoting themselves to their "calling." This was the concept that the highest form of moral obligation was to fulfill one's duty in worldly affairs. Weber juxtaposed this religious attitude with the Calvinist practice of rational capitalism. Unlike previous approaches to economic gain, he argued that Calvinists made their money with a disciplined work force and the regular investment of capital. And, unlike previous merchants, Calvinists lived frugal lives, reinvesting rather than indulging in their growing wealth. The simultaneous appearance of Calvin's doctrine of predestination and rational capitalism led Weber to conclude that Calvinism ignited a form of economic activity that ultimately led to industrial capitalism. Moreover, this affinity set in motion a process whereby Calvinists came to see economic prosperity as a sign of Christian salvation.

The experience of Albany's Calvinist Presbyterians conflicts with the

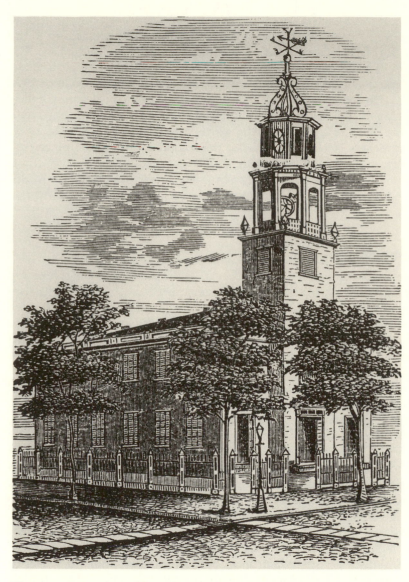

Figure 6. Engraving of First Presbyterian Church. (Collection of the Albany Institute of History and Art. Bequest of Ledyard Cogswell, Jr.)

construal of "independence" of religious ideas in Weber's thesis yet sustains his more general contention that an intimate connection existed between Calvinism and capitalism.[22] Certainly these immigrants may have experienced an "inner loneliness" in response to the precarious state of their religious salvation, and this, in turn, may have motivated their innovative economic activity. But the large and wealthy Dutch congregation subscribed to the same orthodox teachings and, after the war, the Dutch did not demonstrate a similar burst of innovative economic activity. Unlike the Dutch church, however, Albany's Presbyterian congregation was not the established church of the community. It did not draw its members from the city's wealthy, long-term residents. Instead, the Scotch-Irish immigrants who joined the Presbyterian church immediately after the war were primarily poor young men and women struggling to become a part of a foreign community filled with transient strangers. The "outer loneliness" they experienced in working to secure their physical survival must have been as acute as the "inner loneliness" they experienced as children of a wrathful God. The new immigrants who sought to become members of the Presbyterian church were required to submit to a far greater discipline and moral scrutiny. The extreme discipline needed to manage one's economic affairs in order to survive as a stranger in a hostile town paralleled the rigid moral discipline demanded for one's spiritual salvation. When both the religious ideas and the social circumstances of Albany's Presbyterians are considered, the experience of these young Scotch-Irish immigrants seems to have a close empirical fit with Weber's more general theoretical argument. But religious ideas were not an independent factor. The problems of economic survival and religious salvation confronted by Albany's immigrant Presbyterians worked together to transform the economic life of the town.

We can begin to understand the economic problems faced by these Scotch-Irish immigrants by considering the experience of one young Ulsterman whose name was given to his grandson, the philosopher William James. In 1789, eighteen-year-old William James joined the immigrants from northern Ireland who were searching for a new life in America. With no capital or family connections to aid his start in business, James began his career in Albany as a store clerk. He owed his job perhaps to his elementary education and the Scotch-Irish background he held in common with the store's owner.[23]

Like the population as a whole, throughout the 1790's Albany's business world was constantly expanding while the identity of local shopkeepers and store owners was continually changing. The local newspaper advertisements indicate that the traditional general merchants were rapidly being replaced by more specialized businessmen and manufacturers. These new enterprises more actively took advantage of opportunities to expand local trade.[24] At the same time, partnerships among family members and within ethnic groups were forming and dissolving to create capital to take advantage of this economic growth.[25] One visitor described the Albany marketplace in 1789, the year of William James' arrival, as "an unsociable place" which, he explained, was to be expected: "A heterogeneous collection of people, invested with all their national prejudices, eager in the pursuit of gain, and jealous of rivalship, can not expect to enjoy the pleasures of social intercourse or the sweets of an intimate and refined friendship."[26] Like those of his fellow immigrants who were able to survive in this harsh and demanding marketplace, William James must have been industrious and thrifty. After two years as a clerk, he became a tobacco merchant. He then increased his profits by manufacturing his own tobacco products. Two years later James expanded into the produce business, locating his second store near the water to facilitate the unloading of crops. Next, in 1800, he opened another store with his partner Francis McCabe. In another five years he was trading across the ocean with Ireland.[27] James' business career exemplifies the innovative ideas and economic drive of the Albany Scotch-Irish.

These new business practices contrasted sharply with those of the Dutch merchants. Customarily, they dealt in a variety of goods that came up the river on sloops, selling them to the surrounding farmers in exchange for their grain. Unlike William James and the new merchants, the Dutch continued to use New York City middlemen to purchase European goods. This practice was noted by a visitor in 1795.

> The trade of Albany is very safe, but seems not to be very profitable . . . the ancient customs and confined views of the timid yet covetous Dutchmen, have carefully been preserved in this city. No ship sails from Albany directly to Europe; and yet provision is sent thither from this place. It is evident that, if the inhabitants would take themselves the trouble of exporting their produce, they would save useless interest, and return-freight, and double commission, and would obtain employment for their ships during the time when the navigation to the north is shut up by ice. As ideas of this complexion begin to dawn upon the minds of some merchants, and will no doubt, (they will) produce advantageous changes.[28]

Further criticism was leveled at the local practice of relying on others to produce domestic goods. As recently as the 1780's, one townsperson remarked that Albanians did not have "manufactories of any kind, but depended on importation entirely for every manufactured article."[29] In contrast to the timid practices of the Dutch, William James' generation of merchants parlayed their more rational approach to economic activity into growing fortunes.

Diligence was essential both for worldly success and spiritual salvation. When he abandoned Ireland, William James brought with him a deep conviction of the merits of hard work. His life demonstrated a willingness to leave family and native land, embark on a hazardous ocean voyage, and build a life in the transient mercantile world of Albany. Shortly after his arrival, James was admitted to the Presbyterian church. There he joined a growing enclave of fellow countrymen who willingly submitted to a rigid spiritual discipline that shaped their moral lives while providing a catalyst for their growing worldly welfare.

Albany's immigrant Scotch-Irish joined a church whose merchant leaders had assimilated to the town's pre-Revolutionary way of life. Most of the church's leaders at the time of its re-establishment after the war were Scotch-Irish merchants who had come to Albany before or during the Revolution. Like the merchant-elders of the Dutch church, these Presbyterian leaders were older men who were among the wealthiest 10 percent of the community. A majority served at one time or another on the Common Council, and they shared with all long-term Albanians the experience of the Revolution.[30] In contrast to their leaders, men in the postwar Presbyterian congregation were primarily young adults with, at best, average means and artisan skills who came to Albany after the Revolution.[32] In 1785, 200 of these new immigrants petitioned the Common Council for the use of the abandoned military barracks "to shelter themselves in the Course of this Winter."[31] After the congregation's first communion in 1787, an average of fifteen new members were admitted every six months for the next six years. Many of these young immigrants married within five years after their arrival.[33] In July 1787 the church's leaders called to their pulpit the Scotland-trained Reverend John McDonald, who later recalled that the congregation was "poor, few in numbers, and miserably divided in sentiments and habits." On his departure ten years later, however, they were "in perfect harmony with each other, numerous and extensively respectable."[34] The rigid discipline imposed by the church's leaders helps to account for this change.

Both the Presbyterian and the Dutch churches were founded on the principles of Calvinism. The Presbyterian's Westminster catechism was nearly identical to the Dutch church's Heidelberg catechism and held a similarly central place in the religious education of young and old. Knowledge of the religious principles in the Westminster catechism was essential for Presbyterian church membership. New leaders of the church were examined as to their "resolution in God's strength to support and defend [these principles] against innovation."[35] Unlike the Dutch church, however, Albany's Presbyterian congregation was not the established church of the community. The discipline that the Presbyterian leaders exerted over their poor, immigrant congregation was more severe than the moral supervision of the Dutch church leaders. Moreover, the evidence of piety demanded for admission to communion in the Presbyterian church was in the Dutch congregation required only of those who were chosen for church leadership. Although similar in their religious principles and teachings, these two churches held different social positions in the community. For new immigrants to gain admission to a new immigrant church, they had to submit to a greater discipline and moral scrutiny than those who were already established in the town.

It was as hard for a newcomer to be admitted to the Presbyterian church as it was to remain in the town. In the fall of 1788, for example, twenty-two people applied: twelve were admitted, but nine were postponed.[36] Successful applicants were those who demonstrated to the "Session" (a term used to refer to the governing board of elders, the deacons, and the minister) sufficient knowledge of the doctrine, worship, and discipline of the Established Church of Scotland and gave evidence of sufficient piety, which referred to "the influence of religion on (one's) determination to study an exemplary life in (one's) public deportment and private carriage."[37]

The Christian values that these new immigrants were taught to embrace responded to other-worldly concerns. In his sermon "The Faithful Steward,"[38] Mr. McDonald told his congregation that the church was separate from the world and "subject to her own peculiar laws." It would not admit to its communion, "regardless of talents and possesions, the openly immoral and even those whose reputation labours under suspicion." Rather than look to worldly abilities and wealth as measures of religious salvation, McDonald told his congregation to devote themselves to the "Mysteries of God" and warned them of "the absolute necessity of regeneration, through union to the Son of God." Only regenerated Christians were admitted to communion. Such people displayed "a humble, self-denied walk" that was the "fruit of a meek and lowly spirit." They avoided even "the most distant appearance of levity, of affection, of carelessness, or of influencibility in expression or deportment."

Conformity to this ascetic ideal was rigidly reinforced. In addition to the practice common to the Dutch congregation whereby the minister visited each family once a year, the Presbyterian elders divided the town into four sections; one of the four elders was responsible for the church members in each of these divisions. The elders were required to visit each of their families at least once every month in order to "stir up the [people in] diligence and duty both public and private, crushing every cause of strife, warning them of danger, and exciting their attention to the education of youth."[39] Every month the Session met to hear reports from each division; the trial of offenders against the discipline of the church often consumed the largest portion of these meetings. The most frequent charges included: absence from public worship, violation of promises, severity in the collection of money, unchristian language, and "scandal" (sexual immortality). The usual penalty was suspension from the privilege of communion.[40]

Albany's immigrant Presbyterians believed that the sacrament of communion "preserved a distinction between the children of Christ and the slaves of Satan."[41] Communion was only administered twice a year, and then only to church members whom the elders deemed worthy to participate. These people received tokens at the "preparation" service on the Thursday prior to the liturgy. This procedure allowed the elders publicly to separate the moral from the immoral, casting those suspended into a purgatory of public opinion.[42] The Session penalized those who offended church discipline, but they did not regard those on suspension as outside of the church. They continued to keep a careful watch over them, often appointing a committee to bring them to repentance. Most of those accused of transgressions eventually admitted their sins to the elders and, if the sin was considered quite serious (e.g., "prenuptial fornication"), to the entire congregation. Usually they were then restored to full standing in the church. If they continued on a course of sin, not heeding the admonition and entreaties of their elder, they were warned of excommunication. If they proved utterly unrepentant, the Session proceeded to cast them out of God's church and into the urban wilderness of a foreign town. Under such strict supervision, it was almost impossible for anyone to be guilty of immoralities without the fact becoming known to church leaders. Moreover, as the Session minutes attest, it was similarly difficult for anyone to remain in the town for any length of time after committing a sin against church discipline and continually refusing to repent.[43]

The Session also watched over the preaching of the pulpit. In 1798, for example, a visiting minister was accused of promulgating unsound doctrine. A committee of the Session was appointed to present a report to the area Presbytery that claimed that

> Mr. Camp positively denied the doctrine of imputed guilt asserting that man became guilty of Adam's sins by approving it and not otherwise, which Mr. Camp illustrated by observing that it is in the same manner we become guilty of murder if we as spectators to the perpetration of murder approve of it.[44]

The debate over humanity's responsibility for Adam's original sin would soon be joined by the new Yankee congregants. Prior to that time, Albany's immigrant Scotch-Irish elders defended and protected the teachings of their church in the same way that they guarded over the moral behavior of their flock.

At the same time that the Scotch-Irish were keeping close watch over their "inner" lives, the discipline the men displayed in their "outer" commercial lives influenced their economic prosperity and contributed to the transformation of the community's traditional business practices. A comparison of the 1779 and 1799 tax lists shows that the median tax paid by the Presbyterian congregation as a whole rose from the fifty-third to the sixty-eighth percentile in comparison to the overall population. Moreover, the median tax on the 1799 list for new Presbyterian immigrants whose names first appear on the 1790 census places them in the sixty-ninth percentile of the population.[45] Innovative business practices contributed to this economic prosperity. William James' career demonstrates the cycle of expanding growth and capital reinvestment that was characteristic of these newcomers. His decisions to open a store closer to the unloading of ships at the water's edge, manufacture his own products, and engage in the transatlantic trade were similarly characteristic and radical departures from Albany's traditional business practices. But what of Weber's thesis? Clearly, religious ideas alone were not responsible for this rational capitalist activity; still, what can be said about the relationship of the Presbyterian's "inner loneliness" and their economic growth and innovation? The recollections of William James' son Henry suggest their interdependence.

In his "autobiographical sketches" Henry James indicted the severe religious atmosphere of his Albany boyhood because it lacked "any ideal of action but that of self-preservation."[46] Religion was presented to him as nothing more than a "higher prudence" whose sole purpose was "physical security." Orthodox Calvinism was "the curse of the worldly mind, as of the civic or political state to which it affords a material base." And, at the same time, it was "the curse of the religious mind, as of the ecclesiastical forms to which it furnishes a spiritual base." This was because "they both alike constitute their own ideal, or practically ignore any ulterior Divine end." For Henry James the "outer" and "inner" disciplines of his father's people were directed toward the same end of self-preservation.[47]

In an analysis reminiscent of Max Weber's, Henry James argued that when the child's natural instincts are violently suppressed or driven inward by some overpowering outward authority, a moral feverishness is sure to follow. The unintended result was a premature sense of himself as an individual maintaining moral transactions with God.

> It prematurely forced my manhood, or gave it a hotbed development, by imposing upon my credulous mind the fiction of a natural estrangement between me and God. My sense of individuality, my feeling of myself as a power endowed with the mastery of my own actions, was prematurely vitalized by my being taught to conceive myself capable of a direct—that is of a personal or moral—commerce with the most High.[48]

By placing "the child in a bargaining or huckstering attitude toward God," James concluded, the rigidly enforced moral dogmas of his childhood yielded one of two practical results: "either to make the child insufferably conceited, or else to harden him in indifference to the Divine name."[49] You either kept your accounts in such a way that you always believed yourself to be in God's favor, or you protected yourself by becoming indifferent to orthodox moral discipline. By the early nineteenth century, a more moderate Calvinist theology emerged from this by then Yankee dominated congregation. This new moral thinking moved Calvinism closer to accepting the ideals of the surrounding society by subsuming them within a religious world view. Hence, religious salvation inevitably came to be measured in more worldly terms.

A Yankee Town

Between 1790 and 1810 Albany's population increased nearly threefold as more than 9000 immigrants, most of them New Englanders, moved into town.[50] Coming primarily from the hill towns of western Connecticut and Massachusetts, most of these newcomers had for some time lived outside the institutions of traditional society[51] and tended to view the Dutch as a primitive people. Like William James and the other Scotch-Irish who arrived before them, the Yankees came with ambition. Unlike their Presbyterian predecessors, they claimed more liberty for themselves and allowed less power to traditional authority.

That quintessential Yankee Timothy Dwight, then president of Yale College and arguably the best-known man in Connecticut, offered these remarks on the changes that had taken place in Albany between his visit there in 1792 and after the arrival of the first wave of Yankees in the mid-1790's.

> . . . an essential change has taken place in Albany. A considerable number of the opulent inhabitants, whose minds were enlarged by the influence of the Revolutionary War, and the extensive intercourse which it produced among them and their countrymen, and still more by education, and travelling, have resolutely broken through a set of traditionary customs, venerable by age, and strong by universal attachment. These gentlemen have built many handsome houses in the modern English style; and in their furniture, manners, and mode of living, have adopted the English customs. To this important change the strangers, who within a few years have become a numerous body of the inhabitants, have extensively contributed. All these, from whatever country derived, have chosen to build, and live, in the English manner. . . . Within two generations there will probably be no distinction between the descendants of the different nations.[52]

Dwight went on to attribute the "traditionary customs" of Albany inhabitants to the mores of the Dutch families who, "until within a few years ago," were the sole inhabitants of the city. What he identified as traditionally Dutch were the muddy streets, in which his wagon was once "fairly mired," and the houses with their "high, sharp roofs, small windows and low ceilings. The appearance of which is ordinary, dull, and disagreeable." Dwight also disapproved of the indolence of the Dutch merchants, "[who are] regularly seen sitting in a most phlegmatic composure on the porch, and smoking with great deliberation from morning to night."

These external signs were symptoms of moral problems. As this Connecticut minister explained:

> Uncouth, mean, ragged, dirty houses constituting the body of any town, will regularly be accompanied by coarse grovelling manners. . . . On the inhabitants of such a town it will be difficult if not impossible to work a conviction that intelligence is either necessary or useful. Generally they will regard both learning and science with contempt. Of morals, except in the coarsest form, and that which has the least influence on the heart, they will scarcely have any apprehensions.[53]

Thus, Dwight believed that Albany's Dutch people practiced a primitive form of morality. In contrast, the "improvements" that his countrymen engineered in the town would amount to a loosening of traditional structures.[54] Ambitious young immigrants could no longer be restrained by the town's colonial social institutions. In politics, the economy, and religion, human energies had to be given a larger arena.

This conflict between individual and traditional authority had found its initial release in political agitation. Since the 1760's, Abraham Yates and his less affluent, non-Dutch partisans had employed political ideas derived from New England town meetings to advocate a democratic form of government responsive to the needs of the "common man." After the Revolution, they formed themselves into the Anti-Federalist Party and stepped up their campaign against wealthy aristocrats, whom they accused of using illegitimate hereditary powers to enrich themselves and their friends.[55] The town's leaders, in contrast, mocked this lack of propriety and restraint and attributed it to a want of virtuous principles. Candidates from their Federalist Party were put forward as men of "unblemished virtue" and "respectable abilities" who were "friends of order" and "supporters of religion."[56] Matters came to a head in 1789 when an Anti-Federalist riot disrupted a parade in support of the passage of the Federal Constitution.[57] Although the merchant-elders would remain in power into the next century, the arrival of new immigrants further weakened the colonial understanding of political authority.

Leadership, like liberty, now took on more than one meaning. The familiar belief in the derivation of political authority from God was retained; at the same time, emphasis shifted from the subject's obligation to obey to the ruler's obligation to serve. The ruler was a helper as much as a disciplinarian and should respond to public need. This new understanding reached all the way into the meetings of the Consistory of the Dutch church where, in 1794, several members of the congregation startled the elders with the advice that they were "to acquiesce to the opinion of the majority."[58] Similarly confusing was the tendency to understand liberty as freedom from restraint. Symptomatic of this change were the ubiquitous newspaper advertisements for runaway slaves, servants, apprentices, and even merchants who no longer felt a responsibility to meet their obligations but instead joined the westward rush to freedom and prosperity.[59] The traditional formula for political order was still being offered, but new understandings rendered it less effective.

The conflict between ambition and traditional economic restraints forced an even more far-reaching reappraisal. Traditionally, Dutch merchants controlled the local economy for the benefit of the community as a whole. In the colonial period, they controlled the fur trade and screened those who sought admission to trading privileges. At the same time, the leading merchants customarily paid extraordinary civic expenses as well as more than half of the usual costs incurred by the town. The forced dissolution of the Dutch trade monopoly that began in the 1760's had by 1800 eroded the traditional concern for the community from the marketplace and replaced it with various schemes based on self-interest.

Through benevolent self-interest Albanians hoped to get along together and direct their individual energies toward a collective economic growth that would benefit their society as a whole. The following letter to the Albany newspaper in 1791 suggests this kind of moral thinking.

> . . . of all the qualities of the human mind, its liberality is one of the most amiable . . . Mutual good will—a reciprocity of offices, and a liberal indulgence of each others peculiarities, habits, and foibles, are indispensable ingredients in forming a system of either domestic or public happiness. . . .[60]

Such appeals to the "liberality of the mind" were used to bid for harmony among the city's inhabitants. Social harmony, in turn, would allow everyone to pursue their economic ambitions for the benefit of the community as a whole.

What is most striking about Albany's economy at the turn of the century is how it used this new moral thinking to develop a new relationship with the political order. Prior to the Yankee invasion, the Common Council resisted economic innovations that undercut their traditional authority.[61] As late as 1794, a new Yankee immigrant charged that the Common Council was not moving the city "along as fast as it might."

> Our progress must and will go hand in hand with the country around us. We cannot cherish any longer those illiberal prejudices of our predecessors. To stop wasting time requires all your animations and exertions, especially as in doing this you have the pleasing satisfaction of knowing that you are not only increasing the value of the city in aggregate, but the property of every individual who contributes thereto.[62]

The new Yankee belief that the city's political leaders were not doing enough to promote economic growth coincided with the new political understanding of the role of the ruler as responsive to the needs of the people. If, by pursuing their economic ambitions, the people could best provide for the society as a whole, then the politicians had better do what they can to support economic growth. As the Yankees gained control of the Common Council, this is just what their politicians did. By 1805, a writer in the newspaper crowed that

> The many rapid improvements in this city within a few years past reflect no less honor on the public spirit of its citizens than the fidelity of its corpora-

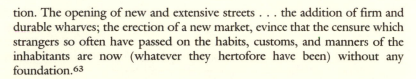

tion. The opening of new and extensive streets . . . the addition of firm and durable wharves; the erection of a new market, evince that the censure which strangers so often have passed on the habits, customs, and manners of the inhabitants are now (whatever they hertofore have been) without any foundation.[63]

To more and more Albanians it was becoming clear that political rulers must serve the people's economic interests.

This new moral thinking that justified political rule by the people and legitimated individual economic ambition introduced tensions and ambiguities into the community's religious life. In colonial times, Albany's Dutch Calvinists believed that the people could not rule themselves because their wills were corrupt. Peace and order required the town's leaders to hold their ground against popular opinion because hierarchical authority was the communal defense against unruly passions. Even though the days of political democracy were still several decades away, a growing postwar recognition of the ability of the individual led the minister of Albany's Yankee Presbyterian church to support individual "improvement."

By the beginning of the nineteenth century, Albany was the state capital and the Presbyterian "Court Church" was the house of worship favored by political dignitaries. Two years earlier the now Yankee-dominated congregation called to its pulpit a twenty-six-year-old Connecticut minister, Eliphalet Nott.[64] Nott supervised the education and morals of the congregation for six years and then, for the next sixty-two was responsible for the moral development of Albany's youth as president of the nearby Union College.[65] Facing from his pulpit such political opponents as Alexander Hamilton and Aaron Burr, Nott rapidly learned how to accommodate and manage the talents of worldly men.

What was so attractive about Mr. Nott, according to one of his hearers, was that

> he was no bigoted sectarian; and in this respect he bore . . . little resemblance to many of his clerical brethren. . . . The narrow dogmas, and common place oratory of the church, were beneath him. His ambition was to make men wise and better, rather than to promote the sectarian interests and speculative tenets of the church.

By the end of his tenure he was hailed as "by far the most eloquent and effective preacher of the period."[66]

First Presbyterian's minister was also known for a dramatic preaching style that assured the rapt attention of his congregation. The Baptist minister Francis Wayland testified to Nott's effect upon his audience.

I sat . . . perfectly entranced, chills running over me from nearly the commencement to the close. When he uttered the Amen, the whole audience experienced a sensible relief. The strain of attention was so great, and as soon as it was over, everyone took a great inspiration, and felt that he could hardly have endured the effect of concentration much longer.[67]

What new ideas did the audience so intently listen to hear?

Like the orthodox Calvinists, Eliphalet Nott insisted on the reality of human depravity and warned of arguments that favored the moral dignity of human nature.

. . . consider that man an enemy who endeavors to make you believe mankind are not depraved, when God and conscience teach you a contrary doctrine . . . much is said, at the present day, of the natural rectitude of man, and the moral dignity of human nature, but these are names without a meaning.[68]

At the same time, however, Nott recognized his hearers were living in a

fascinating but illusive world, where honor flaunts in fictitious trappings; where wealth displays imposing charms, and pleasure spreads her impoisoned banquets. And that too, at a period when the passions are most ungovernable—when the fancy is most vivid—when the blood flows most rapidly through the veins, and the pulse of life beats high.[69]

Given this situation, Nott charged that "Man now turns his eye inward upon himself. He reads 'responsibility . . .' "[70] Taken together, Nott continued the colonial Calvinist emphasis on human depravity, worried over the allure of the new society, yet implored men to act responsibly.

To act responsibly at least meant to take advantage of the new insights gained from natural science and mental philosophy. In keeping with the Enlightenment's embrace of human ability, Nott encouraged his followers not simply to accept their lot, but to "improve" themselves. Rather than turn away from these new ideas, which to some threatened to lead Christians away from the Bible's truth, Nott held that the new knowledge was not opposed to revelation but deepened one's knowledge of it. "Who was it," Nott asked his congregation,

that overleaping the narrow bounds which had hitherto been set to the human mind, ranged abroad through the immensity of space, discovered and illustrated the law by which the Deity unites and governs all things? It was Newton. But Newton was a Christian . . . Who was it that lifted the veil which had covered the intellectual world, analyzed the human mind, defined its powers, and reduced its operations to certain and fixed laws? It was Locke. But Locke too was a Christian.[71]

Education in the sciences was encouraged because science would only affirm the fundamental unity of all truth. So long as the Christian held fast to the belief that ". . . in the vast and perfect government of the universe, vicarious sufferings can be accepted; and that the dread Sovereign, who administers the government, is gracious as well as just,"[72] he was free to learn all that he could about God's world.

This effort to improve oneself through education was part of a larger effort to bring about the kingdom of God on earth. In his sermons Nott charged himself with the task of mapping for Albanians the return route to a lost Eden. Ahead lay that new world he believed would evolve not from the cloister and the church, but from the marketplace, the workshop, and the schools of America. "How am I to be saved?" was the anxious question he heard from the people of Albany. To this he responded that they only had to look about them to see the regenerating spirit at work. Their task was clear; the world must be readied for the millennial jubilee. While affirming moral depravity, Nott's more moderate Calvinism nevertheless moved religious belief closer to the ideals of postwar America by encouraging human ability, the development of science, and the creation of the new society.

*   *   *

Following the Revolution, the people of Albany began a long search for cultural and social definition. The joyous sense of optimism, the flowering of individual creativity and innovation, were countered with the grief of rootlessness and fears of the unknown. Both were results of the individual freedom wrenched from the prerevolutionary communal order.[73] Now the town's inhabitants came and went at an increasingly furious pace. Yankee immigrants accelerated this process, pushing against the collective restraint of Dutch social institutions. Rational economic practices and democratic political agitation introduced tensions and ambiguities into orthodox Calvinist teachings. A more moderate Calvinist theology that subsumed ideals from the surrounding society emerged from this disorder. Despite this moderation of belief, by the second decade of the new century only an elite and largely female minority of the townspeople were members of Albany's Calvinist congregations.

Figure 7. View of Albany in 1818. Print engraved by T. Dixon after a drawing by G. Kane June 4, 1818. (Collection of the New York State Museum, Albany, N.Y.)

Chapter 4

The Twilight of Calvinism

On a Sunday morning in 1813, the Presbyterian minister Arthur Stansbury addressed a congregation of Yankee merchants, master craftsmen, and their families in First Presbyterian Church. These Calvinist leaders of the Albany community believed that God controlled their world. Since the end of the Revolution, however, both they and their community had experienced a disturbing amount of economic, social, and political change that undermined their position as God's moral shepherds over an increasingly godless multitude. Faced with this crisis, Stansbury reminded his people that if they believed, like their New England ancestors, that their God was a "moral governor" whose dealings with them was "a system of discipline calculated in its own nature to instruct and reform them," then they had a role to play. During the first two decades of the nineteenth century, Albany's leading congregations used the methods of their Puritan past to try to slow the course of social change and reinstate conformity to God's law amid the "vice and immorality" of their burgeoning city.[1]

Stansbury's stress on God's "moral government" was a republican rephrasing of the Puritan concept of the national covenant. Both taught that the welfare of society depended on the inhabitants' recognition of their submission to a sovereign God. Puritans created their theory by applying the Old Testament covenant to New England. Stansbury and the Calvinists of his generation did the same for the new Republic. America's constitution and laws came directly from God, and the nation would be punished or rewarded depending on its obedience to His laws. The concept of a moral government retained the Old Testament model for assessing the society of nineteenth-century America. A direct relationship was seen between social unrest and national disaster. It was critical for the church to oversee the moral welfare of the community; without this parental leadership everyone would suffer from the sins of a few.[2] Puritan family government was eroding, but it remained prominent in Albany Protestants' ideas of where authority was to be found and how it should be exercised. Moreover, New York law held heads of families responsible for the actions of their children and dependents.[3]

This attempt to impose traditional order coincided with the last years of real strength for Calvinism in Albany. A growing transient population now undermined the moral authority of the elite. At the same time, from the growing separation of rich from poor, work from family life, and craftsmen from their customers emerged the early industrial class structure. Ideas associated with the manufacturer, mechanic, and journeymen united the artisan community into a rising social class and democratized Albany's political institutions. By the second decade of the nineteenth century, a newly emerging Methodist congregation that embraced the poor and the dislocated challenged the theological supremacy of the Dutch and Presbyterian congregations, which had become pious preserves for an affluent and increasingly female minority of the town's population. These new ideologies offered the towns people various new ways of thinking that together eroded the authority of Calvinism as the world view best able to provide meaning to the people of Albany.

Social Changes

In 1817 Albany was in population, wealth, and trade the second city of the state and the seventh in rank among the cities of the United States.[4] Yankees from the hill country of Massachusetts and Connecticut continued to swarm through the town on their way to the upper Mohawk Valley and over the western slopes of the Catskills.[5] As one observer remarked, "it is doubted if there be a place on this continent which is daily visited by so many teams." The overland passage of migrants spurred an increase in commercial traffic along the Hudson. By the second decade of the century, quays stretched for a mile along the waterfront loading and unloading 80 to 200 sloops and schooners at a time. Albany had rapidly become the focal point of "more extended intercourse . . . than . . . any other place between the Eastern and Western sections of the Union."[6]

The new Yankee merchant elite made the most of this expansion and growth of the town's economy. By 1817 Dutchmen accounted for less than one-quarter of the merchants, manufacturers, and professionals who ranked among the top 10 percent of the town's taxpayers.[7] These included several members of the old and established Dutch families, most notably Philip Van Rensselaer, scion of Albany's oldest and wealthiest family and mayor of the town through most of the first two decades of the nineteenth century. By and large, however, Dutch wealth was inherited, tied up in real estate, or invested in the town's banks. "Though among the most wealthy and respectable," an observer remarked, these "ancient Dutch families . . . were not the most enterprising, nor the most active." In contrast, "the principal merchants of the city . . . those who gave life and character to its business interests—were citizens of a more recent date."[8] Most of these were Yankees. Of the 123 non-Dutch, who accounted for three-quarters of Albany's top decile of taxpayers in 1817, seventy can be traced to their region of birth. Fifty-four percent of these were natives of New England. If we consider only those who came to Albany after 1800, 70 percent were Yankees. And if we add those whose forebearers came to New York from New England, a full 88 percent shared the cultural inheritance of the region's new customers. Albany's wealthiest Yankees gained prosperity by offering shelter (inns) and housing (builders) to their countrymen and supplying their needs for finished goods (crafts and manufacturers).[9]

The needs of the new immigrants turned the town into a manufacturing center. In 1817, 42 percent of the men in the Albany work force were engaged in turning raw materials into finished goods. The 58 workshops and small manufactories listed in the city directory for that year concentrated on supplying the needs of rural life. Wagonmakers, wheelwrights, and harnessmakers provided the traveler with the means for his journey; shoemakers, tailors, and hatters clothed him; while furniture makers, blacksmiths, and several small iron foundries provided the furniture and implements needed for establishing a rural home. Printers and bookbinders provided primers for country schools and reading materials for the entertainment and "improvement" of literate settlers. Their presses produced country editions of local newspapers. Other workshops devoted to watches, jewelry, and silver witnessed the growing prosperity of regional life.[10] By 1820, Albany's largest manufacturing establishments included three tanneries, four breweries, four distilleries, four air furnaces, a prospering tobacco factory, a thriving hatmaking business, and brickyards to fashion the area's better buildings.[11] The Yankee migration into, and through, Albany stimulated this diversification and growth of the town's economy. At the same time, this economic growth accelerated the decline of the town's colonial social order.

Most of the people living in early nineteenth-century Albany were young and transient. In 1817 only 24 percent of all adult male workers were independent proprietors.[12] The largest group in the work force, 35 percent, was made up of the journeyman craftsmen who built the town and manned its workshops.[13] In 1820 58 percent of the population was under twenty-six years of age. Forty percent of the adult male work force in the prime working ages of sixteen to forty-five was under twenty-six.[14] Moreover, of these hundreds of local wage earners living in the city in 1817, fewer than one in five would stay as long as thirteen years.[15] The erosion of the elite's ability to oversee this transient work force can be seen in three areas: the separation of the craftsman from his customer, of work from family life, and of the rich from the poor.

Manufacturing growth during the initial Yankee transformation of Albany separated the craftsman from his customer. Under the traditional handicraft system prevalent prior to the Revolution, the master craftsman made his entire product and sold it directly to the customer. The limited number of customers in town regulated the number of local craftsmen and the size of their shops. From 1799 to 1817, the number of Albany's artisan shops doubled, while the number of skilled workers increased fourfold.[16] For example, George Webster was solely responsible for the town's printing needs for most of the 1790's and, with the assistance of a few journeymen and apprentices, he typeset, bound, edited, and distributed his product. By 1817, however, there were five printing establishments, and Webster had taken in his brother and three nephews as partners, expanded his operation to include a retail bookstore, and distributed his *Webster's Almanac* and school primers to the countryside.[17] Twenty percent of Webster's fellow craftsmen in the Mechanics' Society,[18] formed in 1793 by the town's leading artisans, emulated his new emphasis on the retail aspects of his trade. All were listed as merchants in the 1817 directory. At the same time, a number of merchants who knew little about particular crafts became distributors of manufactured goods. Whether a craftsman devoted more time to the sale of his goods and thus became a merchant, or he contracted with general merchants to market his product, growth in the scale of work forced a division of labor that separated the master craftsman from his traditional role as both producer and distributor, leaving him with less control over his business.

Manufacturing growth also separated the worker from the master's household. Under the traditional system, a craftsman whose business was large enough would employ a journeyman or two, or perhaps an apprentice, who would live in his household. Work, leisure, and domestic life were carried out in the same place and by the same people, and relations between masters and workers transferred easily from the shop to the home. A journeyman in the printing establishment of Jesse Buel described the place of the worker in the craftsman's household as late as 1813.

> In winter we ate breakfast by candlelight, took dinner at 12 (except publication days), supper at 6 . . . and set type until 9. The "eight hour system" was not then in vogue. . . . Everything was systematized by him. In summer he arose with the sun, and his boys (apprentices) likewise. Breakfast was taken at 7 o'clock, dinner at 12 and tea at 6. His boys sat at the same table with him and his family in the order of seniority. . . . His wife and sister were helped first. His apprentices in order next, then his children, who were young, and himself last. . . . These were "old fashioned" republican, patriarchal times, and the old Judge apparently took as much pleasure in having us sit with him, as we did. The modern doctrine of "running against the wind, or this or that man's nobility" was not a part of his system of "Parental Government," for that feeling he tried to inculcate in his boys, and they *did* believe it and gave him respect for it.[19]

This traditional system of "parental government" prevailed in many of the town's mechanic shops, but its authority was undercut by the growing number of master craftsmen whose prosperity allowed them to move out of their shops into private homes and the simultaneous emergence of new boardinghouses for journeymen. More than one-third of the master mechanics whose shops were listed in the 1817 city directory owned separate residences. At the same time, the addresses of the town's journeymen indicate that they lived together in the city's 22 new boardinghouses at least as frequently as in their master's household.[20] This estrangement eroded the latter's parental control while granting the former unprecedented new freedom.

Further evidence of the elite's waning control over their community is indicated by the first signs of residential separation of the rich from the poor. In colonial Albany, the town was one neighborhood. There were no commercial or residential areas based on social class. Most Albanians worked, played, and slept in the same place. The integration of work and family life and of master and wage earner produced a nearly random mix of people and activities in the city. Changes in this arrangement are suggested as early as the 1790's by the construction of the elegant new capitol building at the head of State street and the mushrooming warehouses and larger workshops along the riverfront. The removal of the Dutch church from the intersection of State and Market streets to a nearby neighborhood signaled a broader movement of wealthier proprietors away from their stores and shops and into newly developed residential areas. By 1817, one-third of the top 10 percent of the town's proprietors had retreated to the privacy of separate residences within a few blocks of their businesses in less commercial areas to the west and south. At the same time, the largest numbers of the poorest workers lived on the busiest streets, by the river, and on the town's western and northern periphery.[21] These initial signs of separation between rich and poor were noticed as early as 1819 by a baker who wrote the newspaper to protest the location of the new central market on Howard Street near the capitol. "By this arrangement the rich would have the choice of all the meat and vegetables," Robert Davis exclaimed, because "a working man" would have "to go three quarters of a mile to market."[22] Though rich and poor could still be found on every Albany street, by 1817 there were indications that the estrangement of master and wage earner was being recapitulated in the town's social geography. At the same time, workingmen were not joining the town's elite churches.

Calvinism in the Early Nineteenth Century

By the second decade of the nineteenth century, Calvinist church membership, which bound together nearly all members of the community during the colonial period, had become a haven for an affluent and predominantly female minority of the town's people. In 1817 the two Dutch and four Presbyterian congregations accounted for nearly two-thirds of Albany's church members and more than two-thirds of the church members in the top two deciles of the 1817 tax list.[23] The city's other five churches included the small but influential Episcopal congregation at St. Peter's, a handful of Catholics, a few dozen Lutherans, some Baptists, and a growing group of less affluent journeymen and petty shopkeepers who attended the Methodist church. The unchurched could be found in every economic bracket, but they most noticeably accounted for nearly 75 percent of the 1817 taxpayers with incomes below the community median.[24] In that year, wives and daughters of the elite accounted for more than two thirds of all new Calvinist church members.[25] By the century's second decade, Albany's leading churches were divided from the rest of the community by wealth and gender.

Following the emergence of the new nation, Albany's Dutch and Pres-

byterian congregations became more alike, yet different from their surrounding community. Beginning around 1800, both congregations built
elegant new church buildings and paid their ministers as much or more
than any other church in the state. The traditional Dutch seating arrangement by gender and heredity gave way to the more recent Presbyterian
practice of family pews sold to the highest bidder. Both congregations
increasingly admitted to their membership Christians with cultural backgrounds different from their own.[26] Hastening this intermingling of ethnically different people was their common Calvinist faith and their willingness to act on this ideological unity by opening regional meetings to each
other's representatives, pulpits to each others ministers,[27] and themselves
to each other in monthly "concerts of prayer" for the salvation of the
world.[28]

The persistence of a traditional mentality among the Dutch and Yankee
elite is suggested by the curriculum of the Albany Academy. Begun in 1813
as a preparatory school for their sons, the school's curriculum reflected
that of the Latin grammar school. This was the secondary school of the
seventeenth and eighteenth centuries and the type in which many of the
academy's trustees themselves had been educated. The first objective of
such a curriculum was the mastery of Greek and Latin grammar, essential
skills for those who were to take their place among a cultured elite in an
unchanging world. In contrast, the academy movement, begun by Benjamin Franklin in 1749, saw this narrow classical curriculum as out of step
with the ideas of this-worldly, commercial, optimistic Americans. Franklin's followers, who became legion in the nineteenth century, believed that
the important criterion for the design of a curriculum was practical preparation for leadership in a growing and changing world. The practical effect
was a new concentration on English studies and the introduction of mathematics, science, and related subjects. Latin and Greek were increasingly
seen as ornamental. Such innovations were not fully evident at the Albany
Academy until the curriculum's reorganization based on the Franklin plan
in the late 1820's. Prior to that time courses in mathematics and English
were available, yet parental preference favored the classical curriculum.
Changes in the curriculum did parallel the rise of Yankee influence in
Albany; nevertheless, in the second decade of the nineteenth century the
town's wealthiest citizens prepared their sons for a traditional world.[29]

In addition to their common Calvinist faith, wealthy Yankee merchants
and their Dutch peers shared a respect for traditional roads to wealth.
Those Dutchmen, who accounted for one quarter of the top 10 percent of
Albany's taxpayers in 1817, attained their wealth in the traditional manner

through family, religious, and ethnic ties. Of these thirty-eight people, nineteen shared the same six family names. In all, thirty-four (87 percent) were related to at least one of the other thirty-eight. Thirty-five were members of the Dutch church.[30] A second and smaller group of nine Dutch and non-Dutch newcomers, who were also among the community's wealthiest 10 percent in 1817, followed the traditional pattern of outsiders' upward mobility by marrying into prominent Dutch families and joining their church.[31] The Yankee merchant and manufacturing elite were similarly united by family and faith, though to a lesser degree.

The iron manufacturers John and Isaiah Townsend were typical of the Yankee newcomers. These brothers were descended from Henry Townsend who, with his two brothers, migrated from Norfolk, England, to Massachusetts around 1640. Subsequent generations migrated to New York. Born in the Sterling Iron Works in Orange County, New York, Isaiah married his cousin Anna Townsend, whose father, Solomon, ran a large iron business in New York City as well as in Orange and Suffolk counties. Isaiah arrived with the first great wave of Yankee immigrants in the 1790's and was joined by his brother John in 1802. Five years later they established the city's first iron works. With their brethren at the First Presbyterian Church, they were major promoters and among the first presidents of the first Yankee-controlled banking and insurance companies established to sponsor and protect the increased tempo of the economy.[32] By 1819, Isaiah was serving on the committee that directed the activities of the Albany Sunday School Union,[33] while John was president of the Albany Chamber of Commerce for Public Improvement and would later serve three terms as mayor.[34]

Like the Townsends, successful Yankee merchants in the second decade of the new century were young men in their thirties who joined with their brothers in business and with the Presbyterian church for religion. Six sets of brothers are included among those 38 rich Yankees on the 1817 tax list whose origins can be determined. These six, plus three other pairings of wealthy Yankee merchants and their less wealthy brothers, account for all of the business partnerships contracted by these 38 men.[35] Such fraternal ties expanded available resources and entrusted their use to men who shared kinship as well as contractual responsibilities. Further evidence of family ties among these businessmen is provided by the initial marriages of their progeny. Although they had left older relatives at home and most were too young to have adult children, like the traditional Dutch, they began to intermarry.[36] In all, at least 17 (45 percent) of these 38 wealthy migrants were related to at least one other of their countrymen at the top of the 1817 tax list. And 24 (66 percent) of these 38 became Presbyterians.[37] The road to riches for Albany's prosperous Yankees led first to family ties and then to the sizable resources of the Presbyterian congregation. Although to a lesser degree, the prosperous Yankee shared with the wealthy Dutchman a respect for family ties and shared faith as the basis for a successful career.

Calvinist Women

At the same time that Albany's leading congregations dwindled to include only the most traditional and affluent in the community, they also came to be dominated by women. The growing number of women in the Dutch and Presbyterian churches suggests the changing sexual demographics of church membership and the growing female responsibility for the moral welfare of the community. In 1683, when the Dutch church encompassed nearly the entire community, men and women were equally represented among the town's church members.[38] By 1790, at the beginning of large-scale migration, women accounted for 60 percent of the congregation.[39] By 1815, they accounted for 75 percent of that half of the congregation that became the Second Dutch Reformed Church.[40] In 1816, the membership of the Second Presbyterian Church was also dominated by women.[41] In all, more than two-thirds of the new members of Albany's Dutch and Presbyterian churches were women.[42]

During the first quarter of the nineteenth century, the social position of the town's leading women was changing. In colonial Albany the home was the setting for economic activity and the center of a pattern of socialization characterized by frequent face-to-face contact between relatives associated in a wide range of activities. In this environment, the wife was an agent for her husband when he was called away and a key influence in matters in which her own relatives were involved, and she held the primary responsibility of initiating children and intermarrying newcomers to the traditions by which the family governed itself. When their husbands died, many of these traditional women became the leaders of their households. In 1756, 10 percent of Albany's household heads were women, several of whom were identified as merchants.[43] By 1800, however, fewer women were identified either as heads of households (6 percent) or as businesswomen; now it was primarily impoverished women who received attention in the public records, and they were perceived as pitiful charity cases.[44] Albany's Calvinist women were among the first to be removed physically from the corporate family economy through the separation of workplace and residence and the migration of relatives. A number of women were wealthy enough to purchase rather than make their own household supplies and to employ servants to fulfill domestic needs. For these urban affluent women, involvement in benevolent activities filled the void in their everyday lives. The openness of the rapidly changing city allowed them to experiment with a new social role that would help them recover a position of influence that they had lost due to changes in the town's economic and social relations.[45]

The attempt by Albany's Calvinist men to restore moral order through parental leadership and legal sanctions was aided by the efforts of their wives and daughters in The Ladies Society for the Relief of Distressed Women and Children.[46] Formed in 1804 to fulfill the elite's traditional responsibility to provide "comfort and assistance" to the community's poor, the society was organized, directed, and supported by the wives and daughters of the town's wealthiest Calvinist church members. Even though these women responded to a traditional responsibility of the elite, through the creation and administration of their "Ladies Society" they were able to enlarge the sphere of their influence and create a greater autonomy for themselves. The emergence of this Society signaled a transformation in the domestic life of Albany's elite women that ultimately resulted in a growing majority of women in the leading congregations.

The work of the Ladies Society expanded the influence of Albany's Calvinist women. In colonial times, the deacons of the Dutch church were responsible for the poor. Following the Revolution, this responsibility largely was taken over by the Common Council and delegated to the Overseers of the Poor. Given a mounting chorus of complaints that, by 1804, accused the Common Council of inadequate support and delivery of aid to the poor, it seems that care for the poor, which had once meant assistance to members of one's own church and ethnic group, was only reluctantly extended to the unchurched and destitute strangers who had recently taken up residence in the city. The Ladies Society was created to respond to their need. In its first year of operation, this women's group spent three times more money and aided twice as many people as the Overseers of the Poor.[47] Its board of managers "explored in person the habitations of the sick and poor" and met twice a month to decide on the aid to be given according to the "dimensions of the misery." This assistance was considered emergency relief for people who, through no fault of their own, had become "poor and pitiable."[48] Unlike colonial poor masters, however, they extended their assistance beyond the bounds of their own extended families and ethnic group.

The work of the Ladies Society extended Christian charity to more of the community's poor and, at the same time, created a greater autonomy for the town's leading women. The organizational and financial sophistication these women needed to develop resembled the trading networks and political parties of Albany's merchant capitalists. Throughout the first quarter of the nineteenth century, the members of this women's group elected their own board of managers, met in formal annual meetings, and kept careful accounts much in the manner of meticulous and conservative businessmen. The similarities between these ladies and male merchants were more substantial than analogies between their organizational skills. In fact, 88 percent were the wives and daughters of the merchants and attorneys who were elected to the Common Council and who directed the city's largest economic institutions. Eighty-one percent were members of either a Dutch or Presbyterian church (the rest were Episcopalians).[49] It seems, therefore, that involvement in the Ladies Society was characteristic of the sexual division of labor within Albany's leading families. By joining this society, elite women publicly assumed the moral and religious responsibilities of their mercantile households and an important role in social reproduction. By doing this well they undoubtedly enhanced their own elite status while adding religious reinforcement to the male links in the local trade networks. At the same time, they enlarged their social role in a sphere that was organizationally independent of the male head of the household. The religious leaders of the town applauded the women's new role.

According to the Presbyterian minister Eliphalet Nott, the real purpose of the Ladies Society was to hold together a society that men had torn apart.

> For what object could have been more lovely or commanding, in a city where party reigns, and where the hands of social intercourse in one sex, are by political controversy almost sundered, than an extensive assemblage of disinterested females—an assemblage of mothers and daughters: of individuals of different habits and sentiments, both political and religious, uniting and harmoniously cooperating like bands of sisters for the relief of human misery. Whose influence has been like the influence of morning. At whose approach the horrors of poverty vanish, and the countenance brightens which was overspread by sorrow.[50]

Ann Douglas has suggested that such exaggerated praise for the new role to be played by women in the nascent American society was actually a "compensatory etiquette" in which politeness and reverence for women suggested atonement as much as recognition. Women were honored for the moral sanction they gave to the self-interested business activities of the town's merchant capitalists. Douglas also suggests that at the same time that male rhetoric sought to fix women in their new social role, affluent women, as a rising group seeking increased power and influence, actively and aggressively sought this new status.[51] Both forces seem to have been at work in early nineteenth-century Albany. In any event, among the Calvinist congregations, women were gaining greater autonomy and moral influence. During the second decade of the nineteenth century, these wives and daughters of the town's leaders supported their husbands and fathers in their effort to employ traditional methods to try to bring moral order and discipline to their changing city.

The Moral Society

When Arthur Stansbury preached the importance of restoring God's "moral government" in Albany, he spoke to a Presbyterian congregation of affluent New England merchants and master craftsmen who had been reared under the moral discipline of their traditional faith. During the first fifteen years of the new century, the majority of First Presbyterian's new male members were admitted "on certificate" from "sister churches."[52] The nineteen men who served between 1810 and 1819 as elders, deacons, or trustees were wealthy (top 20 percent)[53] New Englanders (13), most of whom came to Albany before 1800.[54] First Presbyterian's Yankees came to Albany bearing with them their older religious heritage. Most of their church's leaders were merchants, professionals, and government officials, although more than one-third were master craftsmen. These wealthy tradesmen, such as silversmiths and jewelers who catered to the wealthy, and a few tradesman-entrepreneurs, in highly capitalized enterprises such as breweries and iron foundries, were more akin to their fellow church leaders in wealth and economic interests than they were to their fellow tradesmen. Moreover, within the bonds of an older religious heritage, they shared with the merchants a common responsibility as proprietors. In fact, the leaders and members of Albany's six Calvinist churches accounted for 62 percent of the town's proprietors. Although only one-quarter of the town's mechanics were church members (and less than half of these joined a Calvinist congregation), 60 percent of the local master craftsmen were church members, and two-thirds of these were members of the Dutch and Presbyterian churches. The carriers of Albany's Calvinist religious heritage accounted for a clear majority (62 percent) of the town's proprietors, including nearly half (41 percent) of the master craftsmen.[55] The reforms they enacted were intended to return the city to their moral control.

As founders in 1815 of the "Albany Society for the Suppression of Vice and Immorality," Albany's leading churchmen called on "men in stations of authority, high as well as low" to suppress the many vices in their city that "loudly call upon every good member of society for suppression." In their published proceedings, these church leaders acknowledged the growing tide of secularity even among "men in authority" by addressing their appeal to two groups, "the religious public, and all that description of persons who consider morality as a great chain which binds the interests of society together, and as the main pillar of public and private prosperity." The former group, they stated, was "inexorably bound" by their "obedience" to their "Divine Master" to patronize and support the Moral Society. It was their "duty as Christians" to inculcate "all those virtues without which their religion is a name dead and useless." The latter group was appealed to on the basis of the "best interests" of society. The rationale used by these Calvinist churchmen to appeal to their more worldly peers suggests the kinds of vices they sought to suppress and the type of society they wished to restore.

> That profane cursing and swearing are vulgar vices, calculated to deprave the manners, to corrupt the heart, and to lead to general irreverence toward the Supreme Being, few will deny. That the sabbath is an institution of wisdom and benevolence, well designed to preserve purity in the higher classes, decency and order in the lower, all must acknowledge. . . . Through its influence and the public instruction which it affords, the former are taught those lessons which produce a high minded spirit of honor and integrity, a spirit of mercy and charity to their inferiors; and the latter are instructed in all the duties of order and of industry, of patience and submission to their lot. An establishment bearing in its train so many blessings . . . cannot be uninteresting to the moralist, the philosopher or the statesman.[56]

Whether one was motivated by obedience to God or self-interest, Albany's leading churchmen believed both ends demanded that ill-mannered behavior and sabbath desecration cease so that God's "great cause" or "decency and order" might prevail. While acknowledging the importance of self-interest, these traditional religious leaders continued to appeal to men in authority to preserve their God-ordained hierarchical social structure.

Also like their forefathers, these Calvinist churchmen reinforced their moral rules with legal sanctions. Despite the disestablishment of religion, Albany's elite church members supported the successful passage in 1813 of a state "Act for Suppressing Immorality," which gave the force of law to their code of behavior.[57] Then they formed themselves into committees "to watch on every Sabbath, to discover and take up, detain and report to the magistrates all such as may be found in violation of its sanctity." Of particular concern was the "multitude of youth" who seem to have been "abandoned by the natural guardians of their morals" and therefore "never received such instruction as to the enormity of their crimes." The parents of these youth were to be informed of their children's violations and warned of stiff punishment if their behavior was not reformed. In 1816 an auxiliary branch of this society was formed from the master craftsmen who were also Calvinist church members. This "Mechanics Society for the Suppression of Vice and Immorality an the Promotion of Good Morals" divided its members into separate ward committees and, in particular, made themselves responsible for policing the members of their trade.[58]

As pillars of social stability and advocates of economic growth, Albany's successful postwar Calvinist church members carried within themselves the ideological contradictions inherent in the movement toward a new society. Like traditional church leaders, the members of Albany's moral societies relied on the example and influence of parents and men in authority to restrain the erosion of the old social order. At the same time, however, the city directories show that these successful businessmen were the first to leave their shops and stores for the private comforts of affluent neighborhoods. In so doing, they abdicated their parental obligations to their workers. In effect, Albany's Calvinist church members contributed to the social disorder that their moral societies sought to suppress. By 1820 the failure of these societies to restore traditional order was marked by their dissolution.

The Methodist Ideology

On October 5, 1821, John Chester, minister of Albany's Second Presbyterian Church, offered the Moral Society a theological reason for the failure of their efforts to impose patriarchal control over their city. Despite their efforts and the work of the Ladies Society, Albany remained for them an "immoral" city overrun with transient immigrants. The reason for their failure, Chester declared, could be found in the principles underlying their time-honored methods of reform. "The same defects were found to exist in the system and operations of moral societies. They acted upon wrong principles, and they have accomplished little; not because there was not much to be done, but because they mistook the means by which they might have been successful."[59] Older moral reform efforts, Chester argued, were theologically rooted in the Old Testament emphasis on the external restraint of the Law. In colonial America, much as in the times of the Old Testament, church and state were mutually dependent. "Many of our ancestors were educated under a government in which was an established religion interwoven in the very texture of the constitution." New and successful approaches to moral reform, Chester continued, were theologically rooted in the New Testament. In particular, "public opinion," the spirit of the new nation, "is the precise rule of reformation. We cannot often transcend it. Here we are to devote our strength, if we succeed in convincing the minds of men, there will be little difficulty in improving their morals."[60] The traditional methods of moral reform were based on the Law of the Old Testament. These methods were characterized by the imposition of parental and legal authority. The new methods were based on the Spirit of the New Testament. These were founded on the power of "public opinion" to "convince the minds of men." As Chester saw it, to act as true Christians was to communicate the spirit of one's faith.

Reverend Chester ended his remarks by mentioning several new means for moral reform. These included the effort to "enlighten and instruct men" through Sunday schools, which would "do more to promote good morals . . . than all the associations to enact penal laws that were ever formed." And the "better regulation of charity institutions" so that they might instruct the poor in temperance and industry rather than simply offer them a "reward" for being "idle" and "profligate."[61] Each new method was intended to persuade and educate, not punish, the immoral.

Chester's theological analysis was presented at the same time that new methods of moral reform were appearing. During the second decade of the nineteenth century, at the same time that Calvinist methods of moral reform were meeting with failure, a variety of new approaches led by a diverse assortment of women, mechanics, petty shopkeepers, teachers, and ministers, many but not all of whom were members of the new Methodist church, were showing signs of success.

One example of this new approach is suggested by the Methodist attitude toward the distribution of religious reading. The Methodist Tract Society of Albany was formed in 1811, one year after the creation of the Calvinist-supported Albany Bible Society. Both brought the knowledge of God to the poor. The Methodists, however, emphasized the personal meeting of minds in addition to delivering literature to every doorstep. In contrast, the Bible Society measured its success by the number of bibles it distributed. This difference was highlighted by one of the original members of the Methodist Tract Society.

The distribution of tracts may be the means of incalculable good; but to do the work thoroughly there must be much more than simply the leaving of the tract. The mere presentation of Bibles will not Christianize the world. God has been pleased to employ the living ministry for this work; and so in the tract cause, the living Christian should accompany the papers which he gives with such words and sympathies as alone can awaken corresponding feelings in the breasts of those who receive them. Mind must act on mind; there must be a participation of interest, a fellow-feeling manifested, in most cases, before there will be lodgement of truth.[62]

A similarly personal concern motivated the creation of the town's first Sunday schools.

Albany's Sunday schools began not through the leadership of any one church, though here again the Methodist influence was prominent, but more because of the efforts of individuals who shared the Moral Society's alarm at the desecration of the Sabbath but responded with a different solution. In 1816 Susan Bocking, a Methodist and wife of a baker, and Mrs. George Upfold, an Episcopalian and wife of a teacher, established a Sunday school for the purpose of improving the morals of the city's poor. During the next year, "certain members of the Methodist Church," a "missionary," and a number of "young ladies and gentlemen" established similar schools in the parts of the city where children "habitually broke the sabbath and indulged in vices." Unlike the Moral Society, which not only sought punishment for those who broke the Sabbath but refused these schools financial support, each of these new departures saw education as the key to successful moral reform. And unlike the Ladies Society, which several years before had gone so far as to raise funds for a schoolhouse and the salary of a governess to educate the poor, people like Mrs. Bocking and Mrs. Upfold did not raise funds to build a school but opened their own homes and taught the children themselves. In time the number of these schools multiplied and most affiliated with the city's churches although, as late as 1826, several remained as little missions unto themselves set up in places such as "a carpenter's shop, the benches serving for desks."[63] Rather than seek legal punishment to morally discipline Sabbath breakers, advocates of these new measures set up schools to inculcate their moral views.

The Methodist supporters of these new approaches to moral reform suffered prejudice from the town's leaders throughout the first thirty years of their church's existence. Derisive articles in the local newspapers spoke of "ignorant" Methodist preachers whose

. . . only qualifications . . . are a sanctified face and deportment, and brains enough to commit to memory four or five sermons. . . . With this assumed sanctity and with a long face, they enter the pulpit, and commence with something like dignity, but it is soon changed to a boisterous, ranting nonsense, disgusting to the ear of real religion, the only effect of which is to arrouse enthusiastic weakness, and lead the blind into error.[64]

Similarly subject to "laughter and contempt" were reports of Methodist camp meetings in the surrounding countryside, which were seen particularly as "the poisoned source of depravity of morals in the lower classes of the community." Here "the mild, happy, and peaceful doctrines inculcated by the gospel" were so twisted as to "transform human nature and civilized man, into a state of fury and madness."[65]

In response to such attacks, Tobias Spicer, the local Methodist minister in 1823, accused his church's critics of crying out against camp meetings solely because they were "not conducted precisely according to their views of propriety." He explained that, like the Calvinist congregations, "the Methodists endeavor to do all the good they can in the use of ordinary means," yet they "hold Camp Meetings beside, as means extraordinary." This was because, unlike the Calvinist churches, "we are obliged to take men as they are; and if we cannot get them into the powers of a church, we think it better to get them together somewhere else than to let them perish for lack of knowledge."[66] Albany's Methodist congregation grew to over 100 by 1811 and over 200 by 1817.[67] In that year they were comparable in size to every other local church and were the only church that drew the great majority of its membership (66 percent) from those whose tax assessment was below the community median.[68] Where the Calvinist churches had failed, the new Methodist ideology was showing a stubborn success in gathering together the new immigrant poor.

Methodist ideology appealed to Albany's rising social class. Unlike the Calvinist notion of predestination, which only offered hope to those chosen by God, the belief of Methodism's founder John Wesley in the universality of grace made this grace available to a greater number of people, both rich and poor. And, unlike the Calvinist requirement of knowledge as well as experience for church membership, which emphasized the role of the intellect, Methodist preachers sought a conversion of the heart that opened the way to salvation to the simplest and least educated. In this sense, Methodism removed Calvinism's doctrinal and social barriers. The men who brought this message to Albany's poor were neither wealthy nor educated themselves. And, unlike the more erudite and nuanced sermons of Reformed ministers, they believed it was their duty to speak as luridly as possible about the grim realities of sin, the devil, and the fires of hell so that they might frighten sinners into fleeing the wrath to come. Similarly, the measure of an individual's true conversion was not simply responding to questions from the church's elders, as was the Reformed practice, but also the exhibition of emotional convulsions. Those who made this effort and thus were regenerated by God's grace were invited to join a fellowship of the newly reborn in which all would watch over the spiritual welfare of each.

Albany's First Methodist Society was organized into several smaller classes whose members were taught to believe, act, and dress like Methodists. A tight hierarchical system of discipline that extended from the conference to the district to the circuit and on down to the class assured a clear understanding of authority and centralized control. Unswerving allegiance to the church was rewarded with the opportunity for lay leadership as a class leader, steward, exhorter, or preacher in their local society. Methodism therefore provided both the discipline of hierarchical authority and the opportunity for advancement to people in need of communal bonds and personal advancement. Belief in their salvation and the possibility of attaining a higher life was propounded and reinforced by three services each Sunday, weekly class and congregational prayer meetings, seasonal "Nightwatches" of prolonged evening prayer, annual camp meetings, and winter "protracted meetings" lasting for as long as six weeks. General Rules of Discipline, which stressed living a "humble, consistent, upright life, rich in kindly deeds and in utter loyalty to the church," were taught and reinforced in the classes and by the hierarchy.

The class leader was held responsible for knowing the condition of each member under his care. He would be asked by the circuit rider in open meeting if there were any in the class who were ill, in need of temporal aid, or in need of reproving. Among the actions requiring open reproval were profanity, gossip, drinking, disorderly conduct, lying, and reporting on the misdeeds of a brother or sister without first going to them privately to aid them in resisting evil. Such misbehavior was discouraged through class meetings that opened with fervent singing and praying for the opening of hearts and the challenge to live a higher life. In these meetings the class leader usually read and commented on a passage from the Bible and then asked each member about the state of her or his soul. The reports evoked praise, a series of amens, or prayers for increased strength among members who addressed each other as "brother" or "sister." Plain dress as well as right belief and proper action was part of this early discipline.

Subdued clothing, while intended to help one focus on inner spiritual values as opposed to worldly materialism, had the practical effect of visibly designating them as a people set apart. Unlike the more lenient practices of the Calvinist congregations, Methodists took their religion seriously or they were expelled from the only community they knew into the disorder of the emerging early industrial society.[69]

The Mechanics' Ideology

Like the Methodists, Albany's mechanics held to a world view and way of life that conflicted with that of colonial Calvinism. Despite signs of deterioration in the town's economic relations, tangibly manifest in the estrangement of masters from their journeymen, other noncommercial relations continued to bind the new artisan community together. As Paul Faler has argued, to speak of master craftsman and journeyman, rich and poor, is to speak in economic terms. This identifies a person's particular function in the production and sale of goods and his economic relationship to others, but it does not describe his social relations. The domestic system of craft production and the economic relations within it were but one part of a broader social relationship. Certainly it is misleading to assume that one's occupation and wealth were of no importance in determining relations outside the marketplace. But every economic relationship was formed between members of a society whose institutions and relations softened the harshness of cash transactions. As the economy grew and industrialization progressed, economic relationships did come to affect the entire spectrum of social experience and often led to the development of interests and values at odds with one another. At the same time, however, there was the continuation of a way of life that originated in earlier times. In particular, a set of ideas associated with the manufacturer, mechanic, and journeyman united the mechanic community as a rising social class and underlay the democratization of political institutions.[70]

The identity of many of Albany's postwar newcomers is revealed in the names and aims of the institutions they founded. The first and most fundamental of these, the Mechanics' Society, was formed in 1793 by more than 150 master craftsmen and journeymen representing every local trade. Their purpose was one of "protecting and supporting such of their brethren as by sickness or accident may stand in need of assistance, and of relieving the widows and orphans of those who may die in indigent circumstances, and also of providing the means of instruction for their children."[71] In 1811 they distinguished themselves from the town's merchants by founding their own Mechanics' and Farmers' Bank and stipulating in their charter that only mechanics and farmers could be elected as bank officers.[72] These same people were the moving force behind the establishment in 1812 of a Lancaster School that, unlike the elite-supported Albany Academy, provided for the rudimentary education of the town's less affluent children.[73] The pervasive influence and rising affluence of the members of the Mechanics' Society is suggested by its dissolution in 1826, at a time when its leading members were in positions of authority throughout the city.[74] Important aspects of their ideology, claimed by master and journeyman alike, were now widely accepted.

More than a group of people bound by economic ties, the mechanics represented a substantial new social group that was drawn to political ideas reflecting their growing sense of self-worth as well as the economic value of their crafts. In particular, they supported the growing belief that full rights of citizenship should go to the mechanics and farmers because they were essential for the maintenance of human life. In the inaugural lecture of the Apprentices' Library in 1821, master printer Solomon Southwick told the community's young mechanics, "Your importance to society may be perceived at once, by adverting to the vast utility of those mechanical powers which it is your destiny to wield. But for the operation of mechanical powers, . . . man would everywhere still be doomed to roam a savage in the wilds of nature."[75] From Southwick's perspective, society was composed of different groups of which the most important were the producers: mechanics and farmers. Least important were the nonproducers: landed aristocrats, bankers, lawyers, functionaries, and the idle. They were social parasites who contributed nothing to the preservation of human life. The popularity of this central tenet paralleled the Revolutionary movement for American independence and the subsequent growth of American nationalism.[76] Mechanics were called on to develop their trades and themselves as well in order to become active contributors to the new American society.[77]

The biographies of Albany craftsmen suggest they were reared in this ethos. Unanimously described as ambitious, most of the town's successful craftsmen left their homes as young men, frequently chose an occupation different from that of their fathers, and often bristled under the temporal and paternal restraints of an apprenticeship. Take, for example, the printer Joel Munsell, who went from his father's wagon maker trade in Deerfield, Massachusetts, to serve as a printer's apprentice in Greenfield. He left that position to come to Albany when his master insisted on his presence at all of the family's meals.[78] The bustling metropolis of Albany allowed Munsell and his fellow mechanics an escape from the opinions and pressures of others in their New England villages where, as Nathaniel Hawthorne observed, "we need the opinion of each individual neighbor for every act we do . . . and for every friend that we make or keep."[79]

Freed from these restraints, Albany's craftsmen looked not to advantageous marriages in order to better themselves, like colonial artisans, but instead devoted their energies to cultivating themselves. In Southwick's lecture to the aspiring mechanics he repeatedly impressed on them "the absolute necessity of improving every hour, nay every minute, you can justly claim as your own; in the cultivation of your intellectual and moral powers."[80] Munsell's diaries reflect a daily effort to squeeze some studying into the early morning or late evening hours.[81] One reason for this passion for self-education stems from the very nature of craft work, which required the mastery of physical materials and a technical knowledge that often furthered one's interest in science. This traditional motive was stimulated and broadened by the requirement of the new American nation for all citizens to be active participants in their society. The appearance of the mechanics'-sponsored Apprentices' Library rewarded and encouraged such efforts by providing young mechanics with books and scientific lectures. Southwick saw the library as a harbinger of "a great social improvement . . . among the children of industry."[82]

In keeping with their ideology, the mechanics placed technical knowledge at the center of their education, pushed religion to the periphery, and ignored completely the traditional subjects of Latin and Greek. In his lecture Southwick outlined a curriculum that gave primary importance to mechanical knowledge, a subject that prior to the late 1820's was not even offered at the Albany Academy.

> In the first place . . . let me conjure you to study in earnest . . . the general laws and principles of Mechanics . . . [followed by] the best practical treatises on the particular branches which you are individually bound to understand. . . . You will thus lay a foundation for improvement, of which neither time nor accident can deprive you.[83]

The "Science of Morality" was of secondary importance. Here, also unlike the curriculum of the Albany Academy, yet similar to that of the Lancaster School, Southwick emphasized the "plain practical lessons" of the Bible as a "rational system of conduct to be observed through life." This was in contrast to the speculative refinements of moral philosophers such as Locke, Reid, and Stewart, read at the academy, which Southwick believed would only "serve to waste the time, if not bewilder and mislead" those "whose duty is to be mostly active in the pursuit of mechanical labor." Finally, rather than urge the city's young mechanics to immerse themselves in the world of the classics, Southwick implored them to understand the world of their future by studying "the fundamental constitutions and laws . . . which bind you to your country." The mechanics' curriculum stressed their expanding role as producers and contributors to the welfare of the new society.

Despite Solomon Southwick's claim that the practical education of mechanics would neither "prove unfriendly to subordination" nor "weaken the arm of authority,"[84] the mechanics' ideology conflicted with the moral values of Calvinism that gave the authority of God to the town's colonial social structure. The new emphases on self-improvement and progress threatened Calvinist theology, church membership, and even Christian belief. Eighteen-year-old Joel Munsell wrote in his diary how as a child

> . . . three times I had read the bible through and could see comparatively few of its absurdities and inconsistencies, owing to the early and deep impression that had been made on my mind of their divine origin. But yet many things even then seemed wrong and as I grew older and better informed I rid myself of many of the superstitious notions that had audience among the multitude.[85]

At the same time that he developed this more "enlightened" understanding of Christian teachings, Munsell became critical of how Christianity was practiced. As editor of Albany's satirical journal, the Albany *Microscope,* he regularly lampooned wealthy church members and in particular their "priests" for living handsomely yet doing little to help the poor. Still, Munsell's journals testify that he was frequently a churchgoer but not, at least until late in life, a church member. It is not possible to determine how many of Munsell's fellow mechanics were churchgoers, but it is clear that few, and then mostly master craftsmen, were church members.

Methodists and Mechanics

Both the Methodist and mechanic ideologies appealed to the same constituency of less affluent journeymen, petty shopkeepers, and laborers. The growth in the number of Methodist church members, which made them the largest Protestant denomination in Albany by 1850, paralleled the growing popularity of the mechanics' ideology. The first Methodist church was founded in 1792, at the beginning of the Yankee migration. By

1817 Methodists accounted for 14 percent of the town's church members and 5 percent of the population as a whole. In that year, Methodist men worked as journeymen (58 percent), petty shopkeepers (32 percent), and laborers (11 percent). Their median tax assessment was nearly identical to that of the city's journeymen (42d percentile). And they shared with their fellow immigrants a western New England origin. Along with the members of the Baptist congregation, believers in a progressive new theology accounted for half of all churchgoing mechanics and about one quarter of the mechanic community as a whole.[86] All of this indicates that Methodism found its converts among the same people who were attracted to the mechanics' ideology.

The new Methodist and mechanic ideologies represented two complementary yet contending systems of ideas that grew out of the old social order and, at the same time, accelerated its collapse. Both attracted people who aspired to greater personal autonomy, yet were still deeply attached to traditional values. Methodism appealed to both the Calvinist emphasis on human depravity and the new insistence on individual autonomy. The mechanics' ideology emerged from the craftsman's desire to master his trade and, during the Revolutionary period, combined with ideas that corresponded to his developing sense of self-worth and economic importance. Methodism drew its followers primarily from mechanics, though Methodist preachers sternly rebuked any mechanic who denied humanity's degenerate state. At the same time Methodists were among the staunchest supporters of freedom and democracy yet surrendered themselves to a religious discipline based on submission to hierarchical authority. Both points of view stood for the progressive improvement of society. Together with the Baptists and other new departures such as the rural Shaker community, which sold its produce at the Albany marketplace,[87] they represented new social and ideological communities within the larger society that Albany's townspeople drew upon in various combinations to make sense of their lives. The early nineteenth century in Albany was therefore not a time when an older, well-integrated pattern of shared meanings was replaced by a single, equally well-defined modern cultural system. Instead, the new society that began to emerge carried within it a diversity of contending and complementary ideologies. Calvinist efforts to reform the moral order were enhanced and contradicted by new religious and secular ideologies that grew out of and challenged traditional society while disagreeing among themselves.[88]

Figure 8. View from State Street looking north onto Pearl Street in 1819. Engraved by Jacques Milbert. (Collection of the Albany Institute of History and Art.)

Chapter 5

The Changing Meaning of Nationalism in the Early Nineteenth Century

The meaning of nationalism was changing at the same time that new political and religious ideologies were emerging to challenge the world view of colonial Calvinism. As a local solution for transcending particular ethnic and religious differences that might otherwise divide society, the ideological unity of Albany's inhabitants as Americans and Christians was sufficient to carry them through the Revolution. This new national identity did not immediately draw the townspeople out of their Dutch, English, Scotch-Irish, and Yankee communal orientations. Moreover, the merchant-elders' commitment to the liberty of America did not imply any change in the community's hierarchical social structure. Well into the second decade of the new century the inhabitants affirmed these sentiments by electing their church leaders, now members of the Federalist Party, to the Common Council.

After the completion of the Erie Canal in 1825, different understandings of what it meant to be an American competed for moral and political supremacy. The Calvinist assumptions underlying the merchant-elder Common Council leadership lost their a priori character in the face of accelerating mobility and the growth of the market. New political leaders, more notable for their common economic interests than for ties of religion and kin, were voted onto the Council. They brought with them a new interest in cost-effective management and increased production. These new political values resulted in a new emphasis on "usefulness" and productivity in the rhetoric of the new republic. In contrast, journeymen employed the same republican ideology to secure better working conditions. In short, both manufacturers and journeymen employed the language of the new Republic to advance antagonistic visions of the American future.

The triumph of the Workingman's Party in the 1830 city elections signaled enduring changes in social values. Drawing most of their support from long-term tradesmen and newcomers working in the newest, largest, and fastest-growing occupations, the Workingmen's platform endorsed fair economic competition, democratic political reform, common schools, and individual rights as central elements in their vision of American society. These objectives were conservative in comparison with the social goals of the New York City Workingman's Party, yet they were radical when compared to the elite-dominated Regency Party's designs. At first a party of skilled tradesmen, the Workingmen gradually came to include all those who opposed "aristocracy." The party dissolved in 1831, but not before its central reforms were adopted by large segments of the new society.

Social Changes

The completion of the Erie Canal accelerated the collapse of the old social order. Albany's entrepreneurs had longed dreamed of a system of transportation linking the Hudson River with the lumber lands surrounding Lake Champlain and with the ores and agricultural produce now available from the rich farmland between Albany and Lake Erie. After digging began in 1817, these merchant leaders prepared for the new commerce by constructing a pier, 80 feet wide and stretching down the Hudson 4000 feet from the northern end of the city. Twenty subscribers purchased the pier's 121 lots, which together could harbor 1000 canalboats. Their initiative was rewarded in 1824 when 5734 boats passed through the then completed portion of the canal east of the Gennesee River. Three times that number arrived just 4 years later. By 1825, the town's wholesale trade had quadrupled.[1]

Merchants and master craftsmen expanded their operations in response to the new upriver demand for finished goods. This expansion was not uniform across the trades. Shopkeepers catering to the local market, such as butchers and bakers, or the highly skilled, such as shipbuilders or silversmiths, were least affected by the opening of the Erie Canal. Changes were most apparent in the building trades, iron business, and lumber market. Iron foundries, rope factories, and related manufactories became more prominent along the river to the south and on the town's periphery.[2]

Two examples, print shops and building crews, suggest the nature of these changes.

Market operations expanded the printing business, freeing wage earners from the immediate discipline exerted by household-centered production. In 1817 there were twenty-three printers in town, and they were organized into seven shops. Together, the town's print shops published periodicals, books, government publications, and five weekly newspapers.[3] Only one of these shopowners did not live at his workplace. The rest practiced a "system of Parental Government" with their live-in workers.[4] Thirteen years later the city's workforce included more printers (33) organized into fewer shops (5). A majority of the shopowners (3) now lived away from the workplace.[5]

At the same time that skilled tradesmen left their master's household, the division of labor and technological innovation reduced the demand for their work. The larger printing establishments now were surrounded by subsidiary engraving and bookbinding operations. In these areas, the general knowledge of the printer became less important than the technical knowledge of the specialist. At the same time, the new stereotyping process and steam-driven presses reduced the amount of composing work and increased the speed of the press run.[6] Mechanization reduced the craftsman's skills to that of mere typesetters whose craftsmanship was undervalued through wage reductions. As in the printing trade, in Albany's building trades the skilled work could not be handled by the least expensive laborers, yet the work could be subdivided and subcontracted to increase productivity and reduce costs. In 1828, an estimated 131 new buildings were erected. Of these, seventy-seven were brick. Several were over two stories high.[7] Master builders bid against one another for contracts to build blocks of uniform housing to be sold by speculators. These were the first of several neighborhoods of brick homes that were built periodically through the rest of the century. Building crews supervised by subcontractors put up these new commercial and residential structures as quickly as possible and at the least possible cost. Both trades came under the control of aggressive businessmen who stepped up the regularity, pace, and scale of production. They hired young transients with whom they shared little more than temporary contractual obligations. The result was an expansion in the size of work groups, a dilution of traditional skills, and the evolution of masters into businessmen concerned more with the purchase of labor, raw materials, and the distribution of finished goods than with production.

After 1825, more than 12,000 newcomers took up residence in Albany, increasing the town's population to 28,108 by 1835.[8] Most were young, unmarried men in their twenties[9] who found jobs as laborers and journeymen. Compared to the city directory of 1817, Albany's 1830 inventory lists 75 percent more workers with more than half of these men identified as laborers or skilled workers. Laborers from New England and the countryside, plus Irishmen who had worked on the canals, swarmed to jobs on the docks and in the new industries. The greatest increase among skilled workers was in the building trades. Three times the 1817 number of carpenters, masons, and builders worked to keep pace with the demand for commercial and residential housing.[10] In 1830 it was estimated that 1500 "substantial buildings" had gone up in the past five years.[11] Taking their places at the bottom of the work force, these new workers created even greater tensions in the old social order.

Nowhere was this tension more apparent than in the separation of rich and poor into their own neighborhoods. In 1817 less than one-third of the top decile of taxpayers lived apart from their workplace; by 1830, nearly two thirds did. In all, by 1830 61 percent of the town's independent proprietors lived on residential streets away from their stores, offices, and shops. At the same time the number of boardinghouses that sheltered new workers more than doubled.[12] Newcomers increasingly lived apart from their workplace, residing on rented land on the town's periphery and in working-class neighborhoods in the city's center.

The following map shows that after the completion of the Erie Canal the integration of social classes and of economic and domestic activities broke down dramatically.[13] Distinctly middle-class and working-class streets now appeared adjacent to the busiest commercial thoroughfares. Recent poor immigrants predominated outside the central business district.[14] Business-owning families accelerated their retreat from the commercial district. In 1817, for example, only four of the commercial district's proprietors had moved their families to the less settled end of Division Street, four blocks southwest of the intersection of State and North Pearl. By 1830 along these same blocks an homogeneous neighborhood of sixteen middle-class families welcomed home their merchant, professional, and manufacturer fathers from their workday in the heterogeneous mix of rich and poor, merchant, mechanic, and laborer along the commercial streets.

At the same time that shopowners established separate residences, the self-described "ring-streaked, and speckled, rabble, dirty shirt"[15] crowd moved into their own neighborhoods, north of State Street, and along long stretches of the town's periphery, particularly the waterfront. Here could be found the poorest, least skilled, and most transient of Albany's

☐ Central Business District

■ Middle Class Residential

▨ Mixed Residential

▦ Working-Class Residential

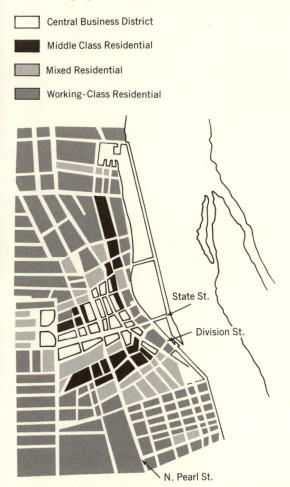

State St.

Division St.

N. Pearl St.

Figure 9. Albany neighborhoods in 1830. Drawn from a map in the 1830 City Directory. (In William Cammeyer Jr. and R. M. Gaw., eds. *The Albany Directory for the Years 1830–1831.* Albany, N.Y.: E. B. Child, 1831.)

workers. The 1828 Common Council Minutes described the city's northern inhabitants as "mostly mechanics" living in "a miserable collection of hovels."[16] In these neighborhoods grocers selling "ardent spirits" concentrated, crime and disorder were most apparent, and most of the more than 300 victims of cholera died in 1832.[17] This further dissolution of Albany's colonial social order occurred at the same time that the lawyers and businessmen who now dominated the Common Council shifted the meaning of nationalism from political unity to economic productivity.

Patriotic Productivity

Prior to 1817, Albany's political parties split along ethnic and religious lines because political relations were an extension of family relations. Federalists found support among the older pre-1800 Dutch, English, and Scotch-Irish merchant and professional families and those dependent on them. These Federalists attended the oldest Dutch, Anglican, and Presbyterian churches. As late as 1804 Dutch merchants, who were also leaders of their church, held a majority of seats on the Common Council. Between 1804 and 1816, they retained their majority in a Federalist coalition with English and Scotch-Irish merchants and professionals. Their colleagues were also leaders in their respective ethnic churches.

The Republican opposition to these Federalists was similarly joined by religion, culture, and kin. The Republican leadership included more recent Yankee merchant, professional, and master craftsman families who belonged to the Presbyterian congregations. Every year between 1799 and 1816 Philip S. Van Rensselaer, scion of the Dutch colony's feudal aristocracy, was chosen by the governor's council of appointment to be their mayor. The "patroon" presided over these two wealthy factions who shared traditional values as trustees of the Albany Academy, participants in interdenominational worship, and supporters of moral societies. Between 1810 and 1816, twenty-nine of the town's thirty-six alderman (81 percent) were members of either the Dutch, Episcopal, or Presbyterian congregations. Eighteen (50 percent) were at some point in their lives ordained by their churches as deacons, elders, or trustees responsible to God for the moral behavior of their fellow Christians.[18]

During the second and third decades of the nineteenth century, this merchant-elder elite lost control over city politics to a variety of newcomers who were less involved in church life and more interested in economic productivity. In contrast to the Common Council alderman of the 1810 to 1816 period, among the thirty-two who served between 1817 and 1823 only two-thirds (22) can be identified with a church and just half of these were leaders within their congregations. Three of these elders were leaders of the growing "minority" Methodist, Baptist, and Roman Catholic churches. A new need to appeal to the popular will, mandated by the 1821 constitutional convention that removed the property requirement for white male suffrage, hastened the decline of religious leaders on the Common Council. After 1820, the majority of Albany's voters were not church members and, as attested by their voting patterns, were less willing to follow the political guidance of church elders. Between 1823 and 1830 less than one-half of the members of the Common Council elected by these voters were members of the elite congregations (45 percent) and only about one-half of these (24 percent) were church leaders.[19] Political decisions were no longer made by the consensus of elders responsible to God but by politicians who offered conflicting interpretations of the popular will. Moreover, these newly elected officials could no longer be easily grouped by culture and kin. Instead, what marked them was their common economic interests as attorneys, merchants, master craftsmen, and allies of local banking establishments.[20]

The increase in Yankee immigrants coupled with the elimination of the property requirement for white male suffrage inevitably led to the decline of the Federalists in city elections. Local political contests then settled down to bickering between republicans over the role of political parties in a popular democracy. The continuing movement within the city's population helps to explain its increasingly mutable politics. A fourfold increase in the population from 1790 to 1820 meant that the individual's status was less fixed by family connections and community norms than in colonial Albany, which projected its social institutions through generations. Political loyalties could not be created through family ties, nor was there time to create and acquire traditional habits with respect to local leaders and parties. Change and uncertainty in political behavior was the rule. Consequently, the democratization of political institutions, which was the major theme in Albany politics during the first three decades of the nineteenth century, did not reflect the triumph of one consistently democratic party against an equally consistent conservative party. Instead, the evolution of political democracy came about through the efforts of politicians of different parties at different times who, in their desire to win elections, supported ideas that would gain the support of voters.[21]

For example, starting in 1817, the young lawyer Martin Van Buren attacked the friends of Governor De Witt Clinton as an aristocratic network of family connections. The Clintonians, ousted in 1820, countercharged that the attempts of Van Buren's followers, who formed the Albany Regency Party, threatened political harmony. Swept from office by a Clinton-led antiparty People's Party in 1824, the Van Burenites continued to insist that, contrary to the more traditional views of their opponents, conflict was necessary in democratic society. The important role played by the Van Buren Regency in the Jacksonian triumph in New York in 1828 supported their view that competition between professional political parties was the only way in which the popular will and public good could prevail. Although leaders of both parties claimed to be "for the people" and "against the aristocracy," neither party represented the coming to power of the city's "common men."[22] But neither were they traditional political leaders willing to impose God's law over the new society.

Following the popular removal of established church leaders from the Common Council, Albany's aldermen responded to appeals for new Christian laws with a studied inattention. On June 12, 1826, the trustees of the First Presbyterian Church scored a minor victory when they were "permitted to erect chains or barriers across Beaver Street and Store Lane" to stop traffic during Sabbath services. But they lost on the larger issue of "closing the marketplace and regulating grocers and victuallers on the Sabbath."[23] When the aldermen in 1828 received a "petition" from "a great number of inhabitants" requesting just such action, they endorsed its underlying contention. "The general disregard of the Sabbath which has hitherto prevailed in our country is calculated to awaken in the bosom of the Christian and the patriot the most alarming apprehensions."[24] But they did not create a new law. In fact, the Common Council did nothing. Subsequent attempts by citizens to stop Sunday work on the construction of the steamboat "De Witt Clinton"[25] and to prohibit the Sabbath passage of boats on the canal[26] were treated with similar disregard. The only other entries in the 1823 to 1830 Common Council Minutes that touched on this subject were several petitions by grocers and tavern keepers for refunds of their fines for selling liquor without a license. All of these appeals were granted. Instead of turning Calvinist morality into city law, the postcanal Common Council embraced political values that encouraged the expanding economy.

The Council's new commitment to cost-effective management was displayed in their new attitude toward the poor. Like the mechanic shops and new manufactories, city government itself expanded. During the 1820's, both the number of city employees and the amount of city revenues more than doubled.[27] But help for the poor was not increased. The city expenditures for the poor in 1830 were the same as they were in 1820.[28] At the same time, care for the poor took on a more economic and impersonal meaning. As recently as the turn of the century, the city officials who served as Overseers of the Poor had functioned like church deacons. They visited the homes of native families who had fallen on hard times due to illness, accident, or death and provided wood, clothing, or money to help them meet their most basic needs. Orphans and the elderly were, wherever possible, placed in homes, and the family head paid a monthly stipend for their care.[29] In contrast to earlier practice, as the number of poor strangers unknown to native inhabitants increased they were placed together in a separate almshouse on the city's outskirts. At the same time, public meetings were held "to consider . . . certain plans, whereby the healthy poor might be enabled and induced to support themselves."[30] Efforts were made to increase their self-sufficiency through vegetable gardens and cottage industries, such as broom making. Reflecting this new fiscal attitude, the Council denied in 1826 a petition for public land to construct an Orphan Asylum.[31] And even when private funds were found, the following objections were made.

> Does not all experience show that the increase in public charities promotes idleness and pauperism; and is not its natural tendency to destroy that incentive to useful and wholesome industry, which moderate pecuniary circumstances?
>
> Are not individual cases of actual suffering from pecuniary want extremely rare, if any at all exists; and if they do exist wouldn't it be better to relieve them through individual contributions rather than through a society where parents might leave their children and continue in idleness and intemperance?[32]

Where only a generation before poverty was accepted and the poor were sustained by family and friends, now the poor were perceived as outcasts, in some way corrupt, and expected to produce for themselves.

This development of a more judgmental and impersonal attitude toward the poor was part of the Common Council's larger effort to make improvements that encouraged productivity. In 1828 items such as the excavation of the canal basin, expansion of public markets, and the constant lengthening, leveling, and paving of city streets held the Council's attention. Manufacturing received the most support. It was promoted as a patriotic act of overriding importance to the nation and worth more than a little social discomfort.[33] On January 7, 1828, for example, the complaints of the inhabitants of Rose Street "occasioned by the delivery of grains at the Brewery of Mssrs. Fidler and Taylor" were denied. Instead, the Council accepted the explanation of the brewers, who found it difficult to supply their numerous customers without interfering with the inhabitants on Rose Street to some degree.[34] Stronger grievances were sustained. Yet even when the complaints of citizens about the noxious fumes from a brick kiln, which "produced serious effects . . . destroying the fruit, vegetables, and some of the Trees" in the neighborhood, were upheld, the Council went out of its way to emphasize the necessity of economic growth.

> [The Council members] are aware of the necessity of encouraging every branch of labour which tends to the improvement of our City, but while this

is taken into consideration we ought not to forget that every Citizen is entitled to the quiet and comfortable enjoyment of his property.[35]

Economic improvement, now envisioned as a patriotic act of citizenship and worthy of more than a little discomfort, was of greater value to the council members than care for the poor and the sanctity of the Sabbath.

The Common Council's linkage of patriotism to productivity suggests a new emphasis within republican ideology. Since the first days of the Republic, patriotism in Albany most importantly had meant the unity of disparate regions and peoples. As the war fervor died down, however, the townspeople joined with the rest of the nation in turning their attention to economic growth. The meaning of patriotic activity now shifted from the political unity of different cultural groups to support for economic productivity. The town's heroes and great men were no longer carved from Revolutionary War lore but from the tales of a growing and expanding society. Eulogists of these fallen leaders exalted their spirit of innovation and enterprise rather than their ability to unite the nation. De Witt Clinton was the first of Albany's new American heroes.

Albanians revered Clinton in a manner rivaled only by the reverence paid to George Washington. Nephew of the state's first governor and son of a major general in the Revolutionary War, Clinton led the successful postwar effort of the Republican Party to replace the Federalist aristocrats with new men committed to economic growth and development of the arts and sciences. As governor, he was universally acclaimed for accomplishing the construction of the Erie Canal. Even his detractors agreed that his lifelong ambition had been to promote the permanent prosperity of the state. The governor's death in 1827 evoked unprecedented public mourning. As one citizen lamented: "Since the day that the FATHER OF HIS COUNTRY was gathered to the tomb of his fathers the public expression of regret for a public loss was never more deep toned or emphatic than when De Witt Clinton died."[36] Numerous eulogies soon poured forth. They all sought to articulate the meaning of Clinton's life by describing him as a transcendent figure, one who was "raised up by Providence to aid in the fulfillment of its grand designs."[37]

If Clinton had been an instrument of God, then God's design was for a nation of "useful" people to apply their skills to greater productivity. The revered governor's name became synonymous with nearly every progressive new departure in the life of the town.[38] The first boat to pass through the Erie Canal[39] and the first train to enter the city's gates[40] were called the "De Witt Clinton". The De Witt Clinton Stove Works,[41] and even De Witt Clinton Fay,[42] son of a trustee of the leading evangelical church, testify to the spirit of innovation and enterprise associated with his name.

Workingmen

Economic expansion forced changes in the social relations between workingmen and their employers that inevitably rendered suspect the unifying appeal of patriotic productivity. As the market continued to expand, these manufacturers increased the speed, size, and regularity of manufacturing while hiring transient workers with whom they shared no more than economic relations. As a result, journeymen in the 1820's experienced harsher conditions and more obvious forms of exploitation than workers in the same trades at the beginning of the century. At the same time, as they lived, worked, and talked with each other, journeymen began to develop a sense of themselves that set them apart from their employers.[43] By the late 1820's, Albany's single society of master craftsmen and journeymen, the Mechanics' Society, had dissolved and in its place were created separate journeymen's societies and similarly exclusive societies of master craftsmen.[44] For a large portion of the town's early nineteenth-century Americans, the businessmen's celebration of productivity seemed to come at their own expense.

The beliefs and forms of social organization of Albany's journeymen first emerged in the years following the canal's completion and their sequestration into working-class neighborhoods. The immediate reason for the town's first labor strike in May 1826 was the carpenters' demand for higher wages.[45] The results of this strike are not known, but it is apparent that over the next several years the carpenters continued to attack the increased competition among master builders that undercut the carpenter's ability to earn a "just wage." To counter this trend, they sought to establish "permanent prices for piece and day work" so that they would no longer be "dupes of our own usefulness."[46] By the 1830's, they had formed their own Journeyman Carpenters' Association.

The Journeymen Carpenters' demand for more money was a symptom of a deeper, more troubling, and internally contradictory concern over the erosion of communal bonds between master and worker. When the Journeyman Painters' Society met in 1831 they made this appeal to their employers: "There is not that degree of reciprocal feeling between the journeyman and his employer which should exist and is highly necessary to both. . . . Unity is the answer. Let the master declare the journeyman's rights and their own inseparable."[47] Sounding like traditional artisans dependent on the leadership and care of their masters, the journeymen only asked that their employers "do justice to themselves and to their journeymen" by agreeing "among themselves to set a price adequate to their labor."[48] Then, in contrast, they asserted their independence by

Figure 10. Engraving of the entrance of the Erie Canal from the Hudson River. (Collection of the Albany Institute of History and Art.)

invoking their newly earned freedom as Americans independent from the subtle economic enslavement practiced by their employers.

> Woe to the power who dares to presume to rob us of the sacred name of freemen—and yet while we risk our lives and fortunes to protect our liberties from foreign invasion and despotic power from abroad. Yet will we nurse the canker in our own bosom which will sooner or later poison or corrode our whole system and render us the fit subjects for tyrants and despots to trample upon.[49]

Like traditional artisans, the journeymen painters were willing to let their masters decide "among themselves" what should be their "just wage." At the same time, they asserted their independence from their employers by phrasing their demand in patriotic terms. "He who deserts his own cause," they concluded, "also deserts his country."[50] The creation of the Workingman's Party in 1830 finally compelled many of the city's master craftsmen, petty shopkeepers, journeymen, and laborers to come to terms with their common political values in a city of obvious inequality.

The origins of the new party can be traced to a meeting of the "Mechanics and Working Men of the City of Albany" in February 1830.[51] On that occasion, 27 men were "appointed by the convention" to serve on the Executive and Corresponding Committee of a new Workingmen's Party. The median income (55th percentile) and occupations of these committee members suggest that they represented a portion of the population that was relatively new and inexperienced in local politics.[52] In fact, less than one-third had previous experience with other political parties. Less affluent newcomers from outside the established structures, they raised issues immediately relevant to their economic and social circumstances.[53]

The participants in the first Workingmen's meeting decided to unite to further their economic and political interests. Their first specific reform effort, to seek a lien law, attests to the character of the party organizers and the membership they hoped to attract. A lien law was a common concern of builders and their journeymen. Among the party's twenty-seven member executive committee were five builders and lumber merchants as well as three journeymen in the building trades. Two of the five builders were listed as masons in the 1817 directory, but they had improved their standing by 1830. These new building masters and contractors were concerned about their legal protection from paying for materials and wages on projects that went bankrupt. At the same time, their employees, such as the members of the Journeymen Carpenters' Association, threatened strikes if they were not paid. The lien law would preserve sound credit and fair competition. In this way, small, speculative builders would be able to advance their interests, journeymen would be spared some of the risks of unemployment, and buyers would have leverage in dealing with the wealthiest builder-capitalists.[54] Shortly after the first organizational meeting of the party, the Correspondence Committee added to their support for the lien law a series of reform objectives that together advocated fair economic competition, democratic political reform, and common schools.

The Workingmen opposed government intervention in the economic sphere so long as individual rights were protected and monopolies restricted. By eliminating the "forced sale of tools" and "imprisonment for debt,"[55] they hoped to protect the journeyman from becoming unable to practice his trade. The party's newspaper particularly struck back at those who saw the debtor as somehow morally corrupt: "the mere fact of being in debt, and being unable to pay, is no evidence of dishonesty or criminality. It does not necessarily involve any moral turpitude. It may be and most frequently is, the consequences of circumstances beyond human control."[56] In addition to securing the individuals' freedom to work at his trade, the party sought to assure him a just wage. By securing "industrious mechanics against fraudulent employers" and "restricting monopolies," they planned to extend to all trades the protection of the lien law. There was nothing in the party's platform that criticized capitalist practices so long as the economic rights of the individual were observed.[57]

A similar respect for the rights of the individual was expressed in the party's demands for political reform. Against the self-aggrandizing tendencies of those now in office, they proposed a "reduction of salaries for public offices," an equalization of property taxes, a reduction in fees charged by the Court of Chancery, and an increase in the salaries paid to jurors—thereby increasing the number of less affluent citizens who could afford to serve. The party's belief in political equality was displayed in their desire to revise the size and number of the postcanal wards so that they were "nearer the people." Newcomers in the fourth and fifth wards, in particular, were underrepresented. And they demanded direct election of the mayor, not his appointment by the elected aldermen. Beyond these economic and political reforms, the most far-reaching goal of the party, and most important following the passage of a lien law, was "public education for every child."[58]

The new party's position on common schools supported universal education of the town's children. In January 1830 both the state legislature and Common Council were petitioned by "a very numerous and highly respectable portion" of the people of Albany who asked that state school aid be used to create common schools. At that time, it was suggested that nearly one half of the city's children of school age were not going to any school and that the majority of state funds for education were lavished on the exclusive Albany Academy.[59] At the same time, the petitioners advocated a new approach to education that placed greater value on human ability. They criticized the Lancaster School for its size, rote methods, and stigma as a charity institution. Instead, they demanded that education give the student a sense of self. "The great moral object of an education," they contended, "is to give the pupil a standing in his own estimation."[60] Two months later the Workingmen argued that both the curriculum and the method employed in the Lancaster School were so dull that "judgment and understanding are not called into exercise, nor the feelings interested."[61] What was needed were inspired and enthusiastic teachers who would teach basic skills and "a love for letters, a desire for higher improvement."[62]

All of the Workingmen's political goals were symbolized in the credo of the party's newspaper, *The Farmers', Mechanics', and Workingman's Advocate,* whose every issue declared: "We hold these truths to be self-evident, that all men are created equal, and that they are endowed by their Creator with certain unalienable rights." In the first issue of April 1830, the editors declared that the party's purpose was to persuade workingmen to dissolve their allegiance to existing parties and "stand up for honesty, justice and equality." They implored:

Farmers, Mechanics, and Workingmen is it not high time that you shed the scales from your eyes; and rend the veil asunder which has for so long beclouded your understanding? Awake. Select men out of your own ranks who have not had their minds tainted and their hearts poisoned.

Such men were to advocate "democratic reform, practical equality," and the "suppression of corruption, intemperance, vice of every kind" so that "all men and women" would become "useful and enlightened members of society."[63] During the summer and fall of 1830, the *Advocate* constantly published the goals that clarified the new party's political agenda. These objectives were conservative in comparison to the more radical goals of the New York City Workingmen's Party, yet they were radical in comparison to the Regency's designs. All positions turned on one's interpretation of the "labor theory of value."

The Labor Theory of Value

The doctrine that all wealth is derived from labor had wide support in the early nineteenth century. It formed the foundation of all Lockean theories of property. Public officials from Andrew Jackson to De Witt Clinton held it as a self-evident truth. In Albany the theory could be heard in Solomon Southwick's admonitions to the readers at the Apprentices' Library, the *Microscope's* denunciation of useless priests, and Abraham Yates' eighteenth-century attacks on usurious Dutch merchants. By the 1820's it had become an axiom of all versions of political economy. Such widespread support was possible because the concept of "labor" was open to interpretation. As Sean Wilentz has argued, "a broad definition might include merchants, professionals, and bankers as productive citizens; a narrow one might exclude all but those who actually worked with their hands. Depending upon one's point of view, the labor theory of value either could be used to defend productive capitalist entrepreneurship or condemn it."[64]

The platform of the Albany Workingman's Party was inspired by the success of a Workingman's Party in the fall of 1829 New York City elections; but it did not agree with the more radical leaders of that party, including Fanny Wright and Thomas Skidmore. These agitators held that American society was fundamentally flawed because of violations of natural law by nonlaboring capitalists who amassed land and charged usurious interest. Skidmore's plan was to redistribute all property equally following an extreme interpretation of the Declaration of Independence's statement that each person had an equal claim on the Creator's endowment. On a visit to Albany, Fanny Wright outlined an equally radical educational system. Like the Albany Workingmen, Wright was critical of elite private schools for the wealthy as well as the rote methods and charity stigma of the Lancaster schools; however, she also wanted to place children under the guardianship of the state in boarding schools and eliminate the "super-stitious" influences of religious education. Through these utopian schools would come a generation to perfect the egalitarian institutions of America.[65]

Following Fanny Wright's October 1829 visit, the first meeting of the Workingman's Party in February 1830, and the subsequent April debut of the *Advocate,* the opposition's newspaper, the *Argus,* began a steady attack on the purported positions taken by the Albany party. On June 9 the editors of the *Advocate* responded, characterizing these attacks as attempts to portray them as a "godless crew of atheists and Jacobian levellers seek-ing a compulsory distribution of property without regard to individual rights of acquisition and seeking to bring in that disastrous sort of equal-ity, which would leave no distinctions for talents, virtue, no incitements to honorable enterprise."[66] Beginning in this issue and continuing in subse-quent numbers, the Workingmen separated themselves from the radical New York city "Workies." Albany Workingmen, they said, were "neither infidels nor agrarians, neither the followers of Fanny Wright, nor any Quixotic reformer, but rather honest men seeking their rights."[67]

At the end of June, the *Advocate* made even plainer the Albany party's differences from the radicals in the New York party by listing their four opposing positions: (1) the Albany party advocated extending education to all children without separating them from the society or control of their parents. "Our opponents wish to have them separated and placed in schools under the guardianship and control of the state"; (2) the Albany party stood for "teaching our children their relationship and accountabil-ity to the Great Author of Nature, and that the present life is only pre-paratory to a future and immortal state of existence." Their New York opponents "deride the idea of the existence of God and of a future life and seek to exclude such instruction from the schools"; (3) in addition, Albany Workingmen were "friends of national liberty and reform" and "opposed to inequality." However, their opponents were going too far in seeking to "extinguish all distinctions between virtue and vice"; (4) finally, they firmly believed that "industry, talent and virtue should be rewarded by the acquisition of honor, wealth and distinction; whereas the New York radi-cals wanted a single-class society. At the same time that the Albany Work-ingman's political agenda differed from a radical interpretation of labor theory of value, their denunciation of aristocracy united their followers in opposition to the town's other political parties.[68]

Between August and October 1830, the Workingmen changed their self-definition from "farmers, mechanics, and laborers" to all those who opposed the principle of aristocracy.

> We see no reason why there should be a distinction between the mechanic who labors with his hands and the lawyer whose means of livelihood exists in the exercise of his brain. But if either of them, or any other person, possessing extra amounts of wealth or having acquired political influence, should attempt to trample upon him who goes honestly about his own business; and endeavors to compel him to become subservient to his political views and interest, we think its savors of aristocracy and ought to be discontinued.

The only people they excluded were those who were opposed to aristocracy, among whom they found "with regret, many who should be on our side—even farmers, mechanics and working men who lend their influence to the support of old abuses, and who are content to remain under the vassalage of party, deprived of their just importance on the social scale." On the other hand, they were surprised to find enlisted in their cause, "many of other professions who might have as much political importance under the present system of things, as they can hope for in the most improved."[69]

> A disproportionate number of this latter group were proposed as candidates for office. It has not been inquired what was a man's occupation, but what were his views in relation to the great objects in view. Lawyers, physicians, farmers, mechanics, merchants, and men of leisure have been indiscriminately selected to conduct the opinions of the party, and proposed as our candidates for the offices of government.[70]

It seems clear from these statements that even though the Workingman's Party saw itself to some extent as representing a particular class, it saw no reason why it could not defer to men of upper class to hold leadership positions in the part so long as they accepted the party's principles.

Social Differences Between the Workingmen and Their Rivals

This raises the question "Were the Workingmen actually workingmen?" Appendix B answers this question. I will summarize those findings here. The Workingmen represented a disparate collection of long-term tradesmen and newcomers in the fastest growing occupations who came from outside the established political structures to advocate liberal political reforms. What united the supporters of the Workingman's Party was a common desire to eliminate aristocratic practices in the economy and politics that discouraged fair competition and individual rights. Journeymen and other less affluent workers, who once had depended on their masters and employers to look out for their best interest, reacted against mistreatment by asserting their economic and political rights. Capitalist entrepreneurs and other workers in the new economy supported the party most committed to loosening aristocratic restrictions on equal economic and political competition. The result was a party united in its support for economic growth, equality, education for all people and, as we will see, committed to temperance as a means for bringing order to the new society. Although the Workingman's Party would exist for no more than a year, its values became widely held as Albany moved into the 1830's.

As the political party best able to harness the growing popular movement for reform, the Workingmen accomplished a number of their political goals before succumbing to a coalition of anti-Regency groups that became the Whig Party in 1834. During the fifteen months of the party's existence, the state legislature enacted a lien law,[71] approved a state-funded common school system,[72] and abolished imprisonment for debt.[73] When the Workingman's mayoral candidate was elected, his first act was to free all the debtors in the city jail by paying their debts. After a week in office, he set up a soup kitchen in the basement of City Hall that daily fed as many as 400 paupers throughout the winter.[74] Such clear enactments of the Workingman's political agenda were undercut, however, by the party's support for established political leaders.

As the Workingman's Party grew in strength, it became less a party of tradesmen and finally not even a party opposed to the Regency. The fall 1830 city elections saw a greater participation by eligible voters (74 percent) than any previous city election and the selection of thirteen of the twenty Workingmen candidates to the Common Council. This triumph, however, was not without irony. Few of the Workingmen candidates were, in fact, workingmen; moreover, they chose as their mayor Francis Bloodgood, a lawyer and president of the New York State Bank. By the spring of 1831 the *Advocate* had stopped publication. Several of the party's objectives were taken up by Regency candidates who were cross-endorsed by the Workingmen. At this time, one of the Workingman's leaders observed that "this party, if it deserves the name of a political party, was too disjointed, and composed of materials too heterogeneous to continue long in existence."[75] By the fall of 1831 the party ceased to exist.

During 1832 and 1833, the major opposition to the Regency was a weak coalition made up of the remnants of the National Republican, Anti-Masonic, and Workingman's parties, which became the basis for the emergent Whig Party in 1834. Charles Gotsch has demonstrated that the overwhelming majority of those members of the Workingman's Party who were subsequently active in Albany were active in the Whig Party. He has also shown that most National Republicans and Anti-Masonic Party members became Whigs, and that the Regency was able to hold onto a majority of its followers. The 1832 to 1834 period ended with the beginning of what was to become a strong two-party system in Albany. The Whig Party carried the elections of 1834 by large percentages, primarily as a result of its appeal to the democratic concerns of the electorate. Subsequently, the Whigs would battle evenly with the Regency in the 1835 and 1836 elections, triumph again in 1837, and remain for some time a strong democratic-leaning alternative to the Regency's quest for political control of the city.[76]

Temperance: Moral Revision and Cultural Change

The rise of the Workingmen signaled enduring changes in social relations that required new moral meaning. None of the new political debates were complete breaks with the benevolent entrepreneurialism that prior to 1825 both masters and journeymen had identified with the mechanics' ideology. Softening the desire for increased profits were the still persisting feelings of obligation and patriotic duty that permitted masters to present themselves as both profit-seeking innovators and benevolent craftsmen. Similarly, the image of the Workingmen as equal and independent tradesmen, mindful of their individual rights, must be balanced with the fact that even these "awakened" tradesmen deferred to their "betters" in choosing their political candidates and that two out of every five politically active tradesmen did not support the Workingman's Party. Certainly an older society was giving way to a new one, but there was as much ambiguity in this transformation as there was awareness of what was to come. The temperance issue provides one avenue for assessing the moral revisions that accompanied this cultural change.

The movement to control drinking in Albany arose as the household economy collapsed. Most of the city's temperance supporters had been drinking all their lives. In colonial Dutch Albany drinking was embedded in social ritual. A house could not be built, a wedding celebrated, a child born, a funeral attended, a military display made, or any business prosecuted without the use of liquor.[77] Moreover, within the system of parental government drinking provided a bond between men who lived and worked together, softening and legitimating social inequality. The informal mixing of work and leisure and of master and wage earner strengthened the employer's parental bond to his employee. During the first quarter of the nineteenth century, masters increased the pace, scale, and regularity of production, moved away from the workplace, and spent their leisure hours among themselves. These same men were the first to attack drinking for its effect on worker productivity and proclaim its central role in social disorder.

The temperance movement was begun by the leading members of the town's Calvinist churches. In 1815 their "Society for the Suppression of Vice and Immorality" spoke out against "petty grocers and taverns" that sold liquor to working people and therefore contributed to all sorts of "contamination and vice."[78] In the late 1820's these same Reformed church leaders created city and state temperance societies that reduced nearly all manner of social disorder to the use of strong drink. Disrespectful and indolent workers, runaway husbands, Sabbath breakers, paupers, brawlers, criminals, and disease carriers all combined in their minds into the collective image of an inebriated working class.[79] The height of such thinking was reached when all but 2 of the 336 adult deaths in the 1832 cholera plague were traced to the same single cause: intemperance.[80]

Despite all the fanfare, as we have seen, the effort to control drinking by reestablishing the elite's parental control over their workers had little success. Much was made of the fact that a few inns began to serve coffee instead of spirits, that the Pioneer Stage solicited business with the promise that its crew was strictly temperate, and that at some city celebrations the traditional "corporation punch" was abandoned. Yet in 1830 a Temperance Society Committee reported that there were still 415 taverns and groceries selling spirits in the city.[81] In 1831 a local newspaper lamented that two of the city's largest liquor merchants, who were also members of Second Presbyterian Church, were "selling more of the poison now than at any previous time." At the same time, the Presbyterian newspaper *The Christian Register* continued to run porter and cider advertisements and recipes for homemade beer.[82]

Support for temperance had more than one meaning. Advocates of the town's workingmen were not opposed to the principle of temperance but to the blatantly economic motives of the parental approach. Rather than attack the character of Albany's working men, these "Temperance Generals" were urged instead to demonstrate to their employees a respect for their human rights. "Make men happy in equality, let them be equals in education, equals in the comforts of life," the worker-supported *Microscope* declared, "and misanthropy, murder, and misery will be eradicated, . . . But as long as your Temperance Generals can screw the poor laborer down to his 4 and 6 shillings a day, traffic in his muscles, riot on his bones—so long will poverty, vice and misery exist."[83] At the same time that the Workingmen rejected the self-interested tyranny of Calvinist church temperance leaders, they nevertheless embraced the principle of temperance as a means to their self-improvement.[84]

Albany's more "enlightened" tradesmen supported temperance as a necessary condition of their growing freedom and independence, while denouncing the parental approach of temperance leaders, which demanded the worker's obedience. The party's endorsement of the issue was couched in the provision that educational reform take precedence over the temperance crusade. This was because education was the key to making "all men and women useful and enlightened members of society."[85] With this larger objective in mind, workingmen signed the temperance pledge at the Apprentices' Society while participating in its weekly lectures and discussions for "mutual improvement."[86] And young men signed the "no ardent spirits" pledge at the Young Men's Society for Mutual Improvement.[87] Moreover, journeymens' societies, established after the breakdown of parental government, formed temperance associations to advance their own interests.[88] For different reasons, then, both the town's Calvinist leaders and its rising skilled workers endorsed the temperance principle. The elimination of strong drink would at once discipline tradesmen and point them along the road to greater independence.

✻   ✻   ✻

The rise and triumph of the Workingman's Party heralded enduring changes in social values. While sharing with the elite-dominated Regency Party an endorsement of economic growth, the Workingmen's successful campaign to attain a lien law suggests a widely held belief in fair economic competition. Moreover, the party's advancement of democratic political reforms, support for common schools, and endorsement of individual rights became central values in the emerging vision of the new American society. Drawing most of their support from newcomers in the newest, largest, and fastest-growing occupations, the Workingmen represented insurgents from outside established structures. Beginning in 1829 and continuing on into the 1830's, their political movement was paralleled by the sudden growth of the town's evangelical Christians who, like the Workingmen, represented newcomers in the expanding economy. By the early 1830's colonial Calvinism had finally given way to these new political and religious movements, who shared many of the same social values.

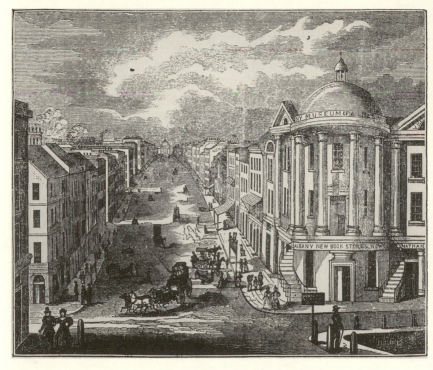

Figure 11. Engraving of a view of State Street from Market Street in the 1830's. (Collection of the Albany Institute of History and Art.)

Chapter 6

The Emergence
of the New Society

One fall morning in 1828, the elders at Second Presbyterian Church summoned their young, temporary preacher, Edward Norris Kirk, to an urgent meeting at the town's most elegant law office.[1] Since his arrival in Albany a few months before, Mr. Kirk had spoken with great feeling and force about God's imminent judgment. Such preaching, the elders believed, "offended the tastes of the congregation." Before responding to this accusation, Mr. Kirk asked if one of the elders would lead them in prayer. They responded, as Kirk recounts, with great consternation.

> I have never been in a besieged city; but I can conceive how people act when the ceiling opens and a bomb-shell strikes the floor. The appearance of those gentlemen was literally comical. Their manner seemed to say, "What! prayer in a lawyer's office in State Street, at nine o'clock in the morning?" The thing is right; but if anyone should come in it would seem very queer. To be sure, it is the King's business, but it will not do to have Him take part in it.[2]

There was a bustling of chairs; an old curtain was drawn to conceal the scene from employees and clients. The elders turned the office over to Mr. Kirk, who prayed that God reveal his will. The next morning, Mr. Kirk was given his wages and expelled from his ministry.[3]

The tensions that Edward Kirk exacerbated soon led to the formation of a new congregation under his leadership. This event was part of the Old School–New School division between and within America's Presbyterian congregations. This fundamental clash, between what George Marsden has called "the two great formative influences in American religious life—

Calvinism and revivalism,"[4] divided what became Kirk's Fourth Presbyterian Church from the rest of Albany's Calvinist congregations and was a harbinger of the divisions that finally formally split the New School from the Old School at the 1837 meeting of the Presbyterian General Assembly. At that meeting Kirk, along with his Troy colleague Nathan S. S. Beman and the evangelist Charles G. Finney, was singled out by the Old School leaders for his heretical beliefs and practices.[5]

Despite exclusion by the Old School patriarchs, the New School leaders succeeded in transforming the central beliefs and practices of Calvinism. Convinced that individual souls must be saved if America was to survive temporally and spiritually, evangelical ministers told their congregations that their own selfishness caused the social evil in the world. They exhorted their listeners to choose good over evil and recruit their neighbors in this great task. Together they had the power to eliminate sin and disorder. Revivalism, moral reform, and interdenominational cooperation would provide the means to realize the millennial power of God in their city. As a leader of this larger movement Kirk, along with his communicants at Fourth Presbyterian Church and his admirers in Albany's rapidly multiplying Methodist and Baptist churches, exemplified the emerging American Protestantism.

Following the 1830's revivals, evangelical Christians predominated in Albany's churches. As late as 1827, and despite a near doubling of the town's population since 1817, only two new congregations appeared. Over the next eight years, church membership increased 89 percent. Nine new congregations were organized to go with the thirteen already established (see Table 6.1). Most of these new Christians (87 percent) joined Fourth Presbyterian Church or one of the new Methodist or Baptist congregations (see Table 6.2). Between 1828 and 1836 these new evangelicals moved from a minority (25 percent) to a majority (54 percent) of the town's Christians.[6]

This great triumph of evangelical Christianity was not without irony. New religious ideas were fashioned from new political ideas and economic practices even while enlightenment humanism was sternly repudiated. Under Mr. Kirk's direction, the radical new Fourth Presbyterian Church congregation broke with the Calvinist doctrine of innate depravity and put in its place a more reasonable commitment to human ability. Respect for individual rights and personal liberty became a Christian duty. Systematic methods for creating and sustaining converts were assimilated from current economic practices. At the same time, social reforms emphasizing education and temperance became benchmarks for measuring the arrival of the millennium.

Table 6.1. Albany Church Growth, 1828–1836

Churches	New Church Founded	1828 Membership	1836 Membership
Established			
First Dutch		250[a]	323[a]
Second Dutch		264	279[a]
Third Dutch	1834		050[a]
First Episcopal		193	203[a]
Second Episcopal	1828		070[a]
First Presbyterian		460	500
Second Presbyterian		365	505[a]
Third Presbyterian		281	162[a]
Evangelical			
Fourth Presbyterian	1829		640
First Baptist		197[a]	350[a]
Second Baptist	1834		400
African Baptist		NA	NA
First Methodist		395[a]	374
Second Methodist	1830		300
Third Methodist	1832		206
Fourth Methodist	1835		137
African Methodist		NA	NA
Other			
Lutherans		100[a]	108[a]
Roman Catholics		NA	NA
Associate Reformed		NA	NA
Universalists	1830		120[a]
Friends	1829		NA

[a] Estimate.

Total number of churches in 1828: 13

Total number of churches in 1836: 22; 69% increase.

Total number of communicants in 1828: 2505.

Total number of communicants in 1836: 4727; 89% increase.

Table 6.2. Established and Evangelical Church Growth, 1828–1836

	Churches in 1828	Churches in 1836	Increase, %	Members in 1828	Members in 1836	Increase, %
Established	6	8	33	1813	2092	15
Evangelical	4	9	125	592	2407	307

Percentage of evangelical Christians in 1828: 25%.

Percentage of evangelical Christians in 1836: 54%.

Percentage of new Christians (1828–1836) who joined Evangelical churches: 87%.

By the end of the 1820's, the theocratic unity of Calvinism was eroding in the face of new political and religious movements whose common ground marked out the values of the new society. Both the Workingmen and the new evangelicals represented insurgents from outside established structures who disagreed among themselves yet together advocated economic growth, democracy, education, and individual rights, which were hailed on all sides as patriotic virtues. The rise of the Workingman's Party and its triumph in the city elections of 1830–1831 signaled that for hundreds of Albany's journeymen and small shop owners something was seriously wrong with the new Republic that required a new political liberalism founded on their individual rights. The birth of Edward Kirk's Fourth Presbyterian Church in 1829 provided capitalist entrepreneurs and women with powerful ethical claims that directed the community's moral reformation. Less than a third of the leaders of Albany's Workingman's Party were church members and only one-quarter of these were evangelicals, yet both the evangelicals and the Workingmen represented newcomers in the new and fastest-growing occupations who embraced the new social values.[7]

Fourth Presbyterian Church

When the young minister Edward Norris Kirk arrived in Albany in May 1828, he observed that the congregation at Second Presbyterian Church had "become crystallized into" an "ecclesiastical formalism" that valued the "prominence" of their members more than "living piety."[8] Like all of the community's Calvinist congregations, the people of Second Presbyterian Church had felt their moral influence wane as each successive wave of new immigrants loosened their control over social morality. At the same time, if the rapidly diminishing evidence of elders' house visits and church trials is any indication, internal discipline had grown lax.[9] Fashion and status, conversely, had become more important. Second Presbyterian Church relied on its identity as the Yankee church, symbolized by the codfish and golden pumpkin on its weathervane, and its elegant new building to attract leading statesmen such as De Witt Clinton and Martin Van Buren, a U.S. senator and soon-to-be-president of the United States. "Such men as these," one observer noted, "would call into their fellowship the young men of prominence, and keep for the organization the position (of pre-eminence) it had gained."[10]

The diminished influence of the Calvinist churches on public life was now apparent. On the occasion of De Witt Clinton's funeral, for example, every eulogist gave a peculiar account of his churchgoing life. One said he was "attached"[11] to the Second Presbyterian Church; another that he was a "respector"[12] of religion; a third remarked that "to the virtues of a truly great mind, (he had) added the faith of a CHRISTIAN."[13] Others vaguely spoke of his "private worth" or "private virtue."[14] All seemed to tack these phrases on, at the end of lengthy statements of his public achievements, as if to assure those who may have been concerned that he indeed was a churchgoer. In all cases, denominational religion was described as something separate and not of great importance to his public life.[15]

One reason for this retreat of Calvinism into private life was the fact that public attitudes now repeatedly contradicted the pessimism of Reformed dogma. Apparently those who held such conflicting beliefs either believed in traditional religious doctrines privately or ignored them entirely. As George Marsden has pointed out, the Reformed church dogma that dominated Presbyterian church councils during the early nineteenth century was increasingly at odds with the popular evangelicalism that was taking hold within the congregations.[16] By the time of Clinton's funeral at the Second Presbyterian Church in February 1828, the full force of this contradiction had yet to hit Albany. Edward Norris Kirk was the catalyst for this confrontation, which challenged not only traditional religious doctrines but a whole way of life. Some measure of the depth of this confrontation is suggested by the words of the senior elder who, after firing Kirk, informed the congregation that "He will never preach in that pulpit again; and I, for one, would wade through blood to my knees, to drive him out of the city."[17]

*   *   *

Edward Norris Kirk was invited to Albany as a temporary replacement while Second Presbyterian Church's current minister, John Chester, was ill. A recent Princeton Seminary graduate, he had been swept up in the revivals at Princeton and Yale in the early 1820's. Following seminary, as an agent for the interdenominational American Board for Foreign Missions, Kirk learned how to translate his Princeton seminary training into practical results by listening to the concerns raised by "common people."

> My professors and teachers had given me religious truth in its abstract forms, as the deepest thinkers had shaped it. This was very well as a foundation. But it was all Saul's armor when I met Goliath in the field. I found the necessity of forging my own weapons, to change the views and guide the actions of the

individual men and women I was meeting daily. . . . I was learning, not what Calvin and Luther and Voltaire might have thought about missions, but what John Jones and Mrs. Williams and "the common people" thought; thus from many individuals, learning exactly what any congregation I might address were thinking of when I should rise to address them; also, what answers were effectual in removing objections and securing their hearty cooperation. Thus mind and heart were being saturated with the subject of Foreign Missions.[18]

In Albany, Mr. Kirk employed his ability to address the concerns of the alienated in the congregation to catalyze the growing evangelical movement.

Following his sudden dismissal from Second Presbyterian Church, the young minister was visited by a "company of gentlemen" who told him "that the present state of things was a climax long desired by many in the church, and by some expected; that the division of the church was now a settled fact; that worldly men had held the church in check too long."[19] When a petition from this dissenting minority to reinstate Kirk was turned down by the elders, they submitted a formal statement entitled "Reasons for Withdrawing from the Second Presbyterian Church." Here the disaffected members of the congregation stated their desire "to enjoy such ministerial labor as we think conducive to our spiritual and eternal interest," and to found a new church organization in order to meet the increasing "spiritual destitution" in the northern part of the city. "Many of my friends in the ministry advised me not to form the church," Kirk later recounted. Yet "duty appeared to me clear, and I lived to see, I believe, every man of them compelled, more or less reluctantly, to leave his own pulpit."[20]

From the outset Kirk's church was strikingly more evangelical than the town's other Calvinist congregations. The new flock made known its intention to convert others to their point of view by opening their church in a hall over an old tannery in the "poor" and newly settled northern suburb of Colonie. This was an area of ramshackle houses and new manufactories dominated by less affluent and more transient journeymen and small shopkeepers.

A temporary staircase led up on the outside of the building. The windows had no glass, and the seats were rough, and had no backs. During the summer months, and through the early autumn, crowds flocked thither. The windowsills, and every other available space, were occupied by eager listeners. . . . It was no place for the merely curious.[21]

The congregation's decision not to charge a rental fee for seats encouraged the acceptance of poor people. Weekly social meetings were held in the different neighborhoods around the church to acquaint the inhabitants with the new minister. At least one nearby resident complained of being "approached like a highwayman . . . on a public street" and "on a week-day" by one of Kirk's zealous followers who asked "Do you love the Lord Jesus Christ?"[22] Interested parties were directed to the constant meetings held in the room above the tannery.

The new Christian message heard in this room denied the doctrine of innate depravity and thereby tied Christian thinking closer to the new society's more reasonable commitment to human ability. The belief in predestination was replaced by a more tangible confidence in the individual will. Evil was no longer the result of innate depravity but of choices made by selfish men and women. Sin and disorder would be eliminated when they chose good over evil and convinced others to do the same. By taking responsibility for one's own actions and the behavior of others, moreover, the convert's ethical focus moved from a belief that "the church and her ministers must not go in advance of public sentiment," as Kirk explained, to a conviction "that it is right for [God's] church to be the pioneer of moral reformations."[23]

Underlying this new moral energy was a new estimation of human ability. As recently as 1830, Second Presbyterian Church's new minister, William Sprague, had insisted that most people were innately depraved. Christians could not change them but could discipline their behavior through parental control.[24] The new Christian thinking, however, taught that social order and human happiness did not result from external authority but from choices made by people who were morally responsible for their actions. This development was most apparent in the Sabbath schools. In the 1820s, children in Second Presbyterian Church's Sunday school were forced to impress "upon their memories texts of scripture, hymns, and prayers."[25] One hundred and forty-three of these scholars recited from memory 17,865 verses in 1826.[26] In the 1830's Fourth Presbyterian Church's Sunday school scholars did not memorize the Bible. Instead, they were given a "small selection of the Scripture, that instead of the mere exercise of memory, every principle must be thoroughly understood and . . . brought home to the conscience."[27] Individuals capable of moral redemption could not be controlled by external authority. They were free moral agents, capable of accepting or rejecting the salvation of God.

At the same time Mr. Kirk offered to his congregation a more reasonable understanding of human ability, he also presented them with a unified vision of Christianity that transcended divisions of creed and theology. Unlike other Calvinist churches, Fourth Presbyterian Church did not require candidates for admission to demonstrate their knowledge of denominationally bound doctrines. Instead, like the Methodists and Baptists, Kirk's only admission requirement was evidence of a conversion experience. Similarly, the theology students he trained at Fourth Presbyterian Church were given a "more efficient" course of study that stressed a "thorough exegetical study of the Bible" yet gave only passing attention to theology. "I had rather throw my theology and philosophy into the ashes," the young minister declared, "than lose my reference to God's preferences . . . in all my actions."[28]

In addition to this more emotional and biblically based Christian world view, Kirk's church adopted economic practices from the new society. In particular, the length of time spent in church activities and the systematic organization of that time were both increased. Unlike the "half day worshippers" at the city's other Calvinist congregations, the Sabbath services throughout Kirk's ministry encompassed the entire day. Two sessions of the Sabbath school, three prayer meetings, and three preaching services were interwoven from eight in the morning until nine at night. For weeks at a time, a prayer meeting was held every morning at six. During the winter months four-day-long continuous meetings of preaching and prayer kept up the pressure of God's demands. In these organized revivals the evangelist was aided by like-minded ministers from throughout the state who took turns speaking directly to the sinner's damnable state while inviting her to come forward and surrender to God. Reports of numerous and constant conversions in Kirk's church led one observer to accuse him of "manufacturing Christians in the dark watches of the night."[29] One hundred and thirty-four inhabitants did enter Fourth Presbyterian Church in 1829, and an average of 125 joined during each of his eight years in Albany.[30]

After conversion a strict moral discipline kept the new vision alive, while systematic renewal through Bible classes, services, and meetings made it real. The discipline demanded by the church's leaders was reminiscent of the early post-Revolutionary War years at First Presbyterian Church. Like those Scotch-Irish immigrants, each of Fourth Presbyterian Church's communicants was visited each month by an elder responsible for their neighborhood. Wrongdoers were punished for irregular church attendance and for the common vices of profanity, dancing, drunkenness, and theatergoing. More serious sins, such as fornication, were confessed to the Sabbath congregation. Unlike First Presbyterian Church, and more like the Methodists, was the division of the entire congregation into weekly

Bible classes and similar gatherings for conversation and prayer. In addition, Fourth Presbyterian Church developed its own rituals and holy days, such as the annual prayer meeting of ladies held on the anniversary of the sorrowful night after the rejection of Mr. Kirk by the elders of the Second Presbyterian Church.[31]

*   *   *

Some of Albany's Old School Presbyterian leaders recognized that the reason for the rapid growth of the new evangelical congregation had as much to do with changes in ecclesiastical order as with theological principles. In December 1830 the editor of the local Presbyterian newspaper, the *Christian Register,* acknowledged that "there are two classes of Presbyterian churches in this city." Kirk's evangelical church was in one group and the others were "those in the older churches that have not manifested their activity and zeal in the cause of Christ nor exercised that holy and extended influence, nor made their progress in piety and members which is expected of them." Rather than "extend their influence" and "progress" in members, the older churches remained "apprehensive of violations of decency and order."[32]

The following year Kirk's close friend and collaborator, Presbyterian minister Nathan S. S. Beman of Troy, tied the differences between the old and new churches more closely to church order. Beman was an important protagonist in the theological divisions that erupted in the 1830 and 1831 meetings of the Presbyterian General Assembly. The debate in both meetings centered on differences between liberal and moderate Calvinists. In an article published in the *Christian Register,* Beman argued that the reasons for schisms, such as that which occurred at Second Presbyterian Church, were primarily ecclesiastical, not theological. The Troy cleric said that the Presbyterian ministers who attended the 1830 General Assembly reflected a variety of doctrinal stances from "moderate to liberal" Calvinism, which could not be neatly subdivided into Old and New School. A much clearer line of division, he suggested, could be found between high church and low church attitudes toward ecclesiastical order. High church ministers resisted the movement toward democracy within church government and the trend toward interdenominational cooperation. They were

> . . . firm and decided adherents to Presbyterian church government and order, without any such relaxation of the provisions of the constitution as will assimilate it to the peculiarities of congregationalism. In the like manner they

insist on managing their educational and missionary concerns without any amalgamation of them with voluntary associations or with any other bodies whatsoever.[33]

In contrast, New School adherents reflected more inclusive attitudes toward church government. They believed that by supporting interdenominational voluntary societies they were replacing a spirit of sectarianism with "a spirit more enlarged and liberal, more philanthropic and diffuse."[34]

At the beginning of the 1830's, Albany's Old School and New School Presbyterian churches reflected these divisions in "ecclesiastical order." The Old School churches gave a cold shoulder to Presbyterian ministers who supported democratic innovations and interdenominational cooperation. Neither Mr. Kirk, nor Nathan S. S. Beman, nor the great revivalist Charles Finney were permitted to speak from any of the Old School pulpits.[35] At the same time, Mr. Kirk was a frequent speaker and fund raiser at the First Baptist and First Methodist churches and was a supporter of the African Baptist and Methodist churches. Similar circumstances prevailed in the financial support given to interdenominational societies. In 1831 Fourth Presbyterian Church was a substantially less affluent congregation than Second Presbyterian Church, yet contributed twice as much money to the interdenominational Home and Foreign Mission Societies.[36] Moreover, in 1830 Fourth Presbyterian Church dismantled the traditionally hierarchical and denominational approach to Christian benevolence and put in its place a more democratic church organization. Following Kirk's directive, the congregation announced several "Resolutions for a Systematic Organization to Aid in Evangelizing the World." According to this plan, all the members of Fourth Presbyterian Church formed themselves into a "Missionary Society" to which each member gave a monthly contribution. Each month the society met to decide by majority vote where their funds should be allocated.[37] Standing beneficiaries of their time and money included the Education Society, Infant School Society, Home Missionary Society, and the American Board for Foreign Missions. Kirk believed that contributions to these societies, each of which stressed interdenominational cooperation, provided him with a true gauge of his congregation's piety.[38] The moral emphases of New School theology inclined its adherent to uncompromising support for social reforms. Humanitarian social movements that therefore became God–directed moral reformations included the campaigns for common school education and total abstinence from alcoholic beverages.

The Workingmen's campaign for common schools became a moral

crusade when its objectives were charged with a Christian purpose. Both the Workingmen's political drive for better education and Kirk's evangelical theology emphasized self-improvement, the duties of citizenship, and one's obligation to God. Evangelical educational reformers, however, placed the mechanic's stress on self-improvement within a larger spiritual effort "to assist the soul" in "its successive stages of heavenly improvement and refinement."[39] The patriot's desire for civic education was similarly subsumed by the evangelical belief that the "moral government of God" continued to "mould the character of the individuals who compose this nation."[40] Educational reform was given a higher moral purpose. Throughout Kirk's 8 years in Albany, he was frequently called on to speak on the topic of education, at one point performing a "tour through many principal cities in this State and Canada, on the subject of common school education."[41] In these addresses, the Presbyterian evangelist spoke of combining the practical and civic education of the common school with the Christian motives of Sabbath schools. Together they would "form and perpetuate a virtuous national character."

Similar to the common school crusade's synthesis of evangelical Christian motives and Workingman aims was Fourth Presbyterian Church's total abstinence campaign. Prior to 1833, Edward Kirk recalled in his journal, temperance reform was "thought by many to be a very good thing. But it was not discreet to introduce the subject into the pulpit and to urge it forward." At the same time, Calvinist efforts to reassert parental control showed few tangible signs of success. Kirk himself said that he found nothing wrong with an occasional brandy and water. Once convinced of the moral necessity of total abstinence, however, the young minister rallied his forces to promote the cause.

Kirk's conversion to total abstinence came only after he had deliberated its effects on his individual rights. In his journal he recalled first reading about this radical temperance pledge in an address given by Dr. Hewitt of Bridgeport, Connecticut, to the 1832 Presbyterian General Assembly. At first, Fourth Presbyterian Church's minister attacked the address as "a fanatical infringement on individual rights and personal liberty." As he recalled:

> I was no drinker—had no special desire to drink intoxicating beverages. But when I saw this man dictating to men what I should eat and drink, and denouncing me as a soul-murderer, I felt my right invaded. And when he pleaded with tears, I could recognize nothing but a fanatic.

Nevertheless, Kirk was moved by Hewitt's descriptions of the social misery that accompanied drinking. These were scenes similar to the ones the evangelist himself witnessed in the neighborhood of his church. Like Kirk, Hewitt "had been made to observe the effects of intoxicating beverages not as a philosophic spectator." Unlike Kirk, however, Hewitt

> . . . understood the subject; he saw its various and vast relations between the individual and social welfare; he felt the pressure of heaven-sent commission. I was sitting in my nutshell, seeing nothing, feeling nothing in the case but my right to drink a glass of brandy and water when I should choose.

Kirk's reflection continued.

> The field of death was soon open to my view. Scenes of domestic misery, the ravings of the mad-house, the reports of police officers, the army of thirty thousand slain annually with this tremendous weapon, the paralysis of industry, the exposure of life and property and all public interests by the drunkenness of drivers, engineers, physicians, legislators, even clergymen. . . .

The connections Mr. Kirk made between total abstinence and social welfare soon transformed the opponent into an advocate.[42]

During the five years from his change of conviction to the close of his pastorate in Albany, Mr. Kirk became a prominent local, state, and national spokesman for the total abstinence campaign. He delivered ninety temperance addresses in forty-nine different towns. He prepared the first total abstinence address ever made in the state of New York and rewrote his address for the president of the New York State Temperance Society as one of the first national addresses on abstinence in the country.[43] Under his influence, Fourth Presbyterian Church made total abstinence a requirement for church membership.[44] Fourth Presbyterian's elders became the presidents of two nearby ward temperance societies.[45] And, over a six-month period in 1834, Kirk was credited with nearly doubling the membership of the Young Men's Temperance Society while elevating the temperance requirement by demanding a total abstinence pledge.[46]

What made the evangelical's temperance argument so persuasive was its powerful millenial vision. More than an assertion of parental control or a means to greater independence, the elimination of alcohol was seen by Albany's evangelicals as a sign that the millennium was near. Said one Methodist minister, it was "at once an harbinger of the millennium, and destined to be one of the most efficient means of its introduction."[47] Taking the pledge, another local evangelist argued, "had a vital bearing on man's eternal salvation."[48] Unlike earlier Calvinist temperance leaders, Albany's total abstinence evangelists saw temperance as a necessary part of a larger effort to bring about the millennium.

During Edward Kirk's eight years in Albany (1828–1836), those who shared his "liberal spirit" became a majority of the community's Christians. One Baptist and three new Methodist churches were built on newly settled land or in working-class neighborhoods. The diverse theologies of these and other new Christian groups, such as the Friends and Universalists, professed a greater variety of religious ideas than the community had heretofore experienced while together they affirmed human ability. Most extended Christian charity by acting inclusively toward people not unlike themselves: the poor, women, and blacks. At the end of his tenure in Albany, Edward Kirk remarked that he was "the living witness to the fact, that the churches in this city will now bear a degree of directness and pungency that would once have been thought intolerable. I am told I have altered. I say, public sentiment has altered."[49]

The Social Background of Evangelicals

The men and women who followed Edward Kirk out of Second Presbyterian Church represented a new generation of the town's Christian leaders. In all, fifty-seven of Second Presbyterians 365 communicants followed the Reverend Kirk into the new Fourth Presbyterian Church. Sixteen married men formed the nucleus of this group, comprising both the new church's original elders and six of the first eight trustees. Compared with other married men in Second Presbyterian Church's congregation, these 16 household heads were upwardly mobile, recent arrivals involved in the newer or rapidly growing occupations. Fourth Presbyterian Church's leaders were half as likely to have been in town in 1817 (32 percent to 59 percent), yet they were more likely to still be in town in 1835 (70 percent to 48 percent). Although less affluent than their Second Presbyterian Church peers in 1817, they were more affluent by 1830. Four of these men made their mark in the new merchant activities of lumber, hardware, and manufacturing; three were general merchants; five were petty shopkeepers; and four were in the building trades. In several instances, they represented a journeyman's break with a master or a son's decision to leave his father's church. And, like more recent immigrants, they settled outside the central city neighborhood of Second Presbyterian Church's communicants. Most established homes in the newly settled northern section near the canal.[50] A new generation of Christian leaders left Second Presbyterian Church to create Fourth Presbyterian Church, leading at least one observer to remark that "Second Church has had a good skimming." "Yes," said another, "It is very important to skim off the cream."[51]

Table 6.3. Evangelical and Established Long-term Male
Church Members

	Evangelical N = 67	Established N = 270
I Merchants, professionals, and public officials	6 (9%)	124 (46%)
II Petty shopkeepers	19 (28%)	51 (19%)
III Skilled workers	29 (43%)	85 (31%)
IV Unskilled workers	13 (19%)	10 (4%)

The men who joined Albany's Methodist, Baptist, or New School Presbyterian evangelical churches during the 1828–1836 revival period were
postcanal immigrants who found work in the expanding trades or directed
that expansion as capitalist entrepreneurs. In the early part of the century,
one in every four Christian men was a Baptist or a Methodist who probably worked as a journeyman. Table 6.3 displays the occupations of all the
town's Christian men who remained in the community between 1817 and
1830. These church members represented 61 percent of all the town's long-
term male residents.[52] As can be seen, the locus of evangelical support was
among skilled workers. In contrast, the old and established Dutch, Episcopal, and Presbyterian churches dominated the elite merchant and professional occupations. Table 6.4 shows that among the Baptist and Methodist
churches the Methodist church had the largest number of long-term community residents and was primarily a denomination of skilled workers.
During the 1830's revivals, most of the male workers who joined evangelical churches were newcomers in the skilled trades and fastest-growing
occupations. Table 6.5 lists the occupations of every male church member

Table 6.4. Occupations of Baptist and Methodist
Long-term Male Church Members

	Baptists N = 13	Methodists N = 51
I Merchants, professionals, and public officials	3 (23%)	3 (6%)
II Petty shopkeepers	5 (35%)	13 (25%)
III Skilled workers	3 (23%)	22 (43%)
IV Unskilled workers	2 (15%)	13 (25%)

Table 6.5. Occupations of Evangelical and Established Male Church Members in 1830

	Evangelicals N = 268	Established N = 457
I Merchants, professionals, and public officials	57 (21%)	198 (43%)
II Petty shopkeepers	54 (20%)	86 (19%)
III Skilled workers	116 (43%)	150 (33%)
IV Unskilled workers	41 (15%)	23 (5%)

whose name appears on an available church list for the 1828 to 1836 revival period and in the 1830 city directory. It divides these workers between evangelical and established church members. The locus of evangelical support remained among the skilled tradesmen. Moreover, newcomers, those whose names did not appear in the 1817 city directory, accounted for 75 percent of the membership of the new evangelical churches. This compares with a 45 percent recent immigrant population in the established churches. Table 6.6 compares the ten most common occupations of evangelical church members with a list of the town's most rapidly expanding occupations. Seventy-one percent of these evangelical churchgoers participated in the expansion of the economy. Moreover, the leaders of their churches were drawn primarily from the ranks of entrepreneurs, petty shopkeepers, and master craftsman.

The men whom Albany's evangelicals chose to wield religious authority in their churches were also among the leaders of the town's expanding economy. Table 6.7 displays the occupations of Baptist, Methodist, and Fourth Presbyterian male communicants in 1830. Within the evangelical churches, Fourth Presbyterian Church drew more merchants into its fold, while the Methodist church was again clearly the home of skilled workers. Table 6.8 shows the distribution of leadership roles by occupations within the evangelical churches. Here the term "leader" includes elders, deacons, trustees, and the peculiarly Methodist class leaders, local preachers, and exhorters. In most instances, leaders were chosen by a majority vote of the men of the congregation. Taken together, evangelical church leaders represented a cross section of the town's merchants, petty shopkeepers, and skilled workers. Table 6.9 enumerates by denomination the relationship between evangelical church leadership and occupation. Merchants were clearly the leaders of the Baptists and evangelical Presbyterians, while

Table 6.6. Expanding Male Occupations and Evangelical Church Membership in 1830

Occupation	1817–1830 Increase, %	Top 10 1830 Evangelical Occupations, %
Manufacturer	2100	8
Dry goods merchant	750	
Lumber merchant	700	5
Hardware merchant	500	
Painter	250	
Cabinetmaker	177	
Teamster	175	
Laborer	174	12
Butcher	160	
Carpenter	118	17
Builder	90	
Mason	83	7
Baker	83	5
Grocer	76	11
Blacksmith	74	6
	Total	$\overline{71}$
	Median 70%	
Physician	67	
Tailor	58	
Printer	55	
Skipper	53	
Shoemaker	52	18
Public employee	50	
Cartman	48	11
Boadinghouse keeper	20	
Attorney	14	
	Total	$\overline{29}$

Table 6.7. Occupations of Male Baptist, Methodist, and Fourth Presbyterian Church Members in 1830

	Baptist N = 40	Methodist N = 148	Fourth Presbyterian N = 77
I Merchants, professionals, and public officials	10 (25%)	20 (14%)	27 (35%)
II Petty shopkeepers	12 (30%)	24 (16%)	17 (22%)
III Skilled workers	14 (35%)	71 (48%)	27 (35%)
IV Unskilled workers	4 (10%)	33 (22%)	6 (8%)

Table 6.8. Occupations of
Evangelical Church Leaders

	All Churches N = 59
I Merchants, professionals, and public officials	20 (34%)
II Petty Shopkeepers	18 (31%)
III Skilled workers	19 (32%)
IV Unskilled workers	2 (3%)

master craftsmen guided Methodist church activities. Table 6.10 charts the specific occupations of each denomination's leaders. It is apparent that Fourth Presbyterian Church and First Baptist Church were led by merchants in such new specialties as lumber, manufacturing, and building, while shoemakers, carpenters, manufacturers, and grocers were chosen by the men of the new Methodist churches to guide their spiritual lives.

Uriah Marvin was the highest-placed community leader to defect to the New School cause. An elder of Second Presbyterian Church, leader of the Kirk dissidents, and acclaimed elder of the new Fourth Presbyterian congregation, Marvin was also a postwar immigrant Yankee who began as a grocer and rose to prominence through the lumber trade. As an elder of Fourth Presbyterian Church, it was his role to supervise the morals of church members in the northeastern section of the city by the canal. While serving as elder, he was also chosen as president of the fifth ward's Temperance Society.[53] This ward was in an area where Marvin had sought previously to create a Marine Bible Society[54] and build a Bethel Church.[55] In that same neighborhood lumberman Marvin, in conjunction

Table 6.9. Occupations of Baptist, Methodist, and Fourth Presbyterian Church Leaders in 1830

	Baptist N = 11	Methodist N = 30	Fourth Presbyterian N = 18
I Merchants, professionals, and public officials	6 (55%)	3 (10%)	11 (61%)
II Petty shopkeepers	3 (27%)	10 (33%)	5 (28%)
III Skilled workers	2 (18%)	15 (50%)	2 (11%)
IV Unskilled workers	0	2 (7%)	0

Table 6.10. Specific Occupations of Baptist, Methodist, and Fourth Presbyterian Church Leaders in 1830

	Baptists	*Methodists*	*Fourth Presbyterian*
I Merchants etc.	Lumber merchant	Glue factory	Lumber merchant (3)
	Builder	Coach factory	Builder
	Dry goods merchant	Physician	Dry goods merchant
	Attorney		Morocco factory
	Merchant (2)		Hardware merchant
			Attorney
			Merchant (2)
			Deputy quartermaster
II Petty shopkeepers	Leather store	Grocer (3)	Druggist
	Flour store (2)	Shoe store (2)	Shoe store
		Hat store	Hat store
		Tabocconist	Paint store
		Clothing store	Flour store
		Skipper	
		Fruiterer	
III Skilled workers	Tailor	Shoemaker (4)	Baker
	Butcher	Baker (2)	Carpenter
		Carpenter (2)	
		Cooper (2)	
		Tailor	
		Hairdresser	
		Jeweller	
		Blacksmith	
		Currier	
IV Unskilled workers		Laborer	
		Crockery packer	

with his fellow elder and canal businessman Israel Smith, led the "impulse for northern improvements in the city."[56] Between 1826 and 1830 Marvin and Smith petitioned the Common Council for sewage facilities, leveling and paving of streets, and the construction of "sixteen foot wide sidewalks" on Lumber Street for the loading and unloading of timber.[57] Smith was also a founding member in 1829 of the Canal Bank.[58] Along with other leading members of Fourth Presbyterian Church, Marvin and Smith supported efforts to dredge the river and excavate the canal basin to insure the safe passage and harbor of the ships that carried their goods.[59] In their activities as moral disciplinarians, civic-minded citizens, and entrepreneurial businessman, these original elders of Fourth Presbyterian Church displayed the zeal characteristic of this new generation of Christian leaders.

Leaders of the new Baptist and Methodist churches were similarly energetic in their support of the new society. Among the Baptist leaders, Eli Perry and Friend Humphrey were the most well known. Both men came to Albany as journeymen in the early nineteenth century and became successful businessmen. Perry began as a butcher in the early 1820's and was listed as such in the 1830 city directory.[60] By 1830, however, he employed more than 70 men who slaughtered 10,000 cattle each winter in the city's largest beef-packing business.[61] Humphrey began as a tanner, rose to foreman of a large tanning establishment at the northern end of the city, and by 1817 was listed as a leather merchant in the city directory.[62] Each man was elected alderman and then mayor in the 1840's and 1850's. Both were leaders of First Baptist Church. Humphrey served as deacon, elder, and an early temperance advocate. Perry was the superintendent of First Baptist's Sunday School.[63] James P. Gould was the most conspicuous Methodist church member during the precanal period. He was a young Yankee coachmaker when he came to town around 1810 and joined the Methodist church. He later served as a class leader and a trustee.[64] In 1817 Gould established the Albany Coach Manufactory, which turned out the city's finest stage coaches, carriages, and sleighs. In 1831 the factory expanded to include railroad cars.[65] Like Fourth Presbyterian Church's elders, the leaders of Albany's Baptist and Methodist churches shaped the moral and economic life of the new society.

*   *   *

Albany's Christian women contributed significantly to this reformation. Throughout the revival period there was no greater witness to the changing place of Christianity in public life than the predominance of women in every Albany church. By the 1830's joining a church was as much a female phenomenon as holding a job, and *not* joining a church was a male pattern. If the 1830 census is used as a measure, 74 percent of Albany's male work force did not belong to a church. In that same year 72 percent of the members of all churches were women.[66] Largely female congregations were as much the rule for the old and established First and Second Presbyterian churches as they were for the young and growing Methodist churches. And this did not reflect any imbalance in the number of men and women in the community.[67] This separation of women from men corre-

Table 6.11. Women and Church Membership at Second Presbyterian and Fourth Presbyterian Churches in 1831

How Entered	Second Presbyterian *N = 101*	Fourth Presbyterian *N = 188*
Woman alone	21 (21%)	63 (34%)
Man alone	8 (8%)	25 (13%)
Total who follow or enter with women	31 (31%)	61 (32%)
Total who follow or enter with men	11 (11%)	13 (07%)
Total who enter as couples or nuclear families	30 (30%)	26 (14%)

sponded with the growing belief throughout the first half of the nineteenth century that women played a special role in maintaining the moral welfare of the community.[68] At the same time, women displayed a greater autonomy in choosing to become church members and influencing others to do the same.

Women played a decisive role in expanding church membership.[69] Second and Fourth Presbyterian churches kept detailed annual accounts of the names and family relations of all their new members. Women accounted for 69 percent and 71 percent, respectively, of the new members in these churches during the 1829 to 1832 revival period.[70] Table 6.11 presents the relationship between women and church admission in 1831 for each of these churches. At Second Presbyterian Church, 21 percent of the congregation's new members consisted of women who entered the church without any family relations already present. Most of these (13 of 21) were married women. Another 31 percent of these new members either followed or entered the church with their mother, sister, or daughter. All together, 52 percent of Second Presbyterian Church's new members were women who displayed either greater autonomy in entering alone or increased responsibility in influencing the decisions of others. These tendencies were even more striking at Fourth Presbyterian Church. There 34 percent of the congregation's new members were women who entered alone. Another 32 percent followed or came with female relations. In all, 64 percent of the new members of Fourth Presbyterian Church in 1831 were women who either chose to enter on their own or recommended it to other women. As recognized moral leaders in the home and community, more than a few of these women must have believed with Mr. Kirk that "the hopes of human society and the hopes of the Church of God are to be found in the character, in the views and in the conduct of mothers."[71]

Mr. Kirk offered Albany's young mothers a powerful Christian purpose for their lives that, at the same time, encouraged their autonomy. "There is more moral power in a mother," Fourth Presbyterian's minister told them,

> . . . than the world has begun to conceive of, than even Christian mothers have yet begun to fully comprehend. And as they . . . become intelligent in those great purposes of his moral government . . . we have no question that the moral power of the mother will rise.[72]

Not only were women morally powerful and encouraged to develop that power, but as they grew into the Christian way of life they were to escape their traditional degradation.

> And just as far as we get away from Paganism, and all its degradation of the female sex—just as far as we get away from the foolish and romantic ideas of women, that prevailed in the days of chivalry—we shall come to the clear and glorious light of Christianity, and women will be what God meant she should be in his hand, the regenerator of the human race.[73]

Women were to be the primary moral force within the family and the community.

With this concept of the new evangelical role for women in mind, Kirk created a maternal association within his congregation that advised mothers of their critical and peculiarly female role in the Christian development of their child. As Kirk said: "There is an affinity between the feelings of a mother and a child, that does not exist in kind or degree between the father and child, indicating a peculiarity of duty and a peculiarity in the responsibility." The special character of maternal love, Kirk believed, "could not have been unintended. . . . It is one of God's great instruments, for fitting [woman] to reach man in those periods of his existence, when everything is tender in his body and in his soul."[74] Women's new role was to "convey to the heart and understanding of a child" the conviction of sin and that "Christ alone is his help."[75]

The members of the maternal association also played a critical role in evangelizing the town. Kirk told his young female followers that "it is for the enlightened Christian mother (to) go to the habitation of her poor and uninstructed sister, and teach her how to bear her burden, how to train her family."[76] Acting on their own or in response to such advice, young women from several congregations led the effort to educate the young children of the poor in an Infant School.[77] An Orphan Asylum begun in

1831 had a similar origin and purpose.[78] More than one husband of these crusading women must have shared the following lament of a Methodist spouse.

> My wife has lately been promoted to a high rank in one of these societies, and she begins to assume domestic prerogatives that excite some alarm. I am occasionally warned of the necessity of my being home at a named hour, to take charge of our domestic concerns, as my wife's attendance at a meeting of the society is required upon very important business.[79]

Woman's social role placed her squarely within the home. Yet she was there to fulfill a powerful moral purpose that, ironically, encouraged her to gain for herself a greater autonomy through choosing and advocating church membership and serving in voluntary societies.[80]

*   *   *

Evangelical Christianity triumphed in Albany because it moved Christian beliefs and practices closer to the political and economic ideals of the new society. New estimations of human ability, endorsements of democratic procedures, and the inclusion of outsiders were subsumed by an evangelical crusade to create the kingdom of God on earth. New economic values that emphasized systematic work routines geared to increased productivity were assimilated into revival methods of attracting and sustaining converts. Most of the new evangelical men were postcanal immigrants who worked in the new or rapidly expanding trades. They were joined by women who in the moral education of children and the evangelization of the townspeople found a larger moral purpose for their lives. These men and women responded to a rapidly changing social order with new beliefs and practices more attuned to the ideals of the new society.

Workingmen and Evangelicals

By the early 1830's the theocratic unity of colonial Calvinism had given way to new political and religious movements whose overlapping values shaped the new society. Both the Workingmen and the new evangelical men were newcomers working in the newest, largest, and fastest growing occupations. Both groups advocated economic growth, democracy, education, and individual rights. Only a third of the leaders of the Workingman's Party, however, were members of churches and only one quarter

Table 6.12. Church Membership and Political Activism

	Regency N = 244	Workingmen N = 254	Anti-Masons N = 46	National Republicans N = 30
All churches	77 (32%)	87 (34%)	21 (46%)	9 (30%)

Total political activists: 574.
Total church members who were politically active: 194.
Percentage church members who were politically active: 34%.

of these church-going Workingmen joined evangelical churches. Nevertheless, it is clear that Christian Workingmen represented the mechanics' interest in every Albany church.

Several tables demonstrate the relationship between political party and denominational membership for the leaders of all political parties in 1830.[81] Table 6.12 shows that only 34 percent of Albany's political leaders in 1830 were church members. Table 6.13 demonstrates that among the political activists who did join churches, 27 percent joined the Baptist, Methodist, or Fourth Presbyterian evangelical churches. Moreover, there is no obvious correlation between party and denominational affiliation. As Table 6.14 indicates, there was support for each party within each denomination. Presbyterians were the strongest political supporters of all four parties, and there was substantial support for both the Workingmen and Regency in every congregation. What apparently divided the church-going supporters of the two major political parties actually had less to do with denomination than with occupation. This was particularly true of the established churches.

United by their membership in established churches, Albany's politically active Christians were divided by occupation. Table 6.15 divides by occupation the supporters of the Workingmen and the Regency who were members of the Dutch, Presbyterian and Episcopal churches. Skilled workers made up the largest contingent of Workingman supporters in

Table 6.13. Political Activity and Denominational Membership

	Baptist	Methodist	Fourth Presbyterian	Dutch	Episcopal	Presbyterian
N = 194	10 (5%)	28 (14%)	14 (7%)	41 (21%)	26 (13%)	75 (39%)

Evangelical church members who were politically active: 52 (27%).
Established church members who were politically active: 142 (73%).

Table 6.14. Political Party and Denominational Membership

	Baptist	Methodist	Fourth Presbyterian	Dutch	Episcopal	Presbyterian
Workingmen N = 87	3	11	4	20	8	41
Regency N = 77	4	14	7	17	13	22
Anti-Masons N = 21	2	2	3	2	4	8
Nat. Republicans N = 9	1	1	0	2	1	4

these churches; merchants accounted for the majority of Regency supporters. The tensions that finally split Second Presbyterian Church and caused disruptions in other established congregations are suggested by these divergences in occupation and political ideology within the traditional churches.

George Marsden has stated that most established churches "were divided in spirit, if not in body, between traditionalists and evangelicals during the early nineteenth century."[82] In Albany, this was particularly true of Second Presbyterian Church, but there are indications of similar tensions in the other denominations. First Dutch Church indicated sympathy with the New School cause by offering its vestry for the first organizational meetings of Kirk's church.[83] The new Third Dutch Church (1834) struggled financially for years in an underdeveloped part of the city.[84] The founder of this church, Reverend Isaac Ferris, was a well-known spokesman for progressive Sunday Schools that stressed an

Table 6.15. Occupations of Workingmen and Regency Supporters in the Established Churches

	Workingmen N = 70	Regency N = 47
I Merchants, professionals, and public officials	21 (30%)	29 (62%)
II Petty shopkeepers	13 (19%)	6 (13%)
III Skilled workers	32 (46%)	11 (23%)
IV Unskilled workers	4 (6%)	1 (2%)

active inner spirit.[85] The new St. Paul's Episcopal Church (1827) was founded, according to their historian, by "an evangelical movement within the church which sought new members from the growing population."[86] Isolated members of all these churches could be found participating in interdenominational societies. Unlike Second Presbyterian, none of these other established churches experienced turmoil leading to schism, yet class and ideological tensions were probably present in all their congregations. Although it is certain that few of the Workingman's supporters were evangelicals, it is also clear that those Workingmen who were Christians represented the mechanic's interest in all the town's churches.

*   *   *

To Joel Munsell and his freethinking fellow editors at the Albany *Microscope,* the idea that their morals should be regulated by a "crowd of young women" was simply another sign of the tyranny and fanaticism of all the town's churches. Between 1819 and 1848, this scathingly anticlerical weekly held the attention of a loyal readership in a town where dozens of other new newspapers and periodicals failed.[87] The *Microscope* incited older republican fears of a new evangelical union of church and state that would subvert the reason and therefore the independence of the common man. At the same time, the editors offered their readers rationalist ideas on universal salvation. The newspaper approved of economic growth and technological improvement. In addition, the editors firmly supported the principle of temperance. Rather than encourage church membership, however, these freethinkers wanted to replace the traditional habits of the workshop with their own societies of mutual improvement. What they offered Albany's young, unchurched men was a way of knowing that limited the influence of evangelical thought while providing them with an intellectual setting of their own. The pages of the *Microscope* provide one avenue for a closer examination of the differences between these two social groups.[88]

Joel Munsell was one among the thousands of post-canal immigrant Yankee men who made Albany their home. Arriving in 1827, Munsell worked in several print shops before settling down with the *Microscope,* rising to co-editor and publisher by 1834.[89] As a newly employed printer, he counted among his boardinghouse friends several journeymen who were members of the Universalist Church.[90] These were young Yankee immigrants like himself and probably not unlike the many skilled tradesmen and shopkeepers in town who chose not to follow their wives into denominational church membership. Sensitive to the rights of the common man, they were liberal in their social thinking and their religion. Munsell's own conversion away from established religion was encouraged by his reading of Thomas Paine's *The Age of Reason*.[91] As the leader of a newspaper that broadly represented the views of Albany's "enlightened" immigrant Yankee tradesmen, he and his fellow contributors offer us the best available insight into the world view of the town's unchurched workers.

The *Microscope*'s liberal Christianity was critical of the "superstition" and "sectarian bigotry" of the town's established and evangelical churches. "We belong to no distinct sect," the editors proclaimed.

> We are partial to no particular set of conventional forms. The universe is our church; its creator, the God we worship. Our anthems are the free songs of nature. Our ideal heaven is without walls; it has no gates to close upon our adversaries, nor porters to refuse them admission.[92]

From this perspective, all supporters of the city's denominations were guilty of creating an atmosphere that impeded the critical effort to liberalize and improve the human mind. "It is not that we love the clergy less," the *Microscope* editors proclaimed, "but that we love religion more, that we shall continue our endeavor to hurl the bolts of reason and argument against the votaries of superstition and the images of idolatry."[93] Albany's freethinkers believed that the "enlightenment" gained through study and reflection freed them from dependence on revealed religion. Conversely, they warned that by eliminating reason, revealed religion also removed the believers' ability to come to their own judgments. This denial of their intellectual independence, in turn, made them vulnerable to despotism. Evil-minded politicians could pamper and corrupt a few weak-willed "priests," and gain approval for their desired status as God's elect.

The clergy of the established churches were the constant target of the *Microscope*'s attacks. The paper was least critical of churchgoing Workingmen, whom they chided as dupes of an "exclusive class of men, altogether undeserving of the people's regard."[94] The "corrupt priests" of the established churches, in contrast, were singled out as hypocritical opportunists.

> These pensioned divinity orators, these seventh day glories, who live six days on the wine and marrow of luxury, these "meek and lowly" dwellers in splendid houses, who ride in carriages, who wear black and eschew lean salaries—deem themselves treated with disrespect if we worldly men do not

bow and cringe to them. . . . They rob the widow, they wrong the fatherless, they prey upon the fears of the effeminate, and cajole the weak-minded of their fellow creatures.[95]

The Christian rhetoric of these priests existed purportedly to advance their own selfish interests and those of their congregation. If they did take part in any other Christian duty beyond the preparation of sermons and the administration of the sacraments, the *Microscope* did not aver it. Instead, the paper observed that:

> The greatest part of our priests are handsomely provided for and receive in addition presents of no small amount. This being the case, and having so much time on their hands, is it not surprising how few of them we find visiting the distressed family . . . (or) wiping the tear from the orphan's eye. Would not the clergy be aiding the Christian religion by works, of this, and the like nature, more than by thundering out the terrors of Mount Sinai, and torturing and twisting texts of scripture to support their own peculiar tenets. Would not good works and philanthropy silence the scoffer at religion.[96]

Because of their apparently selfish and hypocritical behavior, Albany's established clergymen were despised by the *Microscope*'s editors. Kirk and his evangelical followers, however, were perceived as more of a threat.

Instead of viewing missionary societies, maternal associations, and Sabbath Schools as at least social improvements if not signs of the millennium, the *Microscope* saw evangelical social activism as a threat to the independence of the common man. "There is not a day passes," the editors state in 1829,

> . . . in which we do not (in the very community in which we live) . . . see a belief in miracles and fanaticism, that would disgrace the understanding of an idiot, held up as unquestionable truth, and hundreds . . . of professional deceivers . . . succeed in carrying away the admiration of the multitude, and bearing down every attempt at inquiry or the discovery of truth.[97]

Kirk, in particular, was singled out as one who had "acquired a most powerful influence over the minds of a large portion of this community; but especially over the unwary and the uneducated."[98] By limiting the reason of the unsophisticated, evangelical leaders were thought to increase their political power. "All of these religious societies," the *Microscope* concluded, "are under the control of a sect seeking civil power."[99]

Albany's freethinkers were not interested in obeying the godly authority of a few: they wanted the rights they believed that God had given to all. "Was our Saviour crucified and his system of religion introduced for the purpose of forming a hierarchy," they asked, "or was he manifested to break the oppressor's yoke, to unbind the heavy laden, and set the captive free?"[100] Evangelicals threatened to destroy this God-given freedom through their missionary societies and Sabbath regulations that violated the constitutional separation of church and state. To counter this threat, the freethinkers supported their own liberal educational institutions, which they saw as alternatives to the evangelicals' churches and Sabbath schools. In this way they hoped to hasten the arrival of their own rationalist kingdom. This was a world free of religious tyranny, where men would truly be able to think and act for themselves.

The Albany of the 1820's and 1830's offered disciplined, self-motivated freethinkers abundant opportunities to improve their minds. The Young Men's Society for Mutual Improvement provided a focal point for these activities. Munsell was an original subscriber to this new society and shared their pride in bringing together "the young of all ranks, professions, sects, and pursuits for their mutual benefit."[101] Here, for a small membership fee, any young man of the city could come to attend "Literary and Scientific Lectures," discuss issues in formal debates, or chat about city affairs. Lecture topics in 1834 included geology, phrenology, American literature, and American history. Debaters competed to answer such questions as: "Is the love of wealth a more powerful incentive than the love of fame?" "Have the Crusades been beneficial in an intellectual or moral point of view?" "Is genius innate?" "Are theatrical exhibitions beneficial?"[102] Members were encouraged to write essays on subjects of their own choosing, the best of which were read publicly. A reading room, which offered a wide variety of newspapers and magazines, kept the rising generation abreast of current affairs; and a library, that later became the basis for the public library system,[103] gave them the resources to expand their knowledge. In the society's first year, more than 750 young men took advantage of these opportunities and became members.[104] In addition to this society, the Albany Institute for History and Art provided the public with yet another arena for the advancement of knowledge.[105] The *Microscope* itself sponsored guest speakers and reading groups. These cultural and educational institutions provided Albany's freethinkers with an intellectual setting distinct from the churches and Sabbath schools. Here they could nurture arguments that challenged revealed religion and moral reformers on their own ground.

Ironically, however, Albany's "infidels" endorsed many of the same values as their evangelical rivals. Although divided over the world's ultimate metaphysical foundations and the goals of social reform, both groups were united in their support for commercial prosperity and technological improvement. In keeping with Paine's perspective, the *Microscope* was reluctant or unwilling to explain how economic and social changes might also have contributed to what they saw as the loss of American liberty. Even while ridiculing Kirk and his followers, the *Microscope* stood with them in welcoming economic growth. The newspaper itself was a profitable business that kept up with new developments in printing. Munsell displayed the discipline and management skills that would eventually gain him community-wide respect and a comfortable, middle-class livelihood.[106] Together, freethinkers and evangelicals endorsed the new economic values.

Like their evangelical adversaries, the freethinkers stressed to their adherents the importance of temperance. The sinful nature of drinking did not bother them nearly as much as its deleterious effect on the tradesman's reason and independence. Even though the *Microscope* regularly and scathingly criticized the selfish motives of "Temperance Generals" and the political objectives of Kirk's total abstinence campaign, this did not prevent the editors from believing that temperance was a "good cause."[107] At the same time, for example, that the *Microscope* attacked Fourth of July temperance parades as undercutting their celebration of liberty, the editors also decried the uncontrolled drinking of that day.[108] Drinking worried Albany's "enlightened" tradesmen because of the dependence it could bring.

Education, a cause championed by Mr. Kirk, was no less a necessity for freethinkers. Only through reason and reflection, the *Microscope* declared, could "the frail cobwebs of the imagination be swept away, and the intellectual rays of the great orb of knowledge" appear.[109] Both groups stressed the importance of common school education and the central role of the "Young Men's Society" in developing the faculties of young minds. Both Munsell and Kirk were among the first subscribers to this society. Kirk lectured there and never withheld his assistance.[110] Whether intended to dispel the "cobwebs of the imagination" or discern the "attributes of God," both evangelicals and freethinkers shared the new society's high regard for education.

In the end, the *Microscope* offered its followers a liberal Christian understanding of post-canal Albany that differed radically from the available Christian denominational explanations yet endorsed the central values of the new society. However heated the warfare, both Joel Munsell and Edward Kirk were young newcomers caught up in the excitement and arduous effort to create a new way of life. Kirk went on to a long and successful tenure at Boston's Mt. Vernon Church. Munsell created a suc-

cessful printing establishment in an age of keen competition. Late in life he
became a trustee of the local Lutheran church. When Catholics began
pouring into the country, both men became nativists. Though antagonists
in their youth, over time they expanded their common ground.[111]

*   *   *

By the early 1830's, the theocratic unity of Calvinism had collapsed under
the combined assault of new political and religious movements. Each of
these movements represented insurgents from outside established structures. Long-term resident tradesmen combined with capitalist entrepreneurs and newcomers in the fastest growing occupations to create
the Workingman's Party. Their platform sought to eliminate aristocratic
practices in the economy and politics that discouraged fair competition
and individual rights. Entrepreneurs and immigrant women became evangelical Christians. Together they moved religious beliefs and practices
closer to the "spirit" of the age by enveloping the Workingmen's social
concerns with a Christian moral purpose. Freethinking skilled tradesmen,
at the same time, set rational limits on the influence of revealed religion
while creating intellectual settings to improve the reason and independence of the individual. Despite differences among themselves, all of these
new movements advocated the values of economic growth, democracy,
education, and individual rights that were central to the emerging vision
of the new American society.

Conclusion

This account of cultural and social change in Albany, New York, has four implications for the study of religion and social order in American history. First, religion plays an important role in the creation of social life. Second, to understand this role we must adopt a stronger concept of religion as a cultural system. Third, culture influences social order differently in different historical periods. And fourth, by understanding ideology in structural terms, we can see ideological discourse as a form of social action that plays an active role in both the causes and outcomes of social change.

The relationship between religion and social order has formed the central theme of this study. The history of religion in Albany cannot be told solely by tracing ideas. Albany's church members were always immersed in society. The influences between church and society ran both ways. During the colonial period, the Dutch congregation exercised a pervasive influence over the beliefs and social practices of the townpeople. Later, economic and political ideas geared to greater productivity and democratic political processes filtered into the religious language and organization of evangelicals. Moreover, different ideas and social groups complemented and contradicted one another in unpredictable patterns. Witness the peculiar alliance of Dutch traditionalists and immigrant newcomers in opposing the British during the Revolution, the support for temperance shared by Reformed church elders and some mechanics, and the common social values held by Workingmen and evangelicals in support of the new society.

Beyond underscoring the mutual influences between religion and social life, this study demonstrates that culture influences social order differently in diverse historical periods. During the comparatively stable period of the colonial era, culture independently influenced social order, but only by providing limited British and Dutch resources from which people could construct different ways of making sense of their lives. In colonial Dutch Albany, most of the townspeople remained anchored to the Dutch religious and social world, recreating the habits of belief and social practices characteristic of Netherlands trading villages. A number of ex-soldiers crossed the margins into Dutch society by marrying into local family networks. To differing degrees all of the town's merchants learned English, British commercial methods, and something of the common law. As mediators between the local community and provincial authorities, the town's elders were particularly well versed in English ways, yet used this knowledge to protect the autonomy of the local community. In each instance, individual townspeople responded to their particular circumstances by creating meaning for their lives from the available British and Dutch cultural resources. In contrast to cultural action in the colonial period, beginning in the 1760's and continuing at least until the 1830's, Albany's townspeople entered into a period of social and cultural change where explicit ideologies directly influenced social order, though the actual social circumstances in which these ideologies emerged determined which among them survived.

During the 1760's the inner connection between the beliefs of Dutch Calvinism and the economic, political, and social institutions that sustained this world view began to unravel. Population growth, commercialization, and social differentiation placed increased demands on Dutch social institutions. New ideologies emerged to challenge the political and religious world view of Calvinism. Neither the new politics nor the new theology represented complete breaks with the past. Abraham Yates' political party offered its followers a new political ideology based on issues and individual rights. Yet in relying on the support of his own extended family and British ethnic ties, his new alternative remained rooted in the traditional approach to politics based on kinship and patronage. Similarly, Captain Webb's new Methodist preaching, while offering hope to a people in transition, was not accompanied by the strict rules and tight-knit church organization that would characterize the Methodist movement following the Revolution. These new alternatives, however, may have made the town's Dutch people less certain about their traditional way of life. In response, some of the traditional Dutch may have actively defended their world. Hence their older, more taken for granted cultural pattern may have become a self-conscious ideology. During Albany's early Revolutionary period, therefore, some ideologies developed, although they remained rooted in traditional patterns; at the same time, the older Dutch culture perhaps was ideologized. Moreover, during the Revolution these new departures were enveloped by a new political and religious framework for civil unity.

The idea of nationalism took hold in Albany because it responded to the local social problem of heterogeneity compounded by the threat of war. Without immediately affecting the town's hierarchical social structure, leaders of Albany's Dutch, Scotch-Irish, and English ethnic groups created out of their common cultural past a new political and religious framework that redefined the basis for civic ties. The central beliefs of the new nationalism were fashioned from the biblical religion shared by all three groups. As God had delivered his people from Egypt to the "chosen land," these new Americans believed, so too had He delivered them to America. Moreover, God's liberation of America freed Americans not only as a people but also as Christians. Church was separated from state, and the town's leaders affirmed the townspeople's common Christian ties. Coupled with these central beliefs was an enlightenment-spawned commitment to individual freedom and equal rights. Albany's townspeople were no longer united by Dutch ethnicity and Reformed church membership within a social hierarchy. Instead, they were united as Americans and Christians who together asserted the worth and dignity of political equality. The new basis for civic unity did not bring about social equality; neither did it draw the inhabitants out of their communal orientations. Yet it did link them to other communities who together formed a nation. Also, the new nationalism was not able to halt the social trends that underlay the community's tensions. But it did provide the townspeople with a common language, symbols, and rituals for debating their differences. Confronted with the threat of war, the town's heterogeneous leaders had turned to the available resources of their biblical faith and new ideas of individual rights to fashion a civil ideology that would accommodate unprecedented diversity.

Throughout the Revolutionary period Albany's townspeople debated the meaning of America. During the war, America meant first and foremost the unity of disparate regions and people against the invading British Empire. Yet it also had more than one local meaning. For Abraham Yates and his followers, the liberty of America meant an end to the Dutch social institutions that denied their individual rights. In contrast, the community's Dutch elders may well have viewed the Revolution as an opportunity to liberate themselves from the new immigrants whose presence threatened the survival of their social institutions. During the economic expansion of the early nineteenth century, the town's leaders shifted the meaning of nationalism from political unity to economic productivity. America's new heroes were no longer its military leaders but the economic innovators who were leading the way to greater productivity. Yet here again patriotism had more than one local meaning, as journeymen advanced an understanding of America as guarantor of their individual rights. In each instance, Albany's townspeople employed the language of the new civil ideology to debate issues that directly influenced the course of social change. Within this broader nationalism, moreover, mechanic and Methodist ideologies grew out of and challenged Albany's Calvinist world view while disagreeing among themselves.

The new mechanic and Methodist ideologies drew their support from the same constituency of less affluent journeymen, petty shopkeepers, and laborers. The rise of the mechanics' ideology occurred at the same time as the ascendence of the Methodist church. In contrast to the traditional Dutch, both the Methodists and the mechanics emphasized innovation and "improvement" as the pathway to social success. Their belief, that it is within human powers to bring human beings closer to perfection on earth, placed them at odds with the Calvinist belief in the imperfection of human life. Mediating between old and new, Methodism appealed both to the Reformed emphasis on humanity's degenerate state and a new insistence on personal responsibility. The Mechanics' ideology was similarly rooted in yet contended with the ideals of the old social order. It grew out of the artisan's interest in mastering and improving his craft and, at the time of the Revolution, combined with ideas that corresponded to the mechanics' growing sense of worth, respect, and economic importance. During the first half of the nineteenth century, each of these new ideologies, carried by the same immigrant constituency, arose, disagreed with each other, and intermingled as continuations of and challenges to an older cultural system.

The rush of economic activity following the completion of the Erie Canal resulted in the triumph of political and religious movements whose followers shared overlapping social values. Workingmen and evangelicals offered new ways of organizing collective and individual action. The Workingmen consisted of long-term resident tradesmen combined with capitalist entrepreneurs and newcomers in the fastest-growing occupations. Their platform sought to eliminate aristocratic practices in the economy and politics that discouraged fair economic competition, democracy, common schools, and individual rights. The evangelical reformulation of existing cultural ideas enveloped the Workingmen's social concerns with a Christian moral purpose. Evangelical leaders broke with the Calvinist belief that human beings could do nothing to assure their salvation. Instead, they told their followers that by choosing good over evil and recruiting their neighbors in this quest, they would eliminate sin and disorder. At the same time, evangelical leaders incorporated the mechanics' emphasis on productivity and democracy into their religious language and church organization. Consequently, Calvinism moved closer to the ethos of the new political economy.

The post-canal burst of ideological activism represented the experimental efforts of different social groups to create new plans for action in a changed society. Differences in ritual and belief were important because they underscored deep-seated changes in the everyday lives of the town people. Commitment to a new ideology, an event often marked by conversion, was a more conscious act because it represented a break with the patterns of the older culture. Whether actively advocating economic and political rights, the coming of the millennium, or the establishment of a public forum for rational debate, each of these new movements represented a rupture with older cultural patterns. And, although the ends they advocated were not the same, they all agreed that economic growth, democracy, education, and individual rights were important values. By the middle of the 1830's, these values became so uncontested throughout the society that they formed part of the seemingly obvious and natural structure of the new social world.

*   *   *

By rethinking the relationship between religion and social order in American history we can see how our beliefs and actions are the result of debates among a variety of ideologies carried by diverse social groups. If this study of Albany is any indication, the relationship between religion and social order in the American past is as ambiguous and convoluted as life itself. Like the people of Albany, most of us live in a world of complementary and contending world views. How we make sense of our lives is ultimately shaped by moral debates between and among different social groups. By seeing our religious past as a story of tensions and accommodations between different ideologies carried by different social groups, we come closer to understanding that the meaning of our collective life is shaped by this continuing moral conversation.

A Note on Method

As an historical inquiry in the sociology of religion, this study follows the lead of historians and sociologists who in the past two decades have benefited from overlapping research strategies. The use of new evidence such as tax, census, and church lists by historians has provided a social context for intellectual history. More important, the development of social history has brought social and economic factors into play in the interpretation of history.[1] At the same time that historians have made greater use of social data, sociologists have extended their interest in history. A growing number of sociologists have employed historical evidence in their analytic studies. Moreover, they have sought data not merely to affirm preconceived theories but to discover material for new interpretations.[2] The narrowing gap between these two disciplines allows for new perspectives on old topics.

Sociological interpretations of American religious history are in particular need of revision. Despite recent studies by social historians, most of what sociologists know about American religious history is derived from the research of intellectual historians, a school that has relied on literary sources such as sermons, doctrines, and diaries. As a result, sociological analyses have focused on changes in religious ideas rather than fundamental shifts in social order. In addition, by seeking data to affirm theoretical concepts such as "modernization" or "civil religion," these interpretations have obscured the complex relationship between ideology and social experience in the American past. For example, recent studies by social historians have questioned the unilateral erosion of "traditional" colonial society, postulated by modernization theorists, and instead emphasized the persistence of a communal way of life.[3] This suggests that older patterns of religious and social life were not inevitably transformed into new ones, rather that they continued to exist and may even have become lasting characteristics of society. Similarly, the belief that a unifying "civil religion" emerged at the time of the Revolution has been criticized by the discovery of widespread geographic mobility and social diversity during the early national period.[4] These developments indicate that while the national ideology of the Revolutionary generation may have been widely shared, its meaning was differently understood.[5] Sociological analyses of American religious history have placed too much emphasis on theory and the findings of intellectual historians while not paying sufficient attention to the historical record of social change. Consequently, we have no sociological interpretations of American religious history that are grounded in the data of social experience.[6]

The effort to integrate theory and data has been further hampered by disagreements between intellectual and social historians over the relative importance of the minister's sermons in the thought and behavior of the townspeople. Intellectual historians have relied largely on the thought of leading clergymen, particularly as expressed in their sermons, to portray the religious world of colonial Americans. As Harry Stout argues in his study of *The New England Soul,* "the New England sermon" had a "topical and social influence . . . so powerful in shaping cultural values, meanings, and a sense of corporate purpose that even television pales in comparison."[7] In contrast, social historians rarely assume that the religious ideas of a minister represent the world view of the townspeople. The best quantitative data, they point out, indicates that only a small percentage of colonial Americans were members of churches.[8] Moreover, they argue that it is hard to determine who heard what a minister had to say and, more importantly, how the words they heard actually affected their behavior.[9] Clifford Geertz's studies in cultural anthropology offer one possible resolution of this disagreement.

During the past two decades both intellectual and social historians have converged on the writings of Clifford Geertz to develop a new framework for understanding the relationship between religion and social order. William J. Bouwsma has endorsed Geertz's approach as fundamental for a new intellectual history concerned primarily with the "meaning" people gave to their lives.[10] In turn, Richard Beeman has declared that "Geertz's work offers the most plausible starting point . . . for the 'new social historian' in discovering the character of both community 'values' and community 'structure.'"[11] What is appealing about Geertz's approach is his contention that all of social life is shaped by culture, that is, by a range of activities from symbol-laden exercises such as religious rituals to ordinary activities such as building houses or making shoes. "All experience," as Geertz puts it, "is construed experience."[12] Though much has been said both for[13] and against[14] the use of Geertz's approach by historians, his writings remain the starting point for thinking about the cultural dimension of religion.

In looking at the relationship between religion and social order from this cultural perspective, Geertz holds that religious faith is maintained by sacred symbols and social institutions.

> Whatever the ultimate sources of the faith of a man or group of men may or may not be, it is indisputable that it is sustained in this world by symbolic forms and social arrangements. What a given religion is—its specific content—is embodied in the images and metaphors its adherents use to characterize reality. . . . But such a religion's career—its historical course—rests in turn upon the institutions which render these images and metaphors available to those who thus employ them.[15]

Religious faith is rooted in the "conviction that the values one holds are grounded in the inherent structure of reality, that between the way one ought to live and the way things really are there is an unbreakable inner connection."[16] Geertz refers to the ways in which a people explain reality as their "world view." Their general way of life, how they do things, and how they like to see things done is called their "ethos." Religious symbols, therefore, "render the world view believable and the ethos justifiable, and they do it by invoking each in support of the other."[17]

Moreover, when the "inner connection" between different kinds of faith and the images and institutions that have sustained them become unstuck, people respond in various ways.

> They lose their sensibility. Or they channel it into ideological fervor. Or they adopt an imported creed. Or they turn worriedly in upon themselves. Or they cling even more intensely to the faltering traditions. Or they try to rework these traditions into more effective forms. Or they split themselves in half, living spiritually in the past and physically in the present. Or they try to express their religiousness in secular activities. And a few simply fail to notice the world is moving or, noticing, just collapse.[18]

To understand the social and cultural processes that lead to these varied responses, Geertz suggests that the investigator pay attention to a society's history with a particular focus on "the major conceptual themes" as well as "the sort of social order in which such ideas . . . seem inevitable."[19] Working from Geertz's perspective, Ann Swidler has proposed a theoretical framework that provides a cultural approach to studying the relationship between religion and social order in the American past.

In her article, "Culture in Action: Symbols and Strategies," Swidler argues that "Culture influences action . . . by shaping a repertoire or 'tool kit' of habits, skills, and styles from which people construct 'strategies of action.' "[20] Culture, in Swidler's rendering of Geertz, is a "tool kit" of diverse elements such as symbols, stories, and behaviors "which people may use in varying combinations to solve different kinds of problems." "Strategies of action," in turn, are "persistent ways of ordering action through time."[21] Moreover, culture influences action differently in different historical situations.

> In settled periods, culture independently influences action, but only by providing resources from which people can construct diverse lines of action. In unsettled cultural periods, explicit ideologies directly govern action, but structural opportunities for action determine which among competing ideologies survive in the long run.[22]

In settled periods, culture is not a coherent system that pushes actions in a specific direction. Instead, it provides the limiting conditions or range of possibilities, delineating what can, but not what will, happen. Cultural action in settled periods, therefore, involves individual actors and groups choosing from various cultural elements to create diverse strategies of action. In unsettled periods, in contrast, overt political and religious ideologies directly influence action. Ideologies, therefore, represent a phase in the creation of a new cultural system. "Their independent causal influence," however, "is limited," Swidler argues, because, "at least at their origins, ideological movements are not complete cultures, in the sense that much of their taken-for-granted understanding of the world and many of their daily practices still depend on traditional patterns."[23] These movements, moreover, actively compete with other ideologies and with older cultural patterns that, under new historical circumstances, may themselves become ideologies. In "unsettled" periods, therefore, culture independently influences action by making possible new strategies of action. The actual circumstances in which these "strategies" appear, however, determines which ones flourish and which ones survive.

This contrast between "settled" and "unsettled lives," Swidler warns, "is not absolute." Instead, it is

> . . . primarily a distinction between culture's role in sustaining existing strategies of action and its role in constructing new ones. . . . Even when they

lead settled lives, people do active cultural work to maintain or redefine their cultural capacities. Conversely, even the most fanatical ideological movement, which seeks to remake completely the cultural capacities of its members, will inevitably draw on many tacit assumptions from the existing culture.[24]

Still, there are more or less settled periods. The colonial period, particularly prior to 1720, suggests a settled period. During these early years of American history most colonists lived in comparatively isolated, static, homogeneous communities characterized by low population density, immediate access to land, geographic immobility, limited distribution of wealth, little social differentiation, and independence from the market economy.[25] Throughout most of colonial America a patriarchal elite maintained control over economic, political, and religious life. The Revolutionary period, in contrast, beginning as early as the 1740's and continuing at least until the 1830's, represents an unsettled period. During these years the overgrown villages of the colonial era became major urban centers. Population growth, commercialization, and social differentiation, all well underway in most cities by the middle of the eighteenth century, led to factory production, a participatory and contentious civil life, and the emergence of political and religious ideological movements.

This study of religion and social change employs these ideas from Geertz and Swidler to provide a theoretical framework for interpreting Albany's religious past. Geertz's concept of religion as a cultural system best coincides with the colonial world of Dutch Albany. Dutch Calvinism and social institutions provided a world view and ethos that the Albany Dutch assumed to be inherent in the very nature of their world. This analysis extends Geertz's formulation, however, by displaying how the Albany Dutch incorporated British peoples and cultural elements into an increasingly heterogeneous and complex way of life. Moreover, by demonstrating the role that the community's leaders played in mediating between British provincial authority and the needs of the local Dutch community, this inquiry shows how a traditional people employed their knowledge of foreign customs to defend their world. Although Calvinist religious beliefs and social institutions remained at the core of the townspeoples' cultural identity, diverse and contending British cultural elements were also present that the townspeople drew on in various configurations to make sense of their lives.

Ann Swidler's theoretical formulation of cultural action in settled and unsettled periods is similarly affirmed and amplified through interaction with Albany's history. Swidler's conception of the role of ideologies in unsettled periods is particularly helpful in explaining the cultural confusion of Albany's Revolutionary period. This study grounds Swidler's theoretical ideas in the history of one town by describing the specific ways in which Albany's contending republican, Calvinist, mechanic, and evangelical ideological groups actually interacted. Moreover, this inquiry goes beyond Swidler's framework by relating changes in ideology closely to changes in social institutions. By grounding Swidler's theoretical ideas in the historical experience of Albany's diverse social groups and tying their ideologies to changes in the town's social institutions, this study demonstrates how ideological debates among shifting social groups directly influence the course of social change.

Social Differences
Between the Workingmen
and Their Rivals

Charles Gotsch's 1976 doctoral dissertation, "The Albany Workingmen's Party and the Rise of Popular Politics" provides the foundation for this analysis of the social differences between the leaders of Albany's Workingman's Party and their opponents. Gotsch built his quantitative study on a list of 856 members of the four political parties in 1830 to 1831 culled from the city's newspapers. Together these Workingmen, Regency, National Republican, and Anti-Mason activists comprised one-quarter of the eligible voters. By correlating the names of these political activists with city tax lists and occupational directories, Gotsch was able to determine the wealth and occupation of party leaders. In the following analysis I have used Gotsch's list of political activists and his list of all those who held taxable property in 1830. To his data I have added the names and occupations listed in the 1817 city directory and on the 1817 tax list.[1] By considering these data against the background of massive geographic mobility, some of the social divisions that underlay the town's political disputes can be seen.

The rise of the Workingman's Party took place in the midst of a changing society of people in motion. Between the 1825 state census and the 1830 federal census the city's population increased 52 percent. Moreover, 64 percent of the people listed in the 1825 directory had left the city by 1830.[2] For most newcomers, Albany was a place where, as one minister recounted, people "lodged for a while, and remained till perhaps some other agency put them afloat again."[3]

The available social lists offer increasingly accurate means of distinguish-

Table B.1. Political Activity and Community Commitment

	Number	Political Activists N = 856
Adult males in the 1830 census	6337	856 (14%)
Men with occupations listed in the 1830 city directory	2878	572 (20%)
Men with occupations listed in both the 1817 and 1830 city directories	536	209 (39%)

ing those passing through from those who became committed members of the community. Table B.1 compares these measures of community commitment with political activism in 1830. According to the federal census, there were 6338 "Free White Males" living in Albany in 1830. Only 2878 of these men were listed with occupations in the 1830 directory. Men without occupations or somehow not included in the directories accounted for 54 percent of the town's white, male, adult inhabitants. Compared to the men whose names appeared only on the census list, those who had listed occupations and addresses were more likely to have been committed to the community. However, only one-fifth of these men with names in the 1830 directory (536) had lived in the community for at least thirteen years. This is shown by the appearance of their names in the 1817 city directory. Men who held jobs in the community since 1817 were probably more committed to the local society than those who lived there for a shorter time. This commitment is demonstrated by their political activism (39 percent) in comparison to all men who held jobs in 1830 (20 percent) and all those listed on the 1830 federal census (14 percent). These job-holding, long-term community residents represented the base of support for all of the 1830 political parties. Albany's four political parties received between 36 and 41 percent of their support from pre-1817 community residents. In all, 39 percent of the political activists listed in the 1830 directory were also listed in the 1817 directory. As might be expected, the Regency Party had the largest number of supporters among long-term residents (41 percent) and the Workingmen had the least (36 percent). Both parties represented a broad spectrum of occupations, yet each drew the majority of its support from strikingly different occupational groups.

Table B.2 shows the occupations held in 1817 by long-term residents who were members of either the Workingman's or Regency parties in

Table B.2. Support Among Long-term Residents for
the Regency and Workingman Political Parties

	Workingmen N = 85	*Regency* N = 85
I Merchants, professionals, and public officials	16 (19%)	40 (47%)
II Petty shopkeepers	14 (16%)	11 (13%)
III Skilled workers	49 (58%)	29 (34%)
IV Unskilled workers	6 (7%)	5 (6%)

1830. The data on the other two parties, the National Republicans and the
Anti-Masons, is too scanty to include.[4] As can be seen, long-term merchants, professionals, and public officials played a dominant role in the
Regency Party. In contrast, the Workingmen's strength was among skilled
workers. The fact that some merchants and professionals were members of
the party supports the *Advocate*'s position that they were a party of principles, not of manual workers. Still, members of this wealthiest and most
prestigious group were twice as numerous in the Regency. Moreover, as
Table B.3 indicates, most of the merchants and professionals who ran as
Workingman candidates had previous experience with other political parties. In contrast, nearly one half of the Workingman Party's supporters
among established tradesmen and all of the party's supporters among
long-term laborers did not have previous political experience.[5]

To determine the support for the party among newcomers, the relationship between occupations and wealth in the Albany of 1830 first must
be clarified. Table B.4 charts this relationship. This is a ranking of the
average property assessments for each of the twenty-six occupations, with

Table B.3. Long-term Residents Who Were
Workingman Party Supporters in 1830 and Had
Previous Political Experience

I	Merchants, professionals, and public officials	14 (88%)
II	Petty shopkeepers	9 (64%)
III	Skilled workers	27 (55%)
IV	Unskilled workers	0 (0%)

Table B.4. Occupations and Wealth in 1830

Occupation	Average Assessment	Number of Workers	Number with Property	With Property, %
Upper				
Hardware merchant	9579	018	11	61
Merchant	7783	111	61	55
Dry goods merchant	3275	034	09	26
Attorney	2808	057	26	46
Physician	2386	035	14	40
Builder	2151	019	11	58
Public employee	2082	060	24	40
Middle				
Printer	1625	034	06	18
Manufacturer	1461	021	06	29
Baker	0860	033	12	36
Skipper	0746	026	07	27
Lumber merchant	0696	024	10	42
Cabinetmaker	0632	025	06	24
Butcher	0566	026	06	23
Grocer	0485	267	72	27
Lower				
Blacksmith	0325	059	12	20
Boardinghouse keeper	0315	042	03	07
Mason	0307	084	18	21
Carpenter	0238	201	28	14
Teamster	0198	033	03	09
Teacher	0179	022	04	18
Cartman	0177	078	09	12
Tailor	0136	038	07	18
Painter	0120	042	04	10
Shoemaker	0070	131	10	08
Laborer	0032	299	13	04

more than twenty entries listed in the city directory. The number of inhabitants in each occupation, the number in each occupation who owned property, and the percentage of property holders in each occupation is also given. Merchants, the most traditional of Albany's occupations, constituted by far the wealthiest group of the work force. Hardware merchants and dry goods merchants, as well as the up-and-coming lumber merchants, could now be distinguished from general merchants. Seven occupations distinctive for both their average wealth and percentage of property holders constituted an upper class. Aside from hardware merchants, general merchants, dry goods merchants, and the two professional occupations, attorneys and physicians, this group included builders, who were directing the city's physical expansion, and public employees, such as city superintendants and judges who contributed to the capital's growing bureaucracy. Together these seven occupations comprised 18 percent of the work force; all had average property assessments above $1625, and their average number of property holders ranged from 26 to 61 percent.

A middle group of eight occupations represented both the old and new in the economy. Butchers, bakers, and skippers were among the most traditional Albany occupations. Printers, cabinetmakers, and grocers accompanied the post-Revolutionary War Yankee immigration. Lumber merchants and manufacturers were a largely postcanal phenomenon. They accompanied the development of the town's lumber market and the increasing demand for consumer goods. These occupations comprised 25 percent of the work force, all had average property assessments between $485 and $1625, and the average number of property holders ranged from 18 to 42 percent.

The lowest group of 11 occupations was primarily working class. These were the largest and poorest occupations. They comprised 56 percent of the work force. Their average property assessments were all below $325, and no more than 21 percent of the workers in any of these occupations held property. Here the largest and most recent contingent of workers included carpenters and masons in the building trades and laborers on the docks and in the new industries.

Table B.5 charts the relationship between all four political parties and the three groupings of occupation and wealth from Table B.4. Here it can be seen that the Regency, National Republicans, and Anti-Masons drew more than one-half of their support from the traditional elite of merchants, professionals, and public officials. In contrast, the Workingmen were underrepresented in this category and overrepresented in the middle and lower groupings. Even though all of Albany's political parties underrepresented the large number of workers in the town's poorest and most menial occupations, the Workingmen's supporters were drawn from a

Table B.5. Occupations, Wealth, and Political Affiliation in 1830

Group	Workingmen N = 183	Regency N = 187	National Republican N = 16	Anti-Masons N = 28
Upper	55 (30%)	95 (51%)	9 (56%)	15 (54%)
Middle	64 (35%)	39 (21%)	4 (25%)	8 (29%)
Lower	64 (35%)	53 (28%)	3 (19%)	5 (17%)

Table B.6. Occupational Group and Political Affiliation in 1830

	Workingmen N = 182	Regency N = 185	National Republican N = 16	Anti-Masons N = 28
I Merchants	54 (30%)	98 (53%)	9 (56%)	15 (54%)
II Petty shopkeepers	42 (23%)	26 (14%)	3 (19%)	3 (11%)
III Skilled workers	75 (41%)	48 (26%)	3 (19%)	9 (32%)
IV Unskilled workers	11 (06%)	13 (07%)	1 (06%)	1 (04%)

Table B.7. Growth of the Twenty-Six Largest Occupations, 1817–1830

Occupation	Number in 1817	Number in 1830	Percentage Increase, %
Manufacturer	000	021	2100
Dry goods merchant	004	034	750
Lumber merchant	003	024	700
Hardware merchant	003	018	500
Painter	012	042	250
Cabinetmaker	009	025	177
Teamster	012	033	175
Laborer	109	299	174
Butcher	010	026	160
Carpenter	092	218	136
Builder	010	019	090
Mason	046	084	083
Baker	018	033	083
Grocer	152	267	076
Blacksmith	034	059	074
		Median 70%	
Physician	021	035	067
Tailor	024	038	058
Cartman	050	078	056
Printer	022	034	055
Skipper	017	026	053
Shoemaker	086	131	052
Public employee	040	060	050
Boardinghouse keeper	035	042	020
Attorney	050	057	014
Teacher	028	022	−21
Merchant	180	111	−38
(All merchants)	180	187	004

broader cross section of the town's taxpayers than any of the other political parties.

Table B.6 divides all of the political activists of 1830 into occupational groups. Here the findings are similar to those shown in Table B.2 In contrast to all of the other political parties, the Workingmen drew far less support from the elite and substantially more support from petty shopkeepers and skilled workers. Moreover, as Tables B.7 and B.8 demonstrate, the Workingmen best represented the fastest-growing postcanal occupations.

Table B.7 charts the growth of the town's twenty-six largest occupations between 1817 and 1830. Two anomalies need to be explained. The first is the apparent decrease in the number of merchants and the dramatic increase in specific subgroups of merchants such as hardware, lumber, and dry goods as well as manufacturers. These developments can be explained by the ongoing differentiation of merchants as the economy developed. Most of these subgroups were recognized simply as merchants in 1817. When the different subgroups of merchants are added together with those simply described as merchants in 1830, that occupation increased only 4 percent between 1817 and 1830. Second, the decrease in teachers supports the Workingmen's contention that educational institutions were not keeping pace with population expansion.

In looking at Table B.7 a comparatively small growth in the elite occupations of merchants and attorneys and, in contrast, a dramatic increase in laborers and journeymen can be seen. As a whole, Albany's work force expanded 70 percent over these thirteen years. Merchants and attorneys hardly increased; at the same time, the largest growth both in real numbers of new workers and percentage of new workers in each trade occurred among laborers, carpenters, masons, and grocers. These were occupations directly involved in large-scale enterprises and, in the case of grocers, providing food and drink to the new workers. A similarly dramatic growth occurred among the proprietors who employed these new workers. As we have observed, hardware merchants, lumber merchants, dry goods merchants, and manufacturers all greatly increased in numbers, as did builders.

Table B.8 adds a column on the percentage of political activists in each 1830 occupation to the previous table's column on the growth of each occupation between 1817 and 1830. By comparing the growth of each occupation with the percentage of political activists in each occupation, a relationship between expanding occupations and political activity can be determined. The median percentage for political activity in all occupations was 23 percent. In bold are occupations whose political activists numbered

Table B.8. Expanding Occupations and Political Activism in 1830

Occupation	1817–1830 Increase, %	1830 Political Activists, %
Manufacturer	2100	29
Dry goods merchant	750	21
Lumber merchant	700	58
Hardware merchant	500	17
Painter	250	14
Cabinetmaker	177	28
Teamster	175	15
Laborer	174	04
Butcher	160	27
Carpenter	118	10
Builder	090	53
Mason	083	14
Baker	083	18
Grocer	076	18
Blacksmith	074	15
	Median 70%	
Physician	067	26
Tailor	058	11
Printer	055	29
Skipper	053	12
Shoemaker	052	16
Public employee	050	38
Cartman	048	12
Boardinghouse keeper	020	07
Attorney	014	53
Teacher	−21	05
Merchant	−38	38

Median for all political activity in all occupations: 23%.

more than this median. Among those occupations that expanded more slowly than the 70 percent expansion of the work force as a whole, attorneys, merchants, public employees, and printers were most politically active. Among the occupations that expanded more rapidly than 70 percent, lumber merchants, builders, and manufacturers were most politically active.

Table B.9 adds to the data in Table B.8 the percentage of each party's supporters among those politically active in each occupation. Taken together, the Workingman's Party accounted for 58 percent of all political activists among Albany's fastest-growing occupations. Among the new proprietors, all of the manufacturers, 80 percent of the builders, and 64

Table B.9. Expanding Occupations and Party Membership in 1830

Occupation	1817–1830 Increase, %	1830 Activists, %	Workingmen	Regency	National Republican	Anti-Mason
Manufacturer	2100	29	100	00	00	00
Dry goods merchant	750	21	29	14	14	42
Lumber merchant	700	58	64	29	00	07
Hardware merchant	500	17	33	33	00	33
Painter	250	14	67	33	00	00
Cabinetmaker	177	28	43	29	14	14
Teamster	175	15	40	40	00	20
Laborer	174	04	58	42	00	00
Butcher	160	27	57	43	00	00
Carpenter	118	10	62	29	00	00
Builder	090	53	80	20	00	00
Mason	083	14	42	58	00	00
Baker	083	18	67	33	00	00
Grocer	076	18	59	39	00	02
Blacksmith	074	15	89	11	00	00

Median 70%

Occupation	1817–1830 Increase, %	1830 Activists, %	Workingmen	Regency	National Republican	Anti-Mason
Physician	067	26	22	67	11	00
Tailor	058	11	75	25	00	00
Printer	055	29	40	40	00	20
Skipper	053	12	67	33	05	00
Shoemaker	052	16	57	33	05	05
Public employee	050	38	35	61	04	00
Cartman	048	12	44	44	12	00
Boardinghouse keeper	020	07	67	33	00	00
Attorney	014	53	23	57	13	07
Teacher	-21	05	00	100	00	07
Merchant	-38	38	43	50	00	07

percent of the lumber merchants who were politically active were members of the Workingman's Party. The rapidly expanding carpenter, painter, and blacksmith trades gave two-thirds of their political support to the Workingmen. At the same time, the Workingmen were underrepresented in several of the more traditional and slower-growing occupations such as attorneys and merchants.

These data on the Workingmen stand in stark contrast to the information concerning the other three political parties. The Regency, National Republican, and Anti-Mason parties accounted for 70 percent of the political activists in those older occupations less affected by economic growth. Among these occupations the three parties accounted for 79 percent of all attorneys, 65 percent of all public employees, and 60 percent of all merchants who were politically active. Physicians, established printers, and traditional cartmen all gave a majority of their support to parties other than the Workingmen. In sum, the leaders of the Workingman's Party were different from the leaders of the other parties in occupation and wealth, and in the stake they had in Albany's rapidly expanding economy.

Notes

Introduction

1. "Common Council Minutes," 1790, New York State Library, Albany, New York.

2. "Albany As Seen by Dr. Dwight," in Joel Munsell, ed., *Annals of Albany,* 10 vols. (Albany, N.Y.: Munsell, 1850–1859), 8:182; "Conditions and Prospects of the City in 1789," in the *Albany Gazette,* cited in Munsell, *Annals,* 1:338.

3. Gorham A. Worth, "Random Recollections of Albany" in Munsell, *Annals,* 10:191–198.

4. Two articles summarize the advantages and drawbacks of modernization theory. Dean C. Tipps, "Modernization Theory and the Comparative Study of Societies: A Critical Perspective," *Comparative Study of Society and History,* 15(1973):199–222; Peter N. Stearns, "Modernization and Social History, Some Suggestions and a Muted Cheer," *Journal of Social History,* 14(1980):189–210. Tipps concludes that the implicit teleology, limited empirical grounding, and unworkable conceptual apparatus of this approach defeats its benefits. He advocates a "decisive break with the intellectual traditions of modernization theory" and a search for a more fruitful approach. Stearns restates the concept from a sociohistorical approach, urges its utility as a teaching framework, and suggests some limited, empirically grounded research possibilities.

5. Beyond Albany, Randolph A. Roth has arrived at a similar conclusion in his study of postwar Vermont. Political and religious aspirations in Vermont, Roth argues, were "too complex and contradictory to be realized in any straightforward fashion." *The Democratic Dilemma: Religion, Reform, and the Social Order in the Connecticut River Valley of Vermont, 1791–1850* (New York: Cambridge University Press, 1987), 299.

6. This cultural understanding of religion was proposed by Clifford Geertz in "Religion As a Cultural System," *The Interpretation of Cultures* (New York: Basic

Books, 1973), 87–125. For an expanded discussion of the theoretical approach employed in this study, see Appendix A, "A Note on Method."

7. This relationship between culture and social order in different historical periods is developed by Ann Swidler in "Culture in Action: Symbols and Strategies," *American Sociological Review*, 51(1986):273–286. See Appendix A for further discussion.

8. The way in which I am using the term ideology derives ultimately from its use by Karl Marx in the following passage from his *Contribution to the Critique of Political Philosophy* (1859).

> The distinction should always be made between the material transformation of the economic conditions of production . . . and the legal, political, religious, aesthetic or philosophic - in short, ideological — forms in which men become conscious of this conflict and fight it out.

Here ideology means the symbolic forms through which people become aware of the conflict arising from changes in economic production. See Raymond Williams, *Key Words* (New York: Oxford University Press, 1983), 154–156. More immediately my understanding of ideology follows that of Clifford Geertz in "Ideology as a Cultural System." For Geertz, ideologies are variously described as "systems of interacting symbols," "patterns of interworking meanings," or "schematic images of social order" that emerge in times of social change. They respond to a loss of orientation resulting from an absence of adequate cultural resources or "usable models" to explain sociopsychological strain.

> It is a confluence of socio-psychological strain and an absence of cultural resources by means of which to make (political, moral, or economic) sense of that strain, each exacerbating the other, that sets the stage for the rise of systematic (political, moral, economic) ideologies.

By providing new ways of thinking and acting for people in the midst of social change, ideologies attempt to "render otherwise incomprehensible social situations meaningful." "Ideology as a Cultural System" in *The Interpretation of Cultures*, 193–233.

9. This new phase in the town's life has been treated by Brian Greenburg, *Worker and Community: Response to Industrialization in a Nineteenth Century American City, Albany, New York 1850–1884* (Albany: State University of New York at Albany, 1985). L. Ray Gunn discussed the decline of government intervention in his book, *The Decline of Authority: Public Economic Policy and Political Development in New York State, 1800–1860* (Ithaca, N.Y.: Cornell University Press, 1988).

Chapter 1

1. This sociological approach to the study of communities has been developed by Roland L. Warren, "Toward a Reformulation of Community Theory," *Human Organization*, 15 (1956):8–11 and *The Community in America* (Chicago: University

of Chicago Press, 1963), chap. 8. See also Robert Redfield, *Peasant Society and Culture* (Chicago: University of Chicago Press, 1956), chap. 2. Darrett B. Rutman has applied this approach to the study of early American communities. See "The Social Web: A Prospectus for the Study of the Early American Community" in William L. O'Neill, ed., *Insights and Parallels: Problems and Issues of American Social History* (Minneapolis: Burgess Publishing Company, 1973), 57–88 and "Assessing the Little Communities of Early America," *William and Mary Quarterly,* 3d ser., 43(1986):163–178.

2. For an assessment of the contribution of social historians to our understanding of community in colonial New England, see John M. Murrin, "Review Essay," *History and Theory,* 11(1972):226–275. An evaluation of recent studies of the early Chesapeake region is provided by Anita H. Rutman, "Still Planting the Seeds of Hope," *The Virginia Magazine of History and Biography,* 95(1987):3–24.

3. Rutman "The Social Web," 78.

4. Bernard Bailyn, *The New England Merchants in the Seventeenth Century* (Cambridge, Mass.: Harvard University Press, 1955).

5. See Gary Nash's essay, "Social Development," in Jack P. Greene and J. R. Pole, eds., *Colonial British America: Essays in the New History of the Early Modern Era* (Baltimore: Johns Hopkins, 1984), 233–261.

6. The erosion of the communal ideal is discussed in several places. In particular, see Kenneth A. Lockridge, *A New England Town: The First Hundred Years,* enlarged ed. (New York: Norton, 1985), 79–180 and Nash, "Social Development."

7. For some time social historians have been arguing over which of two theoretical positions, one stressing the ascendance of modernity or one emphasizing the persistence of traditional society, best explains community life in colonial America. Kenneth Lockridge's 1970 study of Dedham, Massachusetts, *A New England Town,* was among the first of these social histories that organized its new data around a modernization thesis. In Lockridge's view, Dedham began as a closed, corporate, Christian community where lengthy life expectancy coupled with a low rate of mobility enabled patriarchal authority to hold sway over a united community. Significant changes in Dedham, which led away from the Puritan utopia and toward the privatism and individualism of the provincial town, were driven by rapid population growth and exhaustion of available land. By the third generation, the utopian aura had vanished and everywhere there were signs of capitalist expansion, political factionalism, and loss of religious fervor. In contrast to those who adhere to the modernization thesis, another group of historians has argued for the persistence of the basic values and behavior of early Americans throughout the colonial period. In *Peaceable Kingdoms: New England Towns in the Eighteenth Century* (New York: Alfred A. Knopf 1970), for example, Michael Zuckerman holds that the townspeople of the eighteenth century did not advocate individualism with its values of toleration, pluralism, and majority rule. Instead they saw political factions and religious diversity as destructive. The repeated secession of dissident groups, moreover, permitted the persistence of communal

values in New England towns. This study argues against both positions by seeing social change in colonial America as an interplay between local and extra-local social processes. For further discussion see David G. Hackett, "Culture and Social Order in American History" in David Bromley, ed., *Religion and Social Order: New Directions in Theory and Research* (Greenwich, Conn.: J.A.I. Press, 1991).

8. That trade was the primary motive is well known and best discussed by George L. Smith, *Religion and Trade in New Netherland* (Ithaca, N.Y.: Cornell University Press, 1973), 1–20.

9. Oliver A. Rink, "The People of New Netherlands: Notes on Non-English Immigration to New York in the Seventeenth Century," *New York History* 62(1981):4–42. The story of the appearance of Beverwyck in the midst of Rensselaerwyck is told by Samuel G. Nissenson in *The Patroon's Domain* (New York: Columbia University Press, 1937). For a recent history of the early New York Dutch see Oliver A. Rink, *Holland on the Hudson: An Economic and Social History of Dutch New York* (Ithaca, N.Y.: Cornell University Press, 1986).

10. J. Franklin Jameson, ed., *Narratives of New Netherland 1609–1664* (New York: Charles Scribner's Sons, 1909), 261–262. Relations with the Indians are discussed by Allen W. Trelease in *Indian Affairs in Colonial New York: The Seventeenth Century*, (Ithaca, N.Y.: Cornell University Press, 1960), 204–227.

11. In *Medieval Town* (Princeton, N.J.: Princeton University Press, 1958), 46–47, John H. Mundy and Pieter Riesenberg note that *wyck* was a common eleventh-century northern European term for the commercial area surrounding a fort. The traders outside of Fort Orange created such a mercantile district, and the *bever* was their almost exclusive commodity of trade. I was to lead to this source from a footnote in Alice P. Kenney, "The Dutch Patricians of Colonial Albany," *New York History,* 49(1968):254.

12. Charlotte Wilcoxen, *Seventeenth Century Albany: A Dutch Profile* (Albany, N.Y.: Albany Institute of History and Art, 1981), 6.

13. Hugh Hastings, ed., *Ecclesiastical Records of the State of New York,* 6 vols. (Albany: James B. Lyon, 1901), 1:383.

14. Arnold J. F. Van Laer, trans. and ed., *Minutes of the Court of Fort Orange and Beverwyck,* 2 vols. (Albany, N.Y.: University of the State of New York, 1920–1923).

15. Rink, "The People of New Netherland," 9–42.

16. Kenney, "Dutch Patricians," 257–258.

17. Donna Merwick, "Dutch Townsmen and Land Use: A Spatial Perspective on Seventeenth Century Albany, New York," *William and Mary Quarterly,* 3d ser., 37(1980):53–78.

18. Darrett B. Rutman, *Winthrop's Boston: Portrait of a Puritan Town, 1630–1649* (Chapel Hill, N.C.: University of North Carolina Press, 1965), 68–69, quoted in Merwick, "Dutch Townsmen," 61.

19. For further discussion see Merwick, "Dutch Townsmen."

20. At least 70 percent of Albany's inhabitants prior to 1754 were of Dutch descent. This is true for all available tax, census, and freeholder lists.

21. This is an estimate provided by Stefan Bielinski, Director of the "Colonial

Albany Social History Project." Of the 174 names listed on the 1697 census, 47 names include a man's first name and his father's name but no surname. For example, Frederick Harmanse is actually Frederick Visscher, the son of Harman Visscher. Bielinski arrived at the 150 families figure by making three generations of city residence as the condition for inclusion and by standardizing families by compressing patrinimics, locatives, and occupational names into a single surname. Using this procedure, he identified 153 families, accounting for more than three quarters of the people of colonial Albany.

Funded by the State of New York, the purpose of the "Colonial Albany Social Project" is to develop as complete a picture as possible of Albany inhabitants prior to 1800. The principle resource utilized by Bielinski and his interns is a file consisting of detailed biographical information on any persons who spent any parts of their lives in Albany between 1630 and 1800. The computerized file seeks to include complete "vital information (place, date and particulars of birth, death and marriage); information on all members of households; comprehensive residence, travel and migration data; education and literacy information; religious experience; ethnic identities and background; wealth data (income, real and personal property); legal information; and records of government and military service." Though this project is several years from completion, an early report of its findings can be found in Stefan Bielinski, "The People of Colonial Albany, 1630–1800" in William Pencak and Conrad Wright, eds., *Authority and Resistance in Early New York* (New York: New York Historical Society, 1988).

22. The population in 1697 was 714. "List of the Heads of Families," 1697 in *New York Colonial Manuscripts,* 102 vols., New York State Archives, 42:34. The last reliable city population figure prior to 1757 is 1,136 in 1714. "A List of the Inhabitants and Slaves in the City and County of Albany," 1714, in Joel Munsell, ed., *Annals of Albany,* 10 vols. (Albany, N.Y.: Munsell, 1850–1859) 3:243. My estimate of the number of city residents during the French and Indian Wars is taken from figures given by Abraham Yates for the third ward of the city in 1757. In his "Journal," Yates noted that there were 115 houses, 191 families, and 1,009 people in the third ward. Abraham Yates, Jr., Papers, New York City Public Library. This yields an average family size of 5.25 people. When this number is multiplied by Yates' estimate of 355 houses in all of the city, the population is 1,863. This figure does not include many refugees who lived outside of these established households. For further discussion, see Joseph F. Meany Jr., "Merchant and Redcoat: The Papers of John Gordon Macomb, April 1757–June 1760" (Ph.D. dissertation, Fordham University, 1990), 39–66.

23. Stefan Bielinski, "The Anglicization of a Dutch Village: Population Evolution in Colonial Albany, 1686–1756," (Seminar paper, State University of New York at Albany, 1979), 7–14.

24. This stipulation is a recurrent feature of local Dutch family wills. I am aware of the existence of 245 Albany wills for 1660 to 1776. Pre-1690 wills can be found printed and translated in Arnold J. F. Van Laer, trans. and ed., *Early Records of the City and County of Albany and Colony of Rensselaerwyck,* 4 vols. (Albany, N.Y.: The

State University of New York, 1918). Post-1690 colonial Albany wills can be found in "Will Books I and II" at the Albany Country Records Building and on microfilm in the Special Collections Room of the New York State Library. The best guide to colonial New York wills, though not covering Albany, is David Narrett's "Patterns of Inheritance in Colonial New York City 1664–1775: A Study in the History of the Family" (Ph.D dissertation, Cornell University, 1981). He has an earlier article, "Preparation for Death and Provision for the Living: Notes on New York Wills (1665–1760)," *New York History,* 57(1976):417–437.

25. Codman Hislop, *Albany: Dutch, English, and American* (Albany, N.Y.: Argus Press, 1936), 86.

26. "Dongan Charter," printed in the *Book of City Laws* (Albany, N.Y.: State of New York, 1842), 28.

27. Each householder paid between one and one hundred pounds, with fifteen being the median figure. About than 50 percent of the community paid less than fifteen pounds in taxes and therefore accounted for 15 percent of the city's wealth. A second group comprising 32 percent of the population paid between fifteen and thirty pounds and accounted for 36 percent of the wealth. The richest cluster of taxpayers represented only 20 percent of the population yet accounted for 49 percent of the city's wealth. These wealthiest taxpayers included a few English officials and lawyers, the rest represented merchant families. "City Tax List," 1709. Livingston-Redmond Papers, Franklin Delano Roosevelt Library, New York, N.Y. The tax was used to purchase 1600 stockadoes and 200 loads of wood. Joel Munsell, ed., *Annals,* 5:203–204.

28. Kenney, "Dutch Patricians," 260.

29. These names are listed in the "Deacon's Account Book 1647–1715" and "Pew Records 1730–1770," in Joel Munsell, ed., *Collections on the History of Albany,* 4 vols. (Albany, N.Y.: Munsell, 1865–1872), 1:2–56, 57–80; "Consistory Minutes," 1790–1815, Dutch Reformed Church, Albany, N.Y.; and scattered through both Munsell, *Annals,* and Hugh Hastings, ed., *Ecclesiastical Records of the State of New York,* 4 vols. (Albany, N.Y.: James B. Lyon, 1901).

30. A third category was also present in the work force. Throughout the eighteenth century, Indian, mulatto, and African slaves accounted for about 10 percent of Albany's population and occupied the lowest rank in the town's social hierarchy. The emphasis on trade by New Netherlands' colonists resulted in an enduring lack of laborers that in the Old World was met by servants but here answered by importing slaves. African slaves were considered part of the supplies given to the first Albany settlers by the Dutch West India Company. These slaves were purchased in the West Indies, rather than brought directly from Africa, since the Hudson Valley Dutch needed labor not for plantation gangs but for a variety of tasks that required some knowledge of the culture, language, and expectations of their owners. Albany's slaves, like household servants, were reported to have received the same early childhood treatment as their master's children. Some were baptized and shared in religious instruction. Unlike white servants, however, slaves were given a different, corporal and public, punishment for commiting the same

crimes as white inhabitants. For example, citizens who rode their wagons "immoderate or fast" were fined three shillings. For committing the same crime, slaves were "publicly whipped at the public whipping post." In addition, separate "laws for the regulation of negroes, mulattoes, and other slaves" were created to keep the slaves in their place. These laws were intended to keep all slaves close to their masters' homes, particularly at night, and to prevent their disorderly conduct, especially talking impudently to Christians. United States Department of Commerce. Bureau of Census. *Heads of Families of the First Census of the United States Taken in 1790: New York* (Washington, D.C. Government Printing Office, 1908); Alice P. Kenney, *Stubborn for Liberty* (Syracuse: Syracuse University Press, 1975), 77; George Howell and Jonathan Tenney, "Slavery in Albany" in their *Bicentennial History of Albany, New York from 1609 to 1886* (New York: Munsell, 1886), 300–303; *Laws and Ordinances of the Mayor, Recorder, Aldermen and Commonality of the City of Albany* (Albany, N.Y.: Robertson, 1773).

31. These duties were spelled out in the "The Heidelberg Catechism," the Dutch community's fundamental book of religious instruction. "The Heidelberg Catechism" in *The Psalms of David with Hymns and Spiritual Songs also the Catechism, Compendium, Confession of Faith and Liturgy of the Reformed Church of the Netherlands* (Albany, N.Y.: Webster, 1791), 350–393.

32. Local apprenticeship contracts are translated and printed in Van Laer, ed., *Early Records,* vol. 3.

33. Munsell, *Annals,* 1:97–101.

34. "Deacon's Book," Dutch Reformed Church of Albany, Albany, N.Y. All of the records of the Albany Dutch Reformed Church prior to 1790 were apparently destroyed in a fire in 1938. However, copies of many of these records were made prior to that date. The "Deacon's Account Book" 1647–1715 and "Pew Records" 1730–1770 are in Munsell, *Collections,* 1:2–56, 57–80; a 1683 communicants list is in Munsell, *Annals,* 1:97–101; vital statistics are in Louis Duermyer, ed., *Records of the Reformed Dutch Church of Albany, New York 1683–1809* (Baltimore: Genealogical Publishing Co., 1978); and many items relating to this church can be found in Hastings, *Ecclesiastical Records.* What is missing are the Consistory minutes for the colonial period. Post-1790 Consistory minutes and all other church records are available at the Dutch Reformed Church. Some of these have been photoduplicated and are at the New York State Library.

35. Edmund B. O'Callaghan, comp. and tr., *The Colonial Laws of New York from the Year 1664 to the Revolution,* 5 vols. (Albany, N.Y.: Weed, Parsons, and Company, 1868), 5:585.

36. *Laws and Ordinances,* 28–32.

37. Alice P. Kenney, *The Gansevoorts of Albany* (Syracuse, N.Y.: Syracuse University Press, 1969), 105–106.

38. As in medieval Dutch society, religion pervaded the life of the Albany community. Adherence to doctrinal orthodoxy was understood to be a form of communal loyalty and heresy a dangerous form of sedition. In the late sixteenth century, many Dutch burghers were attracted to the system of theology and

church government worked out by John Calvin in Geneva in the 1540's and 1550's. Calvin was a burgher and a lawyer before he became a theologian, and he devoted a good part of his career to devising religious sanctions for maintaining public order in Geneva. His doctrines underscored God's role as judge and the need for obedience to a moral code of social behavior. Although Calvinism was a minority religion in the Netherlands at the time of the formation of the Dutch West India Company, the principles of Calvinism provided the basis for national unity at the Synod of Dordrecht in 1609. The Dutch Calvinist Reformed Church therefore, directed by its governing body, the Classis of Amsterdam, was the only church permitted in New Netherland. Prior to the English conquest in 1664, Albany's church leaders forcefully resisted the establishment of Lutheran church services and, as recently as the 1760's, resented the practice of "foreign" religions in their town. See Kenney, *Gansevoorts,* xvi–xx, 15, 16.

39. E. T. Corwin, ed., *A Digest of Synodical Legislation* (New York: Reformed Church, 1906). Two sermons were delivered on the Sundays of nonwinter months and all were expected to attend both services. See Kenney, *Stubborn for Liberty,* 130.

40. Dominie Megapolensis, who served the church in the early 1650's, and Dominie Theodorus Frelinghuysen, who was minister in the 1750's, each wrote children's catechisms. Hislop, *Albany,* 85.

41. These inventories are available at the Albany Institute of History and Art, Albany, N.Y.

42. Anne Grant has recounted those years of her childhood spent with the Schuyler family during the French and Indian War. Her father was an officer in the British Army. As an Englishwoman aware of the English system, Mrs. Grant lamented the lack of formal education in Albany. At the same time, she praised the less rational and more symbolic manner in which Dutch children learned their moral principles. "Morals," she stated, "founded in Christianity were fostered . . . by the reverance which children in particular had for their parents, and the young in general for the old, and this was the chief bond that held society together." *Memoirs of An American Lady* (London: Longman, Hurst, Ries and Orme, 1808), 96.

43. "The Heidelberg Catechism," *Psalms of David,* 350–393.

44. Ibid., 355.

45. *Psalms of David,* 479.

46. Corwin, *Digest,* Articles 17, 18, 27, 37.

47. "Consistory Minutes," 1790–1800, Dutch Reformed Church, Albany, N.Y.

48. *Psalms of David,* 480, 452.

49. For example, the first bench had three seats that were occupied by Schuyler men, the third bench had four seats all occupied by Livingston men, and so forth, Munsell, *Collections,* 1:78–80.

50. Gerald F. DeJong, *The Dutch Reformed Church in the American Colonies* (Grand Rapids, Mich.: Eerdmans, 1978), 136–137.

51. Kenney, *Gansevoorts,* 43.

52. Munsell, *Collections,* 1:57–80; "List of Pew Holders," 1790, Dutch Reformed Church, Albany, N.Y.

53. This organization of the Dutch community into generational groups was noticed by Anne Grant as late as the 1750's. As a young girl, she observed that her childhood playmates were divided into "companies" of boys and girls. "All the children of the same age were not in one company; there were at least three or four companies of equal ages, who had a strong rivalry with each other; and children of different ages in the same family belonged to different companies." All through childhood these "companies" competed against each other, and marriages often occurred within the company. *Memoirs,* 89–90.

54. DeJong, *Dutch in the Colonies,* 137–138.

55. Prior to the 1750's Dutch family members rarely moved out of the county. When they did, this may have meant that they had moved beyond the world of the local community and therefore given up their claim to status within that community.

56. Munsell, *Collections,* 1:57–80.

57. Munsell, *Annals,* 3:219.

58. John Calvin, *Commentaries on the Four Last Books of Moses,* Reverend Charles Bingham, trans. and ed., 4 vols. (Grand Rapids, Mich.: Eerdmans, 1950), 4:23–28.

59. Smith, *Religion and Trade,* 23–39.

60. John Calvin, *Commentary on I Corinthians,* John T. McNeil, trans. and ed., 2 vols. (Grand Rapids, Mich.: Eerdmans, 1950), 1:398.

61. *The Colonial Laws of New York from the Year 1664 to the Revolution,* 5 vols. (Albany: James B. Lyon, 1894); *Laws of the State of New York, 1778–1799.* 3 vols. (New York: Thomas Greenleaf, 1792–1800); *Laws and Ordinances of the Mayor, Recorder, Aldermen, and Commonality of the City of Albany* (Albany, N.Y.: Robertson, 1773); *Laws and Ordinances of the Mayor, Recorder, Aldermen and Commonality of the City of Albany* (Albany, N.Y.: Barber, 1791).

62. Calvin, *A Compend of the Institutes of the Christian Religion* (Philadelphia: Westminster, 1939), book 4, chap. 20, 1–6.

63. Kenney, *Gansevoorts,* 13.

64. For further discussion of this larger antagonism see Patricia U. Bonomi, *A Factious People: Politics and Society in Colonial New York* (New York: Columbia University Press, 1971), 39–55.

65. Donna Merwick, "Becoming English: Anglo-Dutch Conflict in the 1670s in Albany, New York," *New York History,* 62(1981):389–414.

66. Merwick, "Anglo-Dutch Conflict," 403.

67. At least fifteen former British soldiers entered the Dutch kinship network through marriage to local Dutch women. Duermyer, ed., *Records of the Reformed Dutch Church of Albany.*

68. "List of the Heads of Families," 1697, *New York Colonial Manuscripts,* 42:34; "A List of the Freeholders in the City and County of Albany in 1720," in Edmund B. O'Callaghan, ed., *Documentary History of the State of New York,* 4 vols. (Albany: Weed and Parsons, 1850–1851), 1:241–242; "List of the Inhabitants of the Citty of

Albany in America with the Number of Troops they can Quarter conveniently within the Stockade and What they can Quarter in case of necessity together with the fire places in Each house and Rooms without Fire, also what appeared in a strett Enquiry made in November 1756. . ." Loudoun Papers, Huntington Library, San Marino, Calif.

69. Bielinski, "Anglicization, 13.

70. Stefan Bielinski, *Abraham Yates, Jr. and the New Political Order in Revolutionary New York* (Albany, N.Y.: New York State American Revolution Bicentennial Commission, 1975), 3.

71. Bielinski, *Yates,* 3–4.

72. "Dongan Charter," 28.

73. Merwick, "Anglo-Dutch Conflict," 393.

74. Ibid.

75. Bielinski, "Anglicization," 10.

76. "City Records," Munsell, *Annals,* 5:114–206. For a discussion of similar legal changes in Connecticut, see Bruce H. Mann, *Neighbors and Strangers: Law and Community in Early Connecticut* (Chapel Hill, N.C.: University of North Carolina Press, 1987).

77. "City Records," *Annals,* 5:120.

78. Kenney, "Dutch Patricians," 259–260.

79. The English governor gave the city corporation one mile of land along the Hudson River and extended that sixteen miles to the west. This encompassed Schenectady, Albany's chief trading rival, until a protest was lodged. The fur monopoly gave Albany the upper hand in competition with several splinter groups of former inhabitants who had established farms and continued the trade in furs at neighboring Coxsacki, Kinderhook, Catskill, Schagitoke, and Saratoga, as well as Schenectady. Although the Common Council paid 300 pounds for this privilege, they quickly recouped their investment by selling some of the new land granted to them by the charter. Hislop, *Albany,* 112–114, "Dongan Charter."

80. Kenney, *Stubborn,* 135–136.

81. "Will Book I," New York State Library, Albany, N.Y. Although not immediately apparent in Albany, the eclipse of Roman-Dutch law also had ramifications for the rights and status of women. See Linda Briggs Biemer, *Women and Property in Colonial New York: The Transition from Dutch to English Law, 1643–1727* (Ann Arbor, Mich.: UMI Research Press, 1983).

82. Bonomi, *A Factious People,* 42. For a broader view of the economics and politics of the fur trade see Thomas E. Norton, *The Fur Trade in Colonial New York, 1686–1776.* (Madison, Wis.: University of Wisconsin Press, 1974).

83. Bonomi, *A Factious People,* 43.

84. George W. Schuyler, *Colonial New York: Philip Schuyler and His Family,* 2 vols. (New York: Charles Scribner's Sons, 1885), 1, chap. 3.

85. Lawrence H. Leder, *Robert Livingston and the Politics of Colonial New York* (Chapel Hill, N.C.: University of North Carolina Press, 1961).

86. Munsell, *Annals,* 2:82–83.

87. Leder, *Livingston,* 57–76.

88. Munsell, *Annals,* 2:136, 169, 171, 233.

89. This encounter is rehearsed in several places. See Arthur James Weisse, *The History of the City of Albany* (Albany, N.Y.: E. H. Bender, 1884), 230–239; Munsell, *Annals,* 2:145; Kenney, *Gansevoorts,* 16–17.

90. O'Callaghan, *Documentary History of the State of New York,* 2:113–114.

91. Munsell, *Annals,* 2:145–146.

92. O'Callaghan, *Documentary History,* 1:690.

93. For a discussion of Anglicization as ethnic aggression in Massachusetts, see John M. Murrin "Anglicizing an American Colony: The Transformation of Provincial Massachusetts" (PhD. dissertation, Yale, 1966).

94. Hastings, *Ecclesiastical Records,* 2:1105–1106.

95. Randall H. Balmer, "The Social Roots of Dutch Pietism in the Middle Colonies," *Church History,* 53(1984):187–199. For an analysis of the tensions and accommodations between the Dutch and the English see his *A Perfect Babel of Confusion: Dutch Religion and English Culture in the Middle Colonies* (New York: Oxford University Press, 1989).

96. Kenney, *Gansevoorts,* 51–54.

97. Don R. Gerlach, *Philip Schuyler and the American Revolution in New York 1733–1777* (Lincoln, Neb.: University of Nebraska Press, 1964), 2.

98. Hastings, *Ecclesiastical Records,* 3:2092.

99. As a rule, the province's Dutch Reformed clergy did not disagree with the English clergy on theological grounds. Writing to the Classis of Amsterdam in the 1680's, the dominies together stated that the English "agree pretty well with us in fundamental truths of our religion, but differ much in spirit, form of Church Government, and usages (or ceremonies)." Hastings, *Ecclesiastical Records,* 2:574.

100. Hastings, *Ecclesiastical Records,* 3:2092.

101. Reverend Thomas Ellison, "The Landed Estate of St. Peter's Church," in the St. Peter's Church Papers New York State Library.

102. Peter Kalm, *Travels in North America,* Adolph B. Benson, ed.(New York: Dover, 1964), 343.

103. Alexander Hamilton, *Gentlemen's Progress: The Itinerarium of Dr. Alexander Hamilton, 1744,* Carl Bridenbaugh, ed. (Chapel Hill, N.C.: University of North Carolina Press, 1948), 63.

104. Kalm, *Travels,* 341–342.

105. Hamilton, *Itinerarium,* 69.

106. Ibid., 73.

107. Kenney, *Gansevoorts,* 65.

108. In the midst of this disorder the Albany Congress of 1754 took place. This meeting of delegates from seven colonies with the Iroquois Indians was marked by Benjamin Franklin's well known presentation of a plan for intercolonial union. Though a significant moment in American political history, the town's leaders played no noticeable role in this Congress. See Munsell, *Annals,* 3:202–204.

109. See Meany, "Merchant and Redcoat," 149–150.

110. David A. Armour, "The Merchants of Albany, New York, 1683–1781." (Ph.D. dissertation, Northwestern University, 1965), 261–263.

111. Ibid., 261–262.

112. Ibid., 262–263.

113. During the 1740's and 1750's, Frelinghuysen, Jr. was a leading figure in the effort to create an American-trained clergy. These actions were opposed by the Albany congregation but were sufficiently extra-local in character to escape considerable dissension within the congregation. See Robert S. Alexander, *Albany's First Church* (Albany, N.Y.: First Church, 1988), 113–129.

114. Anne Grant, *Memoirs*, 192–193.

115. Ibid., 195–196.

116. Ibid., 195–200.

117. Ibid., 200.

Chapter 2

1. Bernard Bailyn, *The Ideological Origins of the American Revolution* (Cambridge, Mass.: Harvard University Press, 1967). Bailyn's *The Origins of American Politics* (New York: Alfred A. Knopf, 1968) supplements the original argument. Several scholars have expanded on and contended with Bailyn's position. For a discussion, see Robert E. Shalhope, "Toward a Republican Synthesis: The Emergence of an Understanding of Republicanism in American Historiography," *William and Mary Quarterly*, 3d. ser., 29(1972):49–80.

2. Nathan O. Hatch, *The Sacred Cause of Liberty* (New Haven, Conn.: Yale University Press, 1977). Historians and sociologists of American religion frequently have converged on this overlapping of religion and politics to consider the implications of Robert Bellah's "civil religion" concept. Robert N. Bellah, "Civil Religion in America," *Daedalus*, 96(1967):1–21. For a discussion of the range and application of Bellah's concept, see Russell E. Richey and Donald G. Jones, eds., *American Civil Religion* (New York: Harper and Row, 1974). John F. Wilson argues against Bellah's claim that a "well-institutionalized" civil religion actually exists by the considering the difficulties involved in finding its social correlates. John F. Wilson, *Public Religion in American Culture* (Philadelphia: Temple University Press, 1979).

3. Edmund S. Morgan, "Conflict and Consensus in the American Revolution," in Stephen G. Kurtz and James H. Hutson, eds., *Essays on the American Revolution* (Chapel Hill, N.C.: University of North Carolina Press, 1973), 303.

4. Gordon S. Wood, *The Creation of the American Republic, 1776–1787* (Chapel Hill, N.C.: University of North Carolina Press, 1969).

5. Eric Foner, *Tom Paine and Revolutionary America* (New York: Oxford University Press, 1976).

6. Rowland Berthoff and John Murrin, "Feudalism, Communalism, and the Yeoman Freeholder," in Kurtz and Hutson, eds., *Essays on the American Revolution*, 256–288.

7. The enduring potential for conflict within this larger consensus is discussed by Morgan in "Conflict and Consensus," 307–309. In a similar vein, John F. Wilson suggests that there is "an open set or cluster of meanings central to American culture." This approach makes it possible to deal with empirical observations that there are subcultures within American society for whom words like "liberty" have different meanings. Wilson, *Public Religion,* 117.

8. Kenneth A. Lockridge, "Social Change and the Meaning of the American Revolution," *Journal of Social History,* 6(1973):415–432; James Henretta, "Economic Development and Social Structure in Colonial Boston," *William and Mary Quarterly,* 3d ser., 22(1965):75–92; Alan Kulikoff, "The Progress of Inequality in Revolutionary Boston," *William and Mary Quarterly,* 3d ser., 28(1971):375–412; Gary B. Nash, "Urban Wealth and Poverty in Pre-Revolutionary America," *Journal of Interdisciplinary History,* 6(1975–1976):545–584.

9. Gary B. Nash, *The Urban Crucible: Social Change, Political Consciousness, and the Origins of the American Revolution* (Cambridge, Mass.: Harvard University Press, 1979), vii.

10. Ibid.

11. Patricia U. Bonomi, *Under the Cope of Heaven: Religion, Society, and Politics in Colonial America* (New York: Oxford University Press, 1986), 5.

12. See the bibliographic essay in Lockridge, *A New England Town,* 193–212.

13. In addition to Nash, *Urban Crucible,* see Dirk Hoerder's study of Massachusetts' crowds, *Crowd Action in Revolutionary Massachusetts, 1765–1780* (New York: Academic Press, 1977). Pauline Maier analyzed the relationship between those crowds and their leaders in *From Resistance to Revolution: Colonial Radicals and the Development of American Opposition to Great Britain, 1765–1776* (New York: Alfred A. Knopf, 1972); and *The Old Revolutionaries: Political Lives in the Age of Samuel Adams* (New York: Alfred A. Knopf, 1980). Richard Alan Ryerson examined the development of the radical committees of Philadelphia and how committee members took and transformed power in *The Revolution Is Now Begun: The Radical Committees of Philadelphia, 1765–1776* (Philadelphia: University of Pennsylvania Press, 1978).

14. Edmund B. O'Callaghan, ed., *Documentary History of the State of New York,* 4 vols. (Albany, N.Y.: Weed and Parsons, 1849–1850) 1:695, 697. In *Landlord and Tenant in Colonial New York: Manorial Society, 1664–1775* (Chapel Hill, North Carolina: University of North Carolina Press, 1978), Sung Bok Kim treats the relationship of the Albany hinterland to the city. See especially 10–11, 17, 20, 33–36, 57–59, 111–114.

15. Both of these figures are estimates. For the first, see note 22 in chap. 1. The three thousand figure for 1779 is computed by multiplying the number of taxpayers (594) on the 1779 city tax list by 5.25, the average family size as defined in note 22 of chap. 1. "City Tax List," 1779, Gerrit Y. Lansing Papers, New York State Library, Albany, N.Y.

16. Most of the county's new immigrants were laborers or farmers. Only one third were trained to work in a trade. These included cordwainers (7 percent),

tailors (6 percent), weavers (5 percent), and blacksmiths (5 percent). "Muster Roll of the Men Rais'd and Pass'd Muster in the City and County of Albany for John Visher's Comp'y Albany May 1762" and "A Muster Roll of the Men Ras'd and Pass'd Muster in the City and County of Albany for Capt'n John de Garemo Company, Albany, June 1762," in *The Annual Report of the State Historian of the State of New York* (Albany, N.Y.: State of New York, 1887), 694–696, 701–702.

17. "List of the Freeholder's in the City of Albany," 1742, in Joel Munsell, ed., *Annals of Albany* 10 vols. (Albany, N.Y.: Munsell, 1850–1859), 2:186–189; The occupations of these freeholders were compiled from various sources by Stefan Bielinski's "Colonial Albany Social History Project" at the New York State Museum, Albany, N.Y.; "List of the Inhabitants of the Citty of Albany in America with the Number of Troops they can Quarter conveniently within the Stockade and What they can Quarter in case of necessity together with the fire places in Each house and Rooms without Fire, also what appeared in a strett Enquiry made in November 1756. . ." Loudoun Papers, Huntington Library, San Marino, Calif.

18. This differentiation may simply have been due to the more detailed eye of the British soldier assigned to this inventory. What is clear is the increase in the number of workers in the artisan trades, the appearance of new trades, and the greater number of tradesmen with British names.

19. Silversmiths were important in Albany for their ability to turn their neighbors' accumulations of silver coins into decorative spoons and bowls. These pieces represented the family's wealth in a safe as well as attractive manner. The monograms on these pieces could not be removed without melting the entire object. Alice P. Kenney, "Private Worlds in the Middle Colonies: An Introduction to Human Tradition in American History," *New York History* 51(1970):5–31.

20. "Loudoun Inventory," Huntington Library; Bielinski, "Anglicization," 16.

21. Munsell, *Annals,* 10:9–52.

22. "Pew Records" 1719–1770, in Munsell, *Collections,* 1:57–80.

23. On his return from Canada in 1750, Peter Kalm noted the friction between these two groups. "Discord had taken firm hold among the inhabitants of Albany. Although they were very closely related through marriage and kinship, they had divided into two parties. Some members of these bore such strong aversion to one another that they could scarcely tolerate the presence of another member, nor could they even hear his name mentioned." Peter Kalm, *Travels in North America,* Adolph B. Benson, ed., (New York: Dover, 1964), 607. These two parties were the old and new generations whose differing interests reflected not only a changing economy but a change in the political and religious leadership of the town as well. For further discussion see Alice P. Kenney, *The Gansevoorts of Albany* (Syracuse, N.Y.: Syracuse University Press, 1969), 33–88.

24. "City Tax List," 1709, Livingston-Redmond Papers, Franklin Delano Roosevelt Library, Hyde Park, N.Y.; "City Tax List," 1767, Schuyler Papers, Box 10, New York City Public Library, New York, N.Y.

25. "City Tax List," 1767, Schuyler Papers.

26. Munsell, *Collections,* 1:81–334.

27. Joseph F. Meany Jr., "Merchant and Redcoat: The Papers of John Gordon Macomb, July 1757–June 1760" (Ph.D. dissertation, Fordham University, 1990), 155.

28. The emergence of political conflict in this way was first suggested to me by Lockridge, "Social Change and the Meaning of the American Revolution."

29. In 1766, the composite Dutch Council member was forty-seven years old, ranked among the community's wealthiest 10 percent, and was an elder of the church. These burghers shared their Council table with John Fryer, a new dram shop owner, Anglican, and resident of a less affluent, heavily British section of the first ward; as well as with the former sheriff, Abraham Yates. Munsell, *Collections*, 1:163; Louis Duermyer, ed., *Records of the Reformed Dutch Church of Albany, New York 1683–1809* (Baltimore: Genealogical Publishing Co., 1978); "City Tax List," 1766, Schuyler Papers, New York Public Library, New York; "Consistory Minutes," 1790–1800, Dutch Reformed Church, Albany, New York; "Record Book," 1720–1770, St. Peter's Church Papers, New York State Library.

30. Much of the information for this discussion of Abraham Yates and the origins of popular politics is taken from Stefan Bielinski, *Abraham Yates Jr. and the New Political Order in Revolutionary New York* (Albany, N.Y.: New York State American Revolution Bicentennial Commission, 1975); and Kenney, *Gansevorts*, 82–87.

31. "Seatings of the Dutch Reformed Church," Munsell, *Collections*, 1:80.

32. For a discussion of Yates' experience of British military abuse during this war, see Joseph Meany, "Merchant and Redcoat," 109–145, 192–206.

33. Kenney, *Gansevoorts*, 82–83.

34. Ibid., 83–84.

35. The presence of the three Yates on the Council so disturbed the city's burghers that Dutch community leaders such as Leendert Gansevoort and Jacob C. Ten Eyck became convinced that the "Yates menace" would have to be eliminated. Stopping Yates became particularly urgent when it seemed that he might attract the support of New Englanders who were now settling in eastern Albany county and challenging the land titles of the area's ruling families. The following year, Abraham Yates was turned out of office in favor of a supporter of the Ten Ecyk-Gansevoort group. Yates' subsequent unprecedented challenge of the election results demonstrated that a significant number of his supporters were barred from voting. Although he paraded these disqualified voters before the Common Council, the results did not change. Between this upheaval and the next election, the Common Council laid down its first specific catalog of residence requirements and other qualifications for voters. The next steps in this growing political controversy were cut short by the Revolution, only to re-emerge in the Federalist versus Anti-Federalist controversies that followed the colonial war for independence. Bielinski, *Yates*, 10–13; Kenney, *Gansevoorts*, 84–86; Munsell, *Collections*, 1:81–354. The classic treatment of New Yorker versus New Englander tensions over borders, sovereignty, land titles, and trade is by Dixon Ryan Fox, *Yankees and Yorkers* (New York: New York University Press, 1940).

36. During the Revolution Yates was chairman of the Committee of the Provincial Convention, which drafted New York's revolutionary constitution in 1777. He also became a state senator under the new government. His papers, published and unpublished, may constitute the largest corpus produced by an Anti-Federalist in the nation. See Staughton Lynd, "Abraham Yates' History of the Movement for the United States Constitution," *William and Mary Quarterly*, 3d ser., 20(1963):224, 226. James Hutson has portrayed the Anti-Federalists as actually having political ideas similar to those of Federalists in that they concurred with their opponents on most of the principles of political theory. The primary difference was that the Anti-Federalists feared the abuse of power by government. James H. Hutson, "Country, Court, and Constitution: Antifederalism and the Historians," *William and Mary Quarterly*, 3d ser., 38(1981):337–368.

37. Abraham Yates as quoted in Lynd, "Abraham Yates," 228.

38. Charles D. Schwartz and Ouida Davis Schwartz, *A Flame of Fire: The Story of Troy Annual Conference* (Rutland, Vt.: Academic Books, 1982), 3.

39. E. Ralph Bates, *Captain Thomas Webb* (London: Pinhorns, 1975), vii.

40. George R. Howell and Jonathan Tenney, *Bicentennial History of the County of Albany from 1609 to 1886* (New York: Munsell, 1886), 764.

41. William C. Kitchin, *Centennial History of First Methodist Episcopal Church, Schenectady* (Schenectady, N.Y.: Official Board of the Church, 1907), 12.

42. Kenneth E. Rowe, *Captain Thomas Webb: Albany Apprentice, It All Started in Albany* (Albany, N.Y.: Public Relations Committee of Trinity United Methodist Church, 1976), 11.

43. Kitchin, *Centennial History*, 12.

44. Bernard Semmel, *The Methodist Revolution* (New York: Basic Books, 1977), 7.

45. Richard W. Pointer, "Religious Life in New York During the Revolutionary War, *New York History*, 66(1985):358–373.

46. Kenney, *Gansevoorts*, 45.

47. Reverend E. P. Rogers, *Historical Discourse on the Reformed Protestant Dutch of Albany* (New York: Board of Publication of the Reformed Protestant Dutch Church, 1858), 30.

48. This reaction of the Albany Dutch to their British rulers is traced by Alice Kenney to the traditional response of medieval Netherlanders to intrusions by the overlords of their region. See Kenney, "The Dutch Patricians of Colonial Albany," *New York History*, 49(July 1968):249–283.

49. When General Burgoyne's army approached the city, special services were held for the entire community to pray for deliverance from the British army. Kenney, *Gansevoorts*, 105–106.

50. "Seatings," in Munsell, *Collections*, 1:57–80.

51. The departure of nearly all of the new British merchants is confirmed through a variety of sources: Reverend Joseph Hooper, *History of St. Peter's Church* (Albany, N.Y.: Fort Orange Press, 1900), 125; "City Tax List," 1779 Gerrit Y. Lansing Papers, New York State Library; Victor H. Paltsits, ed., *Minutes of the*

Commission for Detecting and Defeating Conspiracies in the State of New York: Albany County Sessions 1778–1781, 3 vols. (Albany, N.Y.: University of the State of New York, 1909–1911). For further discussion, see Alice P. Kenney, "The Albany Dutch: Loyalists and Patriots," *New York History,* 42(1961):331–350.

52. During most of the colonial period, the older cultural beliefs and practices of the Dutch were assumed to be inherent in the natural structure of the world. People did not have to reflect upon them or even participate in them yet they knew with certainty that these cultural patterns existed, they framed their world. Under threat of widespread change just prior to the Revolution, the Dutch may well have become more conscious of these previously taken for granted patterns and thus argued for their older way of life as one of several competing ideologies. A similar point is made by Clifford Geertz in his analysis of the loss of religious certainty in modern "ideologized" Islam. People come to "hold" rather than be "held by" their beliefs. *Islam Observed* (Chicago: University of Chicago Press, 1968), 61.

53. Beverly McAnear, "The Albany Stamp Act Riots," *William and Mary Quarterly,* 4(1947):486–498; Roger James Champagne, "The Sons of Liberty and the Aristocracy in New York Politics 1765–1790" (PhD. dissertation, University of Wisconsin, 1960), 93–94; Meany, "Merchant and Redcoat," 35–37.

54. "Constitution of the Sons of Liberty of America and Names of the Signers," *The American Historian* 1(1875):145–147.

55. Ibid., 146.

56. Ibid., 145.

57. Despite anti-British sentiment that led to the closing of St. Peter's Episcopal Church during the war, some of the lay leaders of that church were long-term community residents. They obviously were trusted by the Dutch, who united with them to oppose external aggression. For a history of St. Peter's Church during these years, see Reverend Joseph Hooper, *A History of St. Peter's Church in the City of Albany,* 109–129.

58. Sixty-two men served at one time or another on the Albany Committee of Correspondence. James Sullivan, ed., *The Minutes of the Albany Committee of Correspondence 1775–1778,* 2 vols. (Albany, N.Y.: University of the State of New York, 1923). All but six of these men can be traced to one of the town's three principal churches. Forty-five were members of the Dutch church, nine were from the Anglican church, and seven were Presbyterians.

59. Sullivan, ed., *Albany Committee of Correspondence,* 1:3.

60. Ibid.

61. These figures were derived through a comparison of the lists of 1780 to 1800 Common Council members found in the "Common Council Minutes" at the New York State Library with the membership lists of Albany's Dutch, Anglican, and Presbyterian churches. See the Albany Church Records section of the References.

62. *Albany Gazette,* July 5, 1799.

63. Prior to the Revolution there was little perceived need to print sermons. A small, homogeneous community where face-to-face contacts and the pervasive

principles of the Heidelberg catechism predominated had little need to socialize its people to moral ideas known by all since childhood. Unlike the larger and more heterogeneous New York City, where sermons were published as early as the 1720's, Albany's ministers only began to publish their sermons after the Revolution, when the town's population approximated the size and composition of mid-eighteenth-century New York City. Moreover, the postwar emergence of printing offices coincided with a newly perceived need, as these printers stated, "to promote civil and religious liberty" and advance the "knowledge and instruction" of the people. *Albany Gazette,* November 25, 1791. By articulating the new basis for political and religious unity, the Fourth of July sermons served these ends.

64. The Puritan theme of America as the "New Israel" is discussed in Robert Bellah, *The Broken Covenant: American Civil Religion in Time of Trial* (New York: Seabury Press, 1975), 1–35.

65. John Barent Johnson, *The Dealings of God with Israel and America* (Albany, N.Y.: Charles R. and George Webster, 1798), 14–15.

66. Ibid., 14.

67. Ibid., 18.

68. Ibid., 17.

69. See, for example, Eliphalet Nott, *The Providence of God Towards Israel: A Discourse Delivered in the Presbyterian Church in Albany, the Fourth of July A.D. 1801* (Albany, N.Y.: Charles R. and George Webster, 1801); and John McDonald, *The Duty of America Enforced* (Cooperstown, N.Y.: Phinney, 1799).

70. "Common Council Minutes," 1780–1800, New York State Library.

71. "Subscription List," 1786, Dutch Reformed Church; "Subscription List," 1793, First Presbyterian Church; "Subscription List," 1788–1799, St. Peter's Episcopal Church Papers, New York State Library.

72. "Common Council Minutes," 1790–1800, New York State Library.

73. "Common Council Minutes," 1785–1820, New York State Library. For an observer's account of Albany's ethnic politics at the turn of the century, see Gorham A. Worth, "Random Recollections of Albany," in Munsell, *Annals,* 10:189–218.

Chapter 3

1. Gorham A. Worth, "Random Recollections of Albany," in Joel Munsell, ed., *Annals of Albany.* 10 vols. (Albany, N.Y.: Munsell, 1850–1859), 10:189.

2. Weisse, Arthur James. *History of the City of Albany* (Albany, N.Y.: E. H. Bender, 1884).

3. "Tax List," 1779, Gerrit Y. Lansing Papers, New York State Library, Albany, N.Y.; "Tax List," 1799, Albany Institute of History and Art, Albany, N.Y.

4. United States Department of Commerce. Bureau of Census. *Head of Families of the First Census of the United States Taken in 1790: New York* (Washington, D.C.: U.S. Government Printing Office, 1908); United States Department of Commerce. Bureau of Census. *U.S. Census, Fourth, 1820: New York* (Washington, D.C.: U.S. Government Printing Office, n.d.).

5. William Esmond Rowley, "Albany: A Tale of Two Cities, 1820–1880" (Ph.D. dissertation, Harvard University, 1967), chap. 1.

6. "Pew Holders List," 1790, First Reformed Church; "Pew Holders List," 1786; "Pew Holders List," 1787; "Session Minutes," 1786–1800, First Presbyterian Church, Albany, N.Y.: "Subscription List," 1788–1799; and "Confirmation List," 1791, St. Peter's Church Papers, New York State Library; *First Census, 1790: New York;* United States Department of Commerce. Bureau of Census. *Heads of Families of the Second Census of the United States Taken in 1800: New York* (Washington, D.C.: U.S. Government Printing Office, 1908).

7. "Session Minutes," 1786–1814, First Presbyterian Church. According to First Presbyterian's minister, John McDonald, in 1785 this church was composed of "the members of the former society in union with the strangers of the same denomination who had settled there during and after the war." John McDonald, *Albany Centinel,* November 25, 1800.

8. Richard W. Pointer, *Protestant Pluralism and the New York Experience* (Bloomington, Indiana: Indiana University Press, 1988), chaps. 5–6.

9. Robert S. Alexander, *Albany's First Church and Its Role in the Growth of the City* (Albany, N.Y.: First Church, 1988), 145.

10. "Consistory Minutes," 1790–1800, Dutch Reformed Church.

11. "List of Pew Holders," 1790 and "Membership List," 1816 Dutch Reformed Church; "List of Communicants," 1821, St. Peter's Episcopal Church; "Register of Communicants," 1795–1815, First Presbyterian Church.

12. "Common Council Minutes," 1790–1800, New York State Library; "Consistory Minutes," 1805, Dutch Reformed Church.

13. Reverend Thomas Ellison, "The Landed Estate of St. Peter's Church," St. Peter's Church Papers, New York State Library.

14. "Marriage and Baptism Lists," 1787–1792, St. Peter's Episcopal Church Papers.

15. Ellison, "Landed Estate."

16. "List of Communicants," 1821–1834, St. Peter's Episcopal Church Papers, New York State Library.

17. First Methodist Church: "Marriage and Baptism Records," 1806–1830; "Annual Membership List," 1793–1830; "List of Officers," 1793–1830, Trinity Methodist Church, Albany, N.Y.

18. "Common Council Minutes," 1795, New York State Library.

19. John T. McClintock, "Albany and its Early Nineteenth Century Schools" (M.A. thesis: Harvard University, 1976), 22.

20. George R. Howell and Jonathan Tenney, eds., *Bicentennial History of Albany, New York from 1609 to 1886* (New York: Munsell, 1886), 764.

21. Max Weber, *The Protestant Ethic and the Spirit of Capitalism* (New York: Charles Scribner's Sons, 1958).

22. Although Weber did emphasize the independent influence of Calvinism on the spirit of capitalism, he also believed that social, economic, and technical factors were involved. As many have argued, his study was not intended to replace other studies that emphasized the causal importance of these latter factors but to comple-

ment them with an analysis of the contributing role played by religious ideas. At the conclusion of *The Protestant Ethic,* Weber acknowledges that his study is incomplete because it does not consider these other factors. Moreover, he observes that for a full investigation of religious and economic change "it would also be necessary to investigate how Protestant asceticism was in turn influenced in its development and character by the totality of social conditions, especially economic." *Protestant Ethic,* 183. My theoretical purpose here is to place Weber's thesis into this larger arena by taking both religious ideas and social conditions into account. For an analysis of the social, economic, and technical factors that complement Weber's argument and its implications for Weber's thesis, see David Zaret, *The Heavenly Contract: Ideology and Organization in Pre-Revolutionary Puritanism* (Chicago: University of Chicago Press, 1985).

23. William James, ed., *The Literary Remains of the Late Henry James* (Boston: Houghton and Mifflin, 1884), 146.

24. *Albany Gazette,* advertisements 1790–1800.

25. *Albany Gazette,* legal announcements of the dissolution of partnerships 1790–1800.

26. "Dr. Morse's Descriptions of Albany in 1789," in Munsell, *Annals,* 1:314–315.

27. Howard M. Feinstein, *Becoming William James* (Ithaca, N.Y.: Cornell University Press, 1984), 27.

28. Duke Rochefoucault-Liancourt, "Voyage dans le Etats-Unis," in Munsell, *Annals,* 4:228.

29. "Conditions and Prospects of the City in 1789," in *Albany Gazette,* cited in Munsell, *Annals,* 1:338.

30. "Session Minutes," 1786–1800, First Presbyterian Church, Albany, N.Y.; "City Tax List," 1799, Albany Institute; "Common Council Minutes," 1770–1776, in Munsell, *Collections* 1:211–276; "Common Council Minutes," 1778–1810, New York State Library; James Sullivan, ed., *Albany Committee of Correspondence Minutes;* Paltsits, ed., *Minutes of Commission for Detecting Conspiracies.*

31. "Session Minutes," 1786–1800, First Presbyterian Church; "City Tax List," 1799 Albany Institute of History and Art, Albany, N.Y.

32. "Common Council Minutes," 1785. New York State Library.

33. "Session Minutes," 1786–1835, and "Register of Marriages," 1786–1815, First Presbyterian Church.

34. *Albany Centinel,* November 25, 1800.

35. "Session Minutes," 1785–1790, First Presbyterian Church.

36. "Session Minutes," 1788, First Presbyterian Church.

37. Ibid.

38. John McDonald, *The Faithful Steward: A Sermon Preached at the Ordination of Mr. Aaron Condict* (Albany, N.Y.: Charles R. and George Webster, 1793).

39. "Session Minutes," 1785–1790, First Presbyterian Church.

40. "Session Minutes," 1785–1805, First Presbyterian Church.

41. McDonald, *Faithful Steward,* 24.

42. "Session Minutes," 1785–1805, First Presbyterian Church.

43. Ibid.

44. "Session Minutes," 1798, First Presbyterian Church.

45. "Tax List," 1779, Lansing Papers; "Tax List," 1799, Albany Institute; *First U.S. Census, 1790: New York.*

46. James, *Literary Remains,* 152.

47. Ibid.

48. Ibid., 184.

49. Ibid., 59.

50. The total population increased from 3,498 in 1790 to 10,562 in 1810. *First Census, 1790: New York;* United States Department of Commerce. Bureau of Census. *U.S. Census, Third, 1810: New York* (Washington, D.C.: U.S. Government Printing Office, 1811); Thomas P. Hughes, ed., *American Ancestry,* 9 vols. (Albany, N.Y.: Munsell, 1887).

51. See Richard Bushman, *From Puritan to Yankee: Character and Social Order in Connecticut, 1690–1765* (Cambridge, Mass.: Harvard University Press, 1967), 267–288.

52. "Albany As Seen by Dr. Dwight," in Munsell, *Annals,* 8:182–183.

53. Dwight, *Annals* 8:184.

54. David M. Ellis takes a closer look at these Yankee-Dutch tensions in the Albany area in "Yankee-Dutch Confrontation in the Albany Area," *New England Quarterly,* 40(1972):262–270. Dutch animosity toward New Englanders is most clearly evident in the preferred derivation of the word Yankee. The term is from the Dutch Jan Kees or Kaas, a name given to Dutch pirates of the seventeenth century. Immigrant New Englanders who sought to "improve" the ways of the Dutch were derided as looters or marauders bent on exploiting the local people. H. L. Mencken, *The American Language,* Supplement I (New York: Alfred A. Knopf, 1960); James A. H. Murray, ed., *A New English Dictionary on Historical Principles* (Oxford: Oxford University Press, 1897), I, pt. 2, 14.

55. *Albany Register,* February 4, 1793.

56. *Albany Register,* January 28, 1793.

57. "Celebration of the Adoption of the Federal Constitution," 1788, in Munsell, *Annals,* 1:330–335.

58. "Consistory Minutes," 1790–1800, Dutch Reformed Church.

59. *Albany Gazette,* 1790–1800.

60. *Albany Gazette,* November 1, 1791.

61. This was true as late as 1789, when Elkanah Watson, one of the first Yankees in Albany, argued in vain for the elimination of charges for city trading privileges, the construction of inner-city roads, and the creation of a canal to Lake Erie. Watson, *Men and Times of the Revolution,* 2nd ed. (New York: Dana and Company, 1857).

62. *Albany Register,* August 5, 1793.

63. *The Albany Centinel,* April 16, 1805.

64. For a biography of Nott see Codman Hislop, *Eliphalet Nott* (Middletown, Conn.: Wesleyan University Press, 1980), 1–73.

65. Even though by 1810 Nott rose to the position of Moderator of the Presbyterian National Assembly, his abilities were not immediately perceived by the Scotch-Irish in the congregation. Within a month after his appointment, they formed a committee to challenge his "handling the word of God." In particular, the committee stated that they wanted a minister who will "compose with accuracy, speak correctly, and preach without reading." In addition, concern over changes in the text, meter, and manner of expressing congregational hymns particularly disturbed the dissenters. "Session Minutes," 1798, First Presbyterian Church. A few Scotch-Irish dissenters underscored the continuing importance of ethnic identity by going so far as to form a separate Associate Reformed Presbyterian Church. Reverend J. McClusky Blayney, *History of the First Presbyterian Church of Albany, New York* (Albany, N.Y.: Jenkins and Johnston, 1877), 60–63.

66. Worth, "Random Recollections," in Munsell, *Annals,* 10:208. Albany's Presbyterian church also benefited from the 1801 Plan of Union worked out by New England's Presbyterian and Congregational churches whereby they agreed to cooperate in founding churches on the frontier. Since there was no Congregational church in Albany until the 1830's, most of Albany's early nineteenth century immigrant Congregationalists apparently turned Presbyterian when they crossed the Hudson river.

67. Hislop, *Eliphalet Nott,* 40.

68. Eliphalet Nott, *The Providence of God.*

69. Eliphalet Nott, *An Address Delivered to the Candidates for the Baccalaureate in Union College, at the Anniversary Commencement, May 18, 1805* (Albany, N.Y.: Charles R. & George Webster, 1805), 3.

70. Nott, *Baccalaureate,* 11.

71. Nott, *Baccalaureate,* 29–30.

72. Nott, *Baccalaureate,* 12.

73. Bushman, *Puritan to Yankee,* 288; For a discussion of the relationship of these changes to the Second Great Awakening, see Donald G. Matthews, "The Second Great Awakening as an Organizing Process, 1780–1830: An Hypothesis," *American Quarterly,* 21(1969):23–43.

Chapter 4

1. Arthur Joseph Stansbury, *God Pleading with America* (Goshen, N.Y.: T. B. Crowell, 1813), 4.

2. For further discussion see George M. Marsden, *The Evangelical Mind and the New School Presbyterian Experience* (New Haven, Conn.: Yale University Press, 1970), 21–23.

3. A similar point is made by Paul E. Johnson, *A Shopkeeper's Millenium: Society and Revivals in Rochester, New York, 1815–1817* (New York: Hill and Wang, 1976), 44.

4. Horatio Gates Spafford, *A Gazetteer of the State of New York* (Albany, N.Y.: H. C. Southwick, 1817). Between 1790 and 1840 the population of Albany grew as follows:

Year	Population	Percentage Growth
1790	3,498	—
1800	5,289	51.2
1810	10,562	103.5
1820	12,630	17.4
1830	24,209	91.7
1840	33,721	39.3
1850	50,763	50.6
1860	62,367	22.9

U.S. Department of Commerce. Census Bureau. *U.S. Census, 18th, 1970,* (Washington, D.C.: U.S. Government Printing Office, 1971).

5. The classic treatment of this migration and its accompanying revivals is Whitney R. Cross, *The Burned-Over District: A Social and Economic History of Enthusiastic Religion in Western New York, 1800–1850* (Ithaca, N.Y.: Cornell University Press, 1950).

6. Spafford, *Gazetteer.*

7. "City Tax List," 1817, County Records Office, Albany, N.Y.: *Albany City Directory for 1817* (Albany, N.Y.: Packard and Van Benthuysen, 1817).

8. Gorham A. Worth, "Random Recollections of Albany," in Munsell, Joel, ed. *Annals of Albany.* 10 vols. (Albany, N.Y.: Munsell, 1850–1859) 10:200.

9. "City Tax List," 1817, Country Records Office; Information on the New England ancestry of Albany's Yankee immigrants comes primarily from Jonathan Tenney, *New England in Albany* (Boston: Long Island Historical Society, 1883) and George R. Howell and Jonathan Tenney, *Bicentennial History of Albany, New York from 1609 to 1886* (New York: Munsell, 1886).

10. *City Directory for 1817;* Portions of this section on social changes are indebted to Johnson, *Shopkeeper's,* chaps. 1–2.

11. U.S. Department of Commerce. Census Bureau. *U.S. Census, Fourth, 1820: New York* (Washington, D.C.: U.S. Government Printing Office, n.d.)

12. To derive the number of independent proprietors, I have followed the method used by Paul Johnson in Appendix A of *Shopkeeper's.* Economic information comes from the 1817 city directory and tax list; 1817 is the first year in the nineteenth century for which complete tax records are available. By matching the names and occupations of the directory with the corresponding names and property holdings on the tax list, it is possible to rank occupations and property holdings in relation to each other. Proprietors can be easily identified by stated occupations. Merchants, grocers, and lawyers are proprietors; clerks are employees. But among proprietors there are great differences in degree. Merchants are listed among the very wealthiest of Albany's workers, yet they can also be found in the tenth and lowest decile of taxpayers. Using Johnson's method as a guide, I have collapsed the occupations listed in the 1817 directory into five fundamental categories. Then I have looked for an obvious line separating wealthy businessmen and professionals from less affluent boardinghouse operators and petty shopkeepers.

Distribution of Occupations Within Assessment Deciles (in percent)

	1	2	3	4	5	6	7	8	9	10
Commercial	58	50	50	47	46	25	29	31	15	20
Professional	18	20	9	2	5	2	2	4	2	3
Clerical	4	4	3	6	8	8	7	4	7	7
Skilled	20	26	37	43	42	54	51	48	52	41
Unskilled	0	0	2	2	2	12	11	12	20	20
Number of cases	72	71	70	61	72	62	64	59	52	41

Among the top 50 percent of taxpayers, commercial and professional men account for at least half the total, while below that line their members drop sharply. The fifth decile seems to separate most owners from those listed as grocers and petty shopkeepers. This large number of possible proprietors is reduced sharply, however, if we separate out clearly less affluent grocers from other men of commerce.

	1	2	3	4	5	6	7	8	9	10
Commercial	58	50	50	47	46	25	29	31	15	20
Merchant	56	48	43	35	28	15	13	10	2	14
Grocer	2	2	7	12	18	10	16	21	13	6
Professional	18	20	9	2	5	2	2	4	2	3

Now the third decile marks the line where men of commerce, other than grocers, and professionals account for more than half of the total while below that line the numbers again drop off. This admittedly imperfect process gives us some idea of who the town's white collar proprietors were. These were commercial and professional men in the top three deciles of the city's tax list.

To derive the number of skilled workers who were proprietors I relied on their identification as shop owners in the 1817 directory and added to these the number of skilled workers whose tax assessment was in the top three deciles.

By adding together all the commercial and professional members of the work force whose tax was in the top three deciles and then adding to these the skilled workers who owned their own shops, I arrived at 24 percent as the percentage of Albany's work force who were proprietors.

13. The total number of occupations listed in the 1817 directory is 1643. Of these workers, 1019 are also listed on the 1817 tax list. Using the preceding derivation, this is how the percentage of dependent workers and independent proprietors compare in each occupational category.

Occupation	Total, %	Dependent, %	Independent, %
Commercial	39	24	15
Professional	7	5	2
Clerical	6	5	1
Skilled	41	35	6
Unskilled	7	7	0
Total	100	76	24

14. Department of Commerce, Census Bureau. *U.S. Census, Fourth: New York.*

15. This was derived by determining how many of the journeymen listed in the 1817 directory were listed in the 1830 directory. *City Directory for 1817;* Cammeyer, William, Jr. and R. Gaw, eds., *The Albany Directory for the Years 1830–1831* (Albany, N.Y.: E. B. Child, 1831).

16. Twenty-eight shop owners and ninety-six skilled workers can be identified on the 1799 tax list. Fifty-eight shop owners and 415 skilled workers are listed in the 1817 city directory. "City Tax List," 1799, Albany Institute of History and Art; "City Tax List," 1817, County Records Office; *City Directory for 1817.*

17. *City Directory for 1817;* "Memoir of Charles R. Webster, the Father of Printing in Albany," in Munsell, *Annals,* 5:230–240.

18. "1803 Albany Mechanics' Society Membership List," Albany Collection, American Antiquarian Society, Worcester, Mass.; "Albany Mechanics' Society," in Munsell, *Annals,* 7:240–244.

19. Lewis L. Hoffman, in Munsell, *Typographical Miscellany* (Albany, N.Y.: J. Munsell, 1850).

20. The 1817 directory identifies the shop owners who had separate residences. The directory also lists individual addresses that can be correlated with the addresses of boardinghouses. *City Directory for 1817.*

21. *City Directory for 1817;* "City Tax List," 1817, County Records Office.

22. Robert Davis, "A View of the Albany General Market of the City of Albany, in the Summer of 1819," Albany Institute of History and Art (pamphlet).

23. "City Tax List," 1817 County Records Office; The membership lists for these churches are identified in the Albany Church Records section of the References.

24. The following table offers an overview of the relationship between religion and wealth in Albany in 1817.

> Column One: The 1817 tax list was divided into deciles, the first decile being the wealthiest 10 percent of taxpayers etc.
>
> Column Two: The percentage of the town's total wealth held by each decile of taxpayers.
>
> Column Three: The percentage of taxpayers in each decile who were church members.
>
> Column Four: The percentage of the town's Presbyterians among all church members in each decile.

Column Five: The percentage of the town's Dutch Church members among all church members in each decile.

Column Six: The percentage of Episcopalians among all church members in each decile.

Column Seven: The percentage of Methodists among all church members in each decile.

Wealth Percentile	Total, %	Religious, %	Presbyterian	Dutch	Episcopalian	Methodist
1	45	77	21	28	27	1
2	18	57	16	20	11	9
3	11	51	12	13	16	10
4	8	43	12	11	13	7
5	7	31	8	9	3	11
6	4	36	8	3	10	14
7	3	26	8	4	7	7
8	2	31	5	5	7	14
9	1	27	4	4	1	17
10	1	25	7	2	5	11

Sources: "City Tax List," 1817, County Records Office; Albany Church Records.

25. I have used information on new communicants from the First Presbyterian Church and the Second Dutch Reformed Church to derive this figure. "Register of Communicants," 1796–1816, First Presbyterian Church; "List of Communicants," 1815–1840, Second Dutch Reformed Church.

26. "Consistory Minutes," 1790–1835; "List of Pew Holders," 1790; "Membership List," 1816–1835, First Dutch Reformed Church. "Session Minutes," 1786–1835; "Register of Communicants," 1795–1840, First Presbyterian Church.

27. *Acts and Proceedings of the General Synod of the Reformed Dutch Church in the United States of America in the Year 1800* (New York: Forman, 1800), 11–12.

28. William Buell Sprague, *A Sermon Delivered on Sabbath Morning January 4, 1846 Containing Sketches of the History of the Second Presbyterian Church and Congregation, Albany, During Thirty Years from the Period of Their Organization* (Albany, N.Y.: Pease, 1846).

29. The membership of the first board of trustees, the names on an 1813 subscription list, and the names of the students who actually enrolled all indicate that the school served the sons of the elite. On July 13, 1815 the board of trustees appointed a committee to receive applications for the approaching fall quarter and instructed them to "inquire what course of study the parents or guardians wish to be taught to the applicants." The parents had traditional ideas about education; on November 1, 1815, out of eighty-five students, sixty-two were pursuing classical subjects. John T. McClintock, "Albany and Its Early Nineteenth Century Schools" (M.A. thesis, Harvard University, 1967), 41–42.

30. "City Tax List," 1817, County Records Office; "List of Pew Holders," 1790

and "Consistory Minutes," 1790–1815, First Dutch Reformed Church; "List of Original Members and Officers of the South Albany Dutch Reformed Church," 1815, Second Dutch Reformed Church, American Antiquarian Society, Worcester, Mass.; "List of Communicants," 1815, Second Dutch Reformed Church Records, New York State Library.

31. Ibid., and Tenney, *New England in Albany*.

32. Judith Botch, "A Comparative Analysis of 19th Century Industrialists in Albany, New York" (Seminar paper, Albany Institute for History and Art, 1979), 12–13. Also see Howell and Tenney, *Bicentennial History*, 555–609.

33. Albany Sunday School Society, "Constitution of the Albany Sunday School Society," 1817, American Antiquarian Society, Worcester, Mass.

34. Howell and Tenney, *Bicentennial History*, 663.

35. "City Tax List," 1817, County Records Office; Tenney, *New England*.

36. "Marriage Records," 1785–1816, First Presbyterian Church.

37. "Register of Communicants," 1797–1816, First Presbyterian Church.

38. "1683 Communicants List," in Munsell, *Collections*, 1:97–101.

39. "List of Pewholders," 1790, Dutch Reformed Church.

40. "List of Original Members and Officers of the South Albany Dutch Reformed Church, 1815." Second Dutch Reformed Church.

41. "List of Communicants," 1816–1870, Second Presbyterian Church.

42. This figure was derived from an analysis of the relevant Dutch and Presbyterian church membership lists. See the Albany Church Records section of the References.

43. "List of the Inhabitants of the Citty of Albany in America with the Number of Troops they can Quarter conveniently within the Stockade and What they can Quarter in case of necessity together with the fire places in Each house and Rooms without Fire, also what appeared in a strett Enquiry made in November 1756. . ." Loudoun Paper, Huntington Library, San Marino, Calif.

44. *U.S. Census, Second: New York;* "Common Council Minutes," 1790–1810, New York State Library.

45. For a discussion of these changes in a nearby community, see Mary P. Ryan, *Cradle of the Middle Class: the Family in Oneida County, New York 1790–1865* (New York: Cambridge University Press, 1981).

46. *A Brief Account of the Society Established in the City of Albany for the Relief of Indigent Women and Children* (Albany, N.Y.: Charles R. and George Webster, 1805).

47. "Common Council Minutes," 1804, New York State Library; *Brief Account*.

48. Eliphalet Nott, *A Discourse Delivered in the Presbyterian Church in the City of Albany; Before the Ladies Society for the Relief of Distressed Women and Children* (Albany, N.Y.: Charles R. and George Webster, 1804), 27.

49. These figures are derived from the relevant membership lists in the Albany Church Records section of the References.

50. Nott, *Ladies Society*, 30–31.

51. Ann Douglas, *The Feminization of American Culture* (New York: Alfred A. Knopf, 1977). On controversy surrounding Douglas' thesis see David S. Schuyler. "Inventing a Feminine Past." *New England Quarterly,* 51(1978):291–308 and the rejoinder by David S. Reynolds. "The Feminization Controversy: Sexual Stereotypes and the Paradoxes of Piety in Nineteenth-Century America." *New England Quarterly,* 53(1980):96–106. On the creation of a separate "women's sphere" among early nineteenth century affluent women, see Nancy Cott, *The Bonds of Womanhood: "Women's Sphere" in New England, 1780–1835* (New Haven, Conn.: Yale University Press, 1977).

52. "Register of Communicants," 1796–1816, First Presbyterian Church.

53. "City Tax List," 1817, County Records Office.

54. Tenney, *New England in Albany.*

55. City Directory for 1817; "City Tax List," 1817, County Records Office; Albany Church Records.

56. Albany Society for the Suppression of Vice and Immorality. *Constitution and Proceedings of the Albany Society for the Suppression of Vice and Immorality* (Albany, N.Y.: Churchill and McGlashan, 1815), 7–8.

57. "An Act for the Supressing of Immorality," reprinted in the March 1814 issue of Albany's Presbyterian supported newsletter, the *Christian Visitant.*

58. "Report of the Board of Council of the Albany Society for the Suppression of Vice and Immorality," *Christian Visitant,* November 4, 1814; *Mechanics Moral Society of the City of Albany Associated for the Suppression of Vice and Immorality and the Promotion of Good Morals.* Broadside. (Albany, N.Y.: n.p., 1816)

59. John Chester, *Knowledge and Holiness the Sources of Morality* (Albany, N.Y.: E. & E. Hosford, 1821), 24.

60. Ibid.

61. Ibid., 28–29.

62. *Christian Advocate and Journal,* January 15, 1859.

63. "Origin of Sunday Schools in Albany," in Munsell, *Annals,* 7:178–193.

64. *Albany Microscope,* June 19, 1824.

65. *Albany Microscope,* June 12, 1830.

66. Tobias Spicer, *Camp-Meetings Defended, or a Brief Review of a Pamphlet Lately Published Entitled Camp-Meetings Described and Exposed, and Strange Things Stated* (New Haven, Conn.: T. G. Woodward, 1828), 24.

67. Marriage and Baptism Records," 1806–1830; "Annual Membership List," 1793–1830; "List of Officers," 1793–1830; "History," 1807–1859, Trinity Methodist Church, Albany, N.Y.

68. Ibid.; "City Tax List," 1817, County Records Office.

69. Charles D. Schwartz and Ouida Davis Schwartz, *A Flame of Fire: The Story of Troy Annual Conference* (Rutland, Vt: Academic Books, 1982).

70. This paragraph follows a similar discussion found in Paul Faler, *Mechanics and Manufacturers in the Early Industrial Revolution* (Albany, N.Y.: State University of New York Press, 1981), chap. 3.

71. "Albany Mechanics' Society," in Munsell, *Annals,* 7:240–244.

72. Howell and Tenney, *Bicentennial History,* 529.

73. McClintock, "Albany and its Early Nineteenth Century Schools," 13–20.

74. "Albany Mechanics' Society," in Munsell, *Annals,* 7:240–244.

75. Solomon Southwick, *An Address Delivered . . . at the Opening of the Apprentices' Library* (Albany, N.Y.: John O. Cole, 1821), 9.

76. Ibid.

77. See Faler, *Mechanics,* chap. 3.

78. David S. Edelstein, *Joel Munsell: Printer and Antiquarian* (New York: Columbia University Press, 1950), 51.

79. Quoted in Martin Marty, *Righteous Empire: The Protestant Experience in America* (New York: Harper and Row, 1970), 106.

80. Southwick, *Apprentices' Library,* 12.

81. Edelstein, *Munsell,* 92.

82. Southwick, *Apprentices' Library,* 6.

83. Ibid., 13.

84. Ibid., 7–8.

85. Edelstein, *Munsell,* 56.

86. These figures are derived from comparisons between the 1817 tax list and membership lists of the Methodist and Baptist churches. "City Tax List," 1817, County Records Office; Albany Church Records.

87. Davis, "A View of the General Market," 5.

88. For analysis of a similar situation in France, see Theda Skocpol, "Cultural Idioms and Political Ideologies in the Revolutionary Reconstruction of State Power: A Rejoinder to Sewell" *Journal of Modern History,* 57(1985):86–96.

Chapter 5

1. William Esmond Rowley, "Albany: A Tale of Two Cities, 1820–1880" (Ph.D. dissertation, Harvard University, 1967), chap. 1; George R. Howell and Jonathan Tenney, *Bicentennial History of Albany, New York from 1609 to 1886* (New York: Munsell, 1886), 523–525; Munsell, Joel, ed., *Annals of Albany.* 10 vols. (Albany, N.Y.: Munsell, 1850–1859), 8:125.

2. T. V. Cuyler, ed., *Albany City Directory for 1825* (Albany, N.Y.: E. B. Child, 1825); Cammeyer and Gaw, *Albany Directory for 1830–1831* (Albany, N.Y.: E. B. Child, 1831); State of New York, *Census of the State of New York for 1825* (Albany, N.Y.: State of New York, 1826); "City Tax List," 1830 in Charles Edward Gotsch, "The Albany Workingman's Party and the Rise of Popular Politics" (Ph.D. dissertation, State University of New York at Albany, 1976). 1830 assessment rolls exist for only the first three of Albany's five wards. In his dissertation, Charles Gotsch compiled a list of all those who had taxable property in 1830 by using the available 1830 assessment rolls, the 1831 assessment roll for the fourth ward, and the 1836 roll for the fifth ward. Since the assessed value for the first three wards did not increase substantially from the 1830 to the 1836 assessment, it is probable that the assessment for the fourth and fifth wards also did not increase notably.

3. *City Directory for 1817;* Howell and Tenney, *Bicentennial History,* 699–702; Munsell *Annals,* 5:230–240.

4. Lewis L. Hoffman, quoted in Munsell, *Typographical Miscellany* (Albany, N.Y.: Munsell, 1850).

5. David S. Edelstein, *Joel Munsell: Printer and Antiquarian* (New York: Columbia University Press, 1950), 65–66.

6. Cuyler Reynolds, *Albany Chronicles: A History of the City Arranged Chronologically, from the Earliest Settlement to the Present Time* (Albany, N.Y.: James B. Lyon, 1907), 471; Cammeyer and Gaw, *Albany Directory for 1830–1831;* George R. Towell and Jonathan Tenney, *Bicentennial History of Albany, New York from 1609 to 1886* (New York: Munsell, 1886), 701.

7. Rowley, "Albany: A Tale of Two Cities," 58.

8. State of New York. *Census of the State of New York for 1825* (Albany, N.Y.: State of New York, 1826). State of New York, *Census of the State of New York for 1835* (Albany, N.Y.: Crosswell, Van Benthuysen and Burt, 1836).

9. New York, *1825 Census.*

10. *Albany City Directory for 1817* (Albany, N.Y.: Packard and Van Benthuysen, 1817); Cammeyer and Gaw, *Albany Directory for 1830–1831.*

11. Rowley, "Albany: A Tale of Two Cities," 58.

12. Cammeyer and Gaw, *Albany Directory for 1830–1831.*

13. Following a formula developed by Paul E. Johnson in his Rochester study, *A Shopkeeper's Millenium: Society and Revivals in Rochester, New York, 1815–1817* (New York: Hill and Way, 1576), 48–51, I have classified Albany's streets according to the percentage of independent proprietors that lived on them. At least 70 percent of the residents of middle class streets are proprietors. Working class residential streets have fewer than 30 percent proprietors. Mixed residential streets have between 30 and 69 percent proprietors. Every street with at least twenty addresses listed in the city directory is included.

14. In 1825, the traveler, Anne Royall, described the "compact part of the city" as lying "on two principal streets. . . . Market street is handsome and two miles in length; State Street is quite short and terminates at the capitol: it is, however, a beautiful street, as wide as any of the avenues in Washington." Anne Royall, *Sketches of History, Life, and Manners in the United States* (New Haven, Conn.: By the author, 1826), 273.

15. *Farmers', Mechanics', and Workingman's Advocate,* May 19, 1830.

16. Munsell, *Annals,* 9:178.

17. New York State Society for the Promotion of Temperance, *Fourth Annual Report of the New York State Society for the Promotion of Temperance* (Albany, N.Y.: Packard and Van Benthuysen, 1833), 82.

18. "Common Council Minutes," 1810–1830, New York State Library; Albany Church Records; *Constitution and Proceedings of the Albany Society for the Suppression of Vice and Immorality;* John T. McClintock, "Albany and It's Early Nineteenth Century Schools," (M.A. thesis, Harvard University, 1967).

19. Albany Church Records; "Common Council Minutes," 1810–1830, New York State Library.

20. Lists of the officers of Albany's major banks, businesses, and public works organizations can be found at the end of the 1825 city directory. Cuyler, *City Directory for 1825.*

21. See Alvin Kass, *Politics in New York State* (Syracuse, N.Y.: Syracuse University Press, 1964).

22. Rowley, "Albany: A Tale of Two Cities," 112–116.

23. "Common Council Minutes," June 12, 1826, New York State Library.

24. "Common Council Minutes," March 10, 1828, New York State Library.

25. David O. Mears, *Life of Edward Norris Kirk, D.D.,* (Boston: Lockwood, Brroks, and Co., 1878), 49.

26. Munsell, *Annals,* 9:164.

27. *City Directory for 1817;* Cammeyer and Gaw, *Albany Directory for 1830–1831;* Munsell, *Annals,* 8:132; Reynolds, *Chronicles,* 487.

28. "Common Council Minutes," 1820 and 1830, New York State Library.

29. "Common Council Minutes," 1798–1802, New York State Library.

30. Munsell, *Annals,* 8:85.

31. "Common Council Minutes," March 13, 1826, New York State Library.

32. *Albany Argus,* August 2, 1831.

33. "Common Council Minutes," January 7, 1828, New York State Library.

34. Ibid.

35. "Common Council Minutes," 1828, New York State Library.

36. James R. Manley, *An Eulogium on De Witt Clinton* (New York: Gould and Jacobus, 1828), 21.

37. Citizens of Albany, *Tribute to the Memory of De Witt Clinton* (Albany, N.Y.: Webster and Wood, 1828).

38. Paul E. Johnson alerted me to this relationship between Clinton's name and "progress" in New York.

39. Mears, *Kirk,* 49.

40. Codman Hislop, *Albany: Dutch, English, and American* (Albany, N.Y. Argus Press, 1936), 278.

41. Cammeyer and Gaw, *Albany Director for 1830–1831.*

42. "Communicants List," 1829–1840 Fourth Presbyterian Church, Albany, N.Y.

43. This transformation of the social relations of production is presented in detail by Johnson, *Shopkeeper's,* 37–61.

44. Munsell, *Annals,* 7:240–244.

45. Rowley, "Albany: A Tale of Two Cities," 122.

46. *Workingman's Advocate,* February 2, 1831.

47. Ibid., January 1, 1831.

48. Ibid..

49. Ibid.

50. Ibid.

51. *Albany Argus,* February 12, 1830.

52. Cammeyer and Gaw, *Albany Directory for 1830–1831;* "City Tax List," 1830 in Gotsch, "Albany Workingman's Party and Popular Politics."

54. See Sean Wilentz, *Chants Democratic: New York City and the Rise of the American Working Class, 1788–1850* (New York: Oxford University Press, 1984), 150.

55. Gotsch, "Workingman's Party and Popular Politics," chap. 3.

56. Gotsch, "Albany Workingman's Party and Popular Politics," 58.

57. Rowley, "Albany: A Tale of Two Cities," 116.

58. Ibid., 116–122; Gotsch, "Albany Workingman's Party and Popular Politics," 60–64.

59. Rowley, "Albany: A Tale of Two Cities," 106.

60. Ibid., 107.

61. Gotsch, "Albany Workingman's Party and Popular Politics," 56.

62. *Common School Assistant* (Albany, N.Y.: 1836), no. 1.

63. *Workingman's Advocate,* April 3, 1830.

64. Wilentz, *Chants Democratic,* 157–158.

65. Rowley, "Albany: A Tale of Two Cities," 117.

66. *Workingman's Advocate,* June 9, 1830.

67. Rowley, "Albany: A Tale of Two Cities," 117.

68. *Workingman's Advocate,* June 30, 1830.

69. *Workingman's Advocate,* August 18, 1830.

70. *Workingman's Advocate,* October 16, 1830.

71. Gotsch, "Albany Workingman's Party and Popular Politics," 54.

72. Rowley, "Albany: A Tale of Two Cities," 112.

73. Gotsch, "Albany Workingman's Party and Popular Politics," 59.

74. Rowley, "Albany: A Tale of Two Cities," 127.

75. Jabez D. Hammond, *The History of Political Parties in the State of New York,* 2 vols. (Syracuse, N.Y.: Hall, Mills, and Co., 1852), 2:330–331.

76. Gotsch, "Albany Workingman's Party and Popular Politics," 44.

77. Rowley, Albany: A Tale of Two Cities," 99–100.

78. Albany Temperance Society. "Address and Constitution of the Albany Temperance Society," 2–7, American Antiquarian Society, Worcester, Mass (pamphlet).

79. New York Society for the Promotion of Temperance *Fourth Annual Report of the New York State Society for the Promotion of Temperance* (Albany, N.Y.: Packard & Van Benthuysen, 1833), 82. The *Microscope,* on November 24, 1832, rebuked the Temperance Society's explanation of the relationship between intemperance and the cholera. "The sole object is to paint such a picture of intemperance, by means of the cholera, as will enhance the interests of the Temperance Society, by publishing the most infamous libels upon the characters of almost every individual who was carried off by the pestilence. Never in the annals of moral turpitude has there ever been recorded such damnable falsehoods."

80. Rowley, "Albany: A Tale of Two Cities," 100.

81. Munsell, *Annals,* 9:200.

82. *Christian Register,* November 6, 1830; May 1831.

83. *Microscope,* February 6, 1830.

84. *Workingman's Advocate,* July 14, 1831.

85. *Workingman's Advocate,* June 9, 1830.

86. *Christian Register,* October 25, 1829.

87. Albany Young Men's Society. "A Circular to the Young Men of the State of New York from the Young Men's Society in Albany," 2–4, Albany Institute for History and Art, Albany, N.Y.

88. Notice of the existence of the Journeyman Carpenters Temperance Society was given in the *Argus,* June 7, 1834.

Chapter 6

1. This was the law office of Benjamin F. Butler. He later served as attorney general for the United States. His law partner, Martin Van Buren, was soon to be elected president. Joel Munsell, ed., *Annals of Albany,* 10 vols. (Albany, N.Y.: Munsell, 1850–1859), 8:76.

2. David O. Mears, *Life of Edward Norris Kirk* (Boston: Lockwood, Brooks and Company, 1878), 50.

3. Ibid., 50.

4. George M. Marsden, *The Evangelical Mind and the New School Presbyterian Experience* (New Haven, Conn.: Yale University Press, 1970), 6.

5. Mears, *Kirk,* 66–67.

6. This figure is derived from data provided by the church membership lists in the Albany Church Records section of the References.

7. I partly agree with Nathan O. Hatch's important study, *The Democratization of American Christianity* (New Haven, Ct.: Yale University Press, 1989). I agree with Hatch's view that the rise and growth of evangelical Christianity was primarily the work of people who rebelled against the established order. Antebellum Christian leaders employed extemporaneous preaching and democratic practices that invited common folk to create their own forms of piety. Where I disagree with Hatch is in the limited extent to which he sees the emerging Christian groups assimilating enlightenment, humanism, and economic practices from the surrounding society. For more on this see James Turner, *Without God, Without Creed: The Origins of Unbelief in America* (Baltimore, Md.: Johns Hopkins University Press, 1985), chap. 3. In his eagerness to claim that "the most powerful popular movements in the early republic were expressly religious" (224), Hatch also neglects the role of such non-religious groups as the mechanics whose ideals complemented and contended with popular Christianity in their shared creation of the new society's values.

8. Mears, *Kirk,* 65.

9. "Session Minutes," 1786–1835 First Presbyterian Church; "Session Minutes," 1831, Second Presbyterian Church.

10. Mears, *Kirk,* 62, 45.

11. Citizen of Albany, *Tribute to the Memory of De Witt Clinton* (Albany, N.Y.: Webster and Wood, 1828), 91.

12. Alfred Conkling, *A Discourse Commemortive of the Talents, Virtues and Services of the Late De Witt Clinton* (Albany, N.Y.: Websters and Skinners, 1828), 2.

13. Benjamin Dorr, *A Sermon After the Death of His Excellency De Witt Clinton* (Lansingburgh, N.Y.: n.p., 1828).

14. "Common Council Minutes," 1828. New York State Library.

15. Social scientists often point to this separation of religion from politics as a significant development signaling cultural change. Traditional religion is seen as giving meaning to a patriarchal political structure and to an economy in which rational analysis is not vigorously applied to production for the purpose of maximum yields. This older religious world view is then contrasted with the development within traditional society of a more democratic political structure and more productive means in virtually all economic spheres. What sustains these changes in economic activity is the internalization of new political values that emphasize rationality, specialization, efficiency, and an interest in a future that can be better than the present in material and social terms. Contradictions between these new values and traditional religious beliefs are then displayed. In Albany this contradiction between public values and orthodox dogma became apparent when the Calvinist churches withdrew from public life. See Louis Dumont, *From Mandeville to Marx: the Genesis and Triumph of Economic Ideology* (Chicago: University of Chicago Press, 1977). Also Jacob Viner, *The Role of Providence in the Social Order* (Philadelphia: American Philosophical Society, 1972) and Karl Polanyi, *The Great Transformation* (New York, Farrar and Rinehart: 1944).

16. Marsden, *New School,* 5.

17. Mears, *Kirk,* 51.

18. Mears, *Kirk,* 40.

19. Ibid., 51.

20. Ibid.

21. Ibid., 68.

22. *Microscope,* January 1, 1831.

23. Mears, *Kirk,* 60–99; "Communicants List," 1829–1840, Fourth Presbyterian Church.

24. William B. Sprague, *A Sermon Addressed to the Second Presbyterian Congregation* (Albany, N.Y.: Packard and Van Benthuysen, 1830), 5.

25. Munsell, *Annals,* 7:192.

26. Munsell, *Annals,* 8:165.

27. Isaac Ferris, *A Sermon Preached at the Request of the Board of Managers of the American Sunday School Union* (Philadelphia: American Sunday School Union, 1834), 8.

28. Mears, *Kirk,* 85–90.

29. *Microscope,* January 1, 1831.

30. Mears, *Kirk,* 60–99; "Communicants List," 1829–1840, Fourth Presbyterian Church.

31. Mears, *Kirk,* 69–70.

32. *Christian Register,* December 18, 1830.

33. *Christian Register,* October 8, 1831.

34. Ibid.

35. Mears, *Kirk,* 66.

36. "Session Minutes," 1831, Second Presbyterian Church; "Session Minutes," 1831, Fourth Presbyterian Church.

37. "Session Minutes," 1831, Fourth Presbyterian Church.

38. Mears, *Kirk,* 69.

39. Kirk, "Valedictory Sermon" in *Sermons on Different Subjects Delivered in England and America* (New York: J. F. Trow, 1840), 257.

40. Edward Norris Kirk, *Oration* (Albany, N.Y.: L. G. Hoffman, 1836), 25.

41. Mears, *Kirk,* 99.

42. Mears, *Kirk,* 79–80.

43. "Session Minutes," November 1833, Fourth Presbyterian Church.

44. Ibid.

45. New York State Society for the Promotion of Temperance. *Second Annual Report of the New York State Society for the Promotion of Temperance* (Albany, N.Y.: Packard and Van Benthuysen, 1831), 76, 78.

46. Mears, *Kirk,* 84.

47. *Temperance Recorder* (Albany, N.Y., 1832), 1:1.

48. *Temperance Recorder* (Albany, N.Y., 1832), 1:1:43.

49. Kirk, *Sermons,* 261–262.

50. *Albany City Directory for 1817* (Albany, N.Y.: Packard and Van Benthuysen, 1817); William R. Cammeyer Jr. and R. M. Gaw, eds., *Albany Directory for 1830–1831* (Albany, N.Y.: E. B. Child, 1831); "City Tax List," 1817, County Records Office; "City Tax List," 1830, in Gotsch, "Workingman's Party"; "List of Communicants," 1829–1840 Fourth Presbyterian Church; "List of Communicants," 1816–1870 Second Presbyterian Church. Biographical information in Munsell, *Annals* and George R. Howell and Jonathan Tenney, eds., *Bicentennial History of Albany, New York from 1609 to 1886* (New York: Munsell, 1886).

51. Mears, *Kirk,* 73.

52. The relevant information on church membership listed in the Albany Church Records section of the References has been correlated with the city directories and tax lists for 1817 and 1830 to provide the raw data for these tables.

53. Joel Munsell, ed., *Collections on the History of Albany* 4 vols. (Albany, N.Y.: Munsell, 1865–1872), 2:297.

54. Munsell, *Annals,* 8:87.

55. The Bethel church, intended for waterfront workers, was to be built near a heavily traveled bridge in the canal basin. "Common Council Minutes," October 17, 1826, New York State Library.

56. Munsell, *Annals,* 9:178.

57. "Common Council Minutes," July 19, 1826 and November 8, 1830, New York State Library; Munsell, *Annals,* 9:178.

58. Munsell, *Annals,* 1:295.

59. "Common Council Minutes," April 20, 1829, New York State Library.

60. Howell and Tenney, *Bicentennial History,* 535; Cammeyer and Gaw, *Albany Directory for 1830–1831.*

61. Howell and Tenney, *Bicentennial History*, 546; Munsell, *Collections*, 2:479.

62. Munsell, *Annals*, 6:325, 4:334; *City Directory for 1817*.

63. "Record Book," 1811–1835, First Baptist Church. American Baptist Archives, Colgate-Rochester Divinity School, Rochester, N.Y.

64. "List of Officers," 1793–1830, First Methodist Church. Methodist Church, Albany, N.Y.

65. Howell and Tenney, *Bicentennial History*, 593. Shoemaking was a particularly popular trade among Methodists. During the early pre-canal years at First Methodist Church, two master shoemakers and one shoe store owner accounted for three of the seven class leaders. Moreover, journeyman shoemakers made up one fourth of the congregation's jobholders. For an assessment of the various responses of shoemakers to the new industrial morality, see Paul Faler, "Cultural Aspects of the Industrial Revolution, Lynn, Massachusetts, Shoemakers and Industrial Morality, 1826–1860," *Labor History*, 15(1974):367–394; and Faler and Alan Dawley, "Working-Class Culture and Politics in the Industrial Revolution: Sources of Loyalism and Rebellion," *Journal of Social History*, 9(1976):466–480.

66. U.S. Department of Commerce, Bureau of Census, *Fifth U.S. Census, 1830: New York* (Worthington, D.C.: D. Green 1832); Albany Church Records.

67. According to the 1830 federal census, there were 7110 white males over fifteen years old in Albany and 7175 white females over that same age. U.S. Department of Commerce, Bureau of Census *U.S. Census, Fifth, 1830: New York*. (Washington, D.C.: U.S. Government Printing Office, 1832).

68. See the discussion of Christian women in chap. 4.

69. The following method of analysis loosely follows Mary Ryan's detailed study of the women in Utica's revivals. Mary P. Ryan, "A Woman's Awakening: Evangelical Religion and the Families of Utica, New York, 1800–1840," *American Quarterly*, 30(1978)5:602–623.

70. "List of Communicants," 1829–1832, Second Presbyterian Church, New York State Library; "List of Communicants," 1829–1832, Fourth Presbyterian Church, Albany, N.Y.

71. Kirk, *Sermons*, 105.

72. Kirk, "Maternal Associations," in *Sermons*, 117–118.

73. Kirk, *Sermons*, 118.

74. Ibid.

75. Kirk, *Sermons*, 117.

76. Kirk, *Sermons*, 124.

77. *Proceedings of the Infant School in the City of Albany* (Albany, N.Y.: Christian Register Office, 1829).

78. Henry Phelps, *The Story of the Albany Orphan Asylum* (Albany, N.Y.: Albany Engraving Company, 1893).

79. *Albany Argus*, July 11, 1832.

80. For a discussion of the role of women from different social backgrounds in voluntary societies during the middle decades of the nineteenth century, see Nancy Hewitt, *Women's Activism and Social Change: Rochester, New York 1822–1872* (Ithaca, N.Y.: Cornell University Press, 1984).

81. The following tables use information from Charles Gotsch's dissertation, "The Albany Workingman's Party and the Rise of Popular Politics," and the church membership lists in the Albany Church Records section of the References.

82. Marsden, *New School,* 5.

83. Mears, *Kirk,* 62.

84. Edwin F. See, "Historical Discourse on the Third Reformed Church of Albany," December 21, 1884. Third Dutch Church, Albany, N.Y.

85. Ferris, *Sermon.*

86. Milton W. Hamilton, *St. Paul's Episcopal Church: 150th Anniversary Pamphlet* (Albany, N.Y.: St. Paul's Episcopal Church, 1977).

87. Rowley, "Albany: A Tale of Two Cities," 82–88.

88. My interpretation of freethinkers largely agrees with Wilentz, *Chants Democratic,* 153–157, although I see a greater similarity between evangelicals and freethinkers.

89. Rowley, "Albany: A Tale of Two Cities," 88.

90. Edelstein, *Munsell,* 75. So committed to self-improvement was Munsell that his boardinghouse roommates nicknamed him "Franklin." The Universalist revolt against Calvinism is discussed by Nathan O. Hatch, *The Democratization of American Christianity* 40–42, 170–172.

91. Edelstein, *Munsell,* 56–57.

92. *Microscope,* April 18, 1829.

93. *Microscope,* April 11, 1829.

94. *Microscope,* February 27, 1830.

95. *Microscope,* November 27, 1830.

96. *Microscope,* July 10, 1830.

97. *Microscope,* March 14, 1829.

98. *Microscope,* January 1, 1831.

99. *Microscope,* March 24, 1832.

100. *Microscope,* April 18, 1829.

101. Edelstein, *Munsell,* 112; *Charter of the Young Men's Society for Mutual Improvement in the City of Albany* (Albany, N.Y.: Skinner, 1835), 3.

102. Edelstein, *Munsell,* 112–113.

103. Rowley, "Albany: A Tale of Two Cities," 83.

104. Howell and Tenney, *Bicentennial History,* 690.

105. Rowley, "Albany: A Tale of Two Cities," 83–84.

106. Edelstein, *Munsell,* 376.

107. *Microscope,* November 27, 1830.

108. *Microscope,* May 31, 1834.

109. *Microscope,* May 17, 1834. Kirk saw a more Christian motive, at one point describing the "pure love of knowledge" as resulting in "the admiration of God's attributes." Kirk, *The Greatness of the Human Soul* (Boston: T. R. Marvin, 1844), 21.

110. Mears, *Kirk,* 79.

111. Mears, *Kirk,* chaps. 9–10; Rowley, "Albany: A Tale of Two Cities," 77; Edelstein, *Munsell,* 318, 331–333.

Appendix A

1. Eric J. Hobsbawm, "From Social History to the History of Society," *Daedalus,* 100(1971):20–45.

2. Theda Skocpol, "Sociology's Historical Imagination" and "Emerging Agendas and Recurrent Strategies in Historical Sociology" in Skocpol, ed., *Vision and Method in Historical Sociology* (New York: Cambridge University Press, 1984), 1–21, 356–391.

3. Hal S. Barron, *Those Who Stayed Behind: Rural Society in Nineteenth Century New England* (New York: Cambridge University Press, 1984); Rowland Berthoff and John Murrin, "Feudalism, Communalism, and the Yeoman Freeholder," 256–288 in Kurtz and Hutson, eds., *Essays on the American Revolution* (Chapel Hill, North Carolina: University of North Carolina Press, 1973); Timothy Breen, "Persistent Localism: English Social Change and the Shaping of New England Institutions," *William and Mary Quarterly,* 3d ser., 32(1975):3–28; Robert Gross, *The Minutemen and Their World* (New York: Hill and Wang, 1976); Michael Zuckerman, *Peaceable Kingdoms: New England Towns in the Eighteenth Century,* (New York: Alfred A. Knopf, 1970).

4. See Paul E. Johnson, *A Shopkeeper's Millennium: Society and Revivals in Rochester, New York 1815–1837* (New York: Hill and Wang, 1976) and Sean Wilentz, *Chants Democratic: New York City and the Rise of the American Working Class, 1788–1850* (New York: Oxford University Press, 1984).

5. David G. Hackett, "The Social Origins of Nationalism: Albany, New York, 1754–1835," *Journal of Social History,* 21(1988):659–682.

6. For further discussion, see David G. Hackett, "Sociology of Religion and American Religious History: Retrospect and Prospect," *Journal for the Scientific Study of Religion,* 27(1988):461–474.

7. Harry S. Stout, *The New England Soul* (New York: Oxford University Press, 1986), 3.

8. Jon Butler, "The Future of American Religious History: Prospectus, Agenda, Transatlantique Problematique," *William and Mary Quarterly,* 3d. ser., 42(1985):169–170.

9. Darrett B. Rutman, "New England as Idea and Society Revisited," *William and Mary Quarterly, 3d ser.,* 41(1984):56–57.

10. William J. Bouwsma, "Intellectual History in the 1980s: From History of Ideas to History of Meaning," *Journal of Interdisciplinary History,* 12(1981):288–290.

11. Richard R. Beeman, "The New Social History and the Search for 'Community" in Colonial America,' *American Quarterly,* 29(1977):433.

12. Clifford Geertz, *The Interpretation of Cultures* (New York: Basic Books, 1973) 405.

13. Ronald G. Walters, "Signs of the Times: Clifford Geertz and Historians," *Social Research,* 47(1980):537–556.

14. Darrett B. Rutman, "Encounter with Ethnography: A Review of Isaac's Transformation of Virginia," *Historical Methods Newsletter,* 16(1983):82–86.

15. Clifford Geertz, *Islam Observed* (Chicago: University of Chicago Press, 1968), 2–3.

16. Ibid., 97.

17. Ibid., 97.

18. Ibid., 3.

19. Ibid., 20.

20. Ann Swidler in "Culture in Action: Symbols and Strategies," *American Sociological Review,* 51(1986):273.

21. Ibid.

22. Ibid.

23. Ibid., 279.

24. Ibid., 278.

25. Kenneth A. Lockridge, "Land, Population, and the Evolution of New England Society," *Past and Present,* 39(1968):62–80; Rhys Isaac, *The Transformation of Virginia* (Chapel Hill, N.C.: University of North Carolina Press, 1982) pt. 1.

Appendix B

1. Charles Edward Gotsch, "The Albany Workingman's Party and the Rise of Popular Politics" (Ph.D. dissertation, State University of New York at Albany, 1976), see note 2, chap. 5; *Albany City Directory for 1817* (Albany, N.Y.: Packard and Van Benthuysen, 1817); "City Tax List," 1817, County Records Office.

2. State of New York, *Census of the State of New York for 1825* (Albany, N.Y.: State of New York, 1826); U.S. Department of Commerce, Bureau of Census, *Fifth U.S. Census, 1830: New York* (Washington, D.C.: D. Green, 1832); T. V. Cuyler, ed., *Albany City Directory for 1825* (Albany, N.Y., 1825); William Cammeyer, Jr. and R. M. Gaw, eds., *The Albany Directory for the Years 1830–1831* (Albany, N.Y., 1831).

3. William D. Sprague, *A Sermon Addressed to the Second Presbyterian Congregation in Albany, Sunday Morning August 24, 1854 on the Completion of a Quarter Century from the Commencement of the Author's Ministry Among Them* (Albany, N.Y.: Van Benthuysen, 1854), 11.

4. The Workingman's and Regency parties were the two major political parties in Albany in 1830, together garnering more than 80 percent of the vote. Gotsch found that the National Republicans represented the long-standing Dutch merchant opposition to the Yankee conquest of the city. The Anti-Masons, in contrast, were dominated by New Englanders who opposed the Regency. The Workingmen and the Regency were the two dominant parties in the 1830 and 1831 elections. Their constituency is the focus of this analysis.

5. Gotsch combed Albany's 1823 to 1834 newspapers for the names of the supporters of Albany's political parties. He then developed a list of all the known supporters of Albany's parties in 1830 and their previous political affiliations, if any. These conclusions on previous political experience are drawn from that list.

References

Manuscript Sources

Albany Institute of History and Art, Albany, N.Y. Manuscript Collection.
American Antiquarian Society, Worcester, Mass. Pamphlet, Manuscript, and Newspaper Collections.
Franklin D. Roosevelt Presidential Library, Hyde Park, N.Y. Livingston-Redmond Papers.
Henry E. Huntington Library, San Marino, Calif. Loudoun Papers.
New York Historical Society, New York. Manuscript Collection.
New York Public Library, New York. Abraham Yates Jr. Papers; Schuyler Papers.
New York State Library. Gerrit Y. Lansing Papers; Manuscript and Special Collections.
New York State Archives. Manuscript Collection.

Albany Church Records

Baptist
First Baptist. At the American Baptist Archives, Colgate-Rochester Divinity School, Rochester, N.Y.: "Record Book," 1811–1835.
Pearl Street. At Emmanuel Baptist Church, Albany, N.Y.: "Subscription List," 1834–1840.

Catholic
St. Mary's. At St. Mary's Church, Albany, N.Y.: "Trustees Journals," 1811–1815 and 1823–1848.

Dutch Reformed
North Church (First). At the First Dutch Reformed Church, Albany, N.Y.: "Subscription List," 1786; "Membership List," 1816–1835. "Consistory Minutes,"

1790–1835; "List of Pew Holders," 1790. (The "Deacon's Account Book," 1647–1715 and "Pew Records," 1730–1770 are in Joel Munsell, ed., *Collections on the History of Albany*, 4 vols. Albany, N.Y.: Munsell, 1865–1872, 1:2–56, 57–80. The "1683 Communicants List" is in Joel Munsell, ed., *Annals of Albany*, 10 vols. Albany, N.Y.: Munsell, 1850–1859, 1:97–101. Vital statistics are in Louis Duermyer, ed., *Records of the Reformed Dutch Church of Albany, New York 1683–1809*, Baltimore: Genealogical Publishing Co., 1978; a large number of items relating to this church can be found in Hugh Hastings, ed., *Ecclesiastical Records of the State of New York*, 6 vols. Albany, N.Y.: James B. Lyon, 1901.)

South Church (Second or Madison Avenue). At the New York State Library: "Marriages," 1814–1841; "General Synod Statement of Reformed Church Membership in Albany, 1815;" "List of Communicants," 1815–1840; *Manual and Directory of the Madison Avenue Reformed Church*, Albany, N.Y.: Madison Avenue Reformed Church, 1903. At the American Antiquarian Society, Worcester, Massachusetts: "List of Original Members and Officers of the South Albany Dutch Reformed Church, 1815."

Third Church. At the Third Dutch Reformed Church, Albany, N.Y.: "Marriage Records," 1835–1845; "Baptism Records," 1835–1849; "Consistory Minutes," 1835–1853; Edwin F. See, "Historical Discourse on the Third Reformed Church of Albany," December 21, 1884.

Episcopal

St. Peter's Episcopal Church. At the New York State Library, Albany, N.Y.: "Record Book of St. Peter's Church," 1720–1777; "Marriage and Baptism Lists," 1787–1792; "Subscription List," 1788–1799; "Confirmation List," 1791; "Marriages," 1810–1855;" "List of Communicants," 1821–1834; Reverand Thomas Ellison, "The Landed Estate of St. Peter's Church."

St. Paul's Episcopal Church. At St. Paul's Episcopal Church, Albany, N.Y.: "List of Communicants," 1827–1841; "List of Baptisms," 1827–1841; "List of Marriages," 1827–1841.

Lutheran

First Lutheran Church. At the New York State Library, Albany, N.Y.: First Lutheran Church, "List of Communicants," 1786–1835.

Methodist

First Methodist. At Trinity Methodist Church, Albany, N.Y.: "History of Methodism in Albany," 1765–1791; "Annual Membership List," 1793–1830; "List of Officers," 1793–1830; "Marriage and Baptism Records," 1806–1830; "History," 1807–1859; "Book of Records of the Board of Trustees," 1830–1832; "Burial Records," 1821–1860; "Class Lists," 1835–1838.

West Station. At Trinity Methodist Church, Albany, N.Y.: "Class Lists," 1832–1835.

Presbyterian

First Presbyterian. At First Presbyterian Church, Albany, N.Y.: "Register of Baptisms," 1785–1816; "Register of Marriages," 1785–1816; "Session Minutes," 1786–1835; "Subscription List," 1793; Register of Communicants," 1795–1840;

Second Presbyterian. At the New York State Library, Albany, N.Y.: "List of Communicants," 1816–1870; "Marriages," 1829–1839; "Baptisms," 1829–1840; "Subscription List," 1832. At the Presbyterian Historical Society, Philadelphia: "Catalog of Communicants," 1822; "Session Minutes," 1831.

Third Presbyterian. At the New York State Library, Albany, N.Y.: "List of Associate Reformed Church Members who joined Third Church," 1810–1813; "List of Officers and Elders," 1817–1855.

Fourth Presbyterian. At Fourth Presbyterian Church, Albany, N.Y.: "Communicants List," 1829–1840; "Session Minutes," 1829–1838.

Albany Presbytery. At the Presbyterian Historical Society, Philadelphia: "Minutes," 1810–1838.

Universalist

First Universalist. At the New York State Library, Albany, N.Y.: First Universalist Church "Register," 1830–1840.

Public Records

Albany City Directory for 1817. Albany, N.Y.: Packard and Van Benthuysen, 1817.

"Albany Common Council Minutes," 1780–1840. New York State Library, Albany, N.Y.

Cammeyer, William, Jr. and R. M. Gaw, eds. *The Albany Directory for the Years 1830–1831.* Albany, N.Y.: E. B. Child, 1831.

"The City Records," 1676–1686, in Joel Munsell, ed., *Collections on the History of Albany* 4 vols. Albany, N.Y. Munsell, 1865–1871 and Joel Munsell, ed., *Annals of Albany* 10 vols. Albany, N.Y.: Munsell, 1850–1859.

"City Tax List," 1709. Livingston-Redmond Papers, Franklin Delano Roosevelt Library, Hyde Park, N.Y.

"City Tax List," 1766, 1767. New York Public Library, New York. Schuyler Papers. Box 10.

"City Tax List," 1779. Gerrit Y. Lansing Papers. New York State Library, Albany, N.Y.

"City Tax List," 1799. Albany Institute of History and Art, Albany, N.Y.

"City Tax List," 1817. Albany County Records Office, Albany, N.Y.

Cuyler, T. V., ed. *Albany City Directory for 1825.* Albany, N.Y.: E. B. Child, 1825.

"Dongan Charter" in *Book of City Laws.* Albany, N.Y.: State of New York, 1842.

Hastings, Hugh, ed. *Ecclesiastical Records of the State of New York,* 6 vols. Albany: James B. Lyon, 1901.

Laws and Ordinances of the Mayor, Recorder, Aldermen, and Commonality of the City of Albany. Albany, N.Y.: Robertson, 1773.

Laws and Ordinances of the Mayor, Recorder, Aldermen, and Commonality of the City of Albany. Albany, N.Y.: Barber, 1791.

Laws of the State of New York, 1778–1799, 3 vols. New York: Thomas Greenleaf, 1782–1800.

"A List of the Freeholders of the City and County of Albany in 1720," in Edmund B. O'Callaghan, ed., 4 vols. *Documentary History of the State of New York,* 1:241–242. Albany, N.Y.: Weed and Parsons, 1849.

"List of Freeholders in the City of Albany," 1742. In Munsell, ed. *Annals,* 2:186–188.

"List of the Heads of Families," 1697. In *New York Colonial Manuscripts,* 102 vols. New York State Archives, Albany, N.Y. 42:34.

"A List of the Inhabitants and Slaves in the City and County of Albany, 1714." In Munsell, *Annals,* 3:243.

"List of the Inhabitants of the Citty of Albany in America with the Number of Troops they can Quarter Conveniently within the Stockade and What they can Quarter in case of necessity together with the fire places in Each house and Rooms without Fire, also what appeared in a strett Enquiry made in November 1756. . . ." Loudoun Papers. Huntington Library, San Marino, Calif.

"Muster Roll of the Men Rais'd and Pass'd Muster in the City and County of Albany for John Visher's Comp'y Albany May, 1762." In *The Annual Report of the State Historian of the State of New York,* 694–696. Albany, N.Y.: Wynkoop, Hallenbak, Crawford, and Company, 1897.

"Muster Roll of the Men Rais'd and Pass'd Muster in the City and County of Albany for Capt'n John de Garemo Company Albany June, 1762." In *The Annual Report of the State Historian of the State of New York,* 701–702.

O'Callaghan, Edmund B., comp. and tr. *The Colonial Laws of New York from the Year 1664 to the Revolution,* 5 vols. Albany, N.Y.: Weed, Parsons, and Company, 1868.

———. *The Documentary History of the State of New York,* 4 vols. Albany, N.Y.: Weed, Parsons, and Company, 1850–51.

———. *Documents Relative to the Colonial History of the State of the State of New York,* 15 vols. Albany, N.Y.: Weed and Parsons, 1853–1887.

Palsits, Victor H., ed, *Minutes of the Commission for Detecting and Defeating Conspiracies in the State of New York: Albany County Sessions 1778–1781,* 3 vols. Albany, N.Y.: J. B. Lyon, 1909–1910.

State of New York. *Census of the State of New York for 1825.* Albany, N.Y.: State of New York, 1826.

———. *Census of the State of New York for 1835.* Albany, N.Y.: Crosswell, Van Benthuysen, and Burt, 1836.

Sullivan, James, ed., *The Minutes of the Albany Committee of Correspondence, 1775–1778,* 2 vols. Albany, N.Y.: University of the State of New York, 1923.

United States Department of Commerce. Bureau of Census. *Heads of Families of the First Census of the United States Taken in 1790: New York*. Washington, D.C.: U.S. Government Printing Office, 1908.

———. *Heads of Families of the Second Census of the United States Taken in 1800: New York*. Washington, D.C.: U.S. Government Printing Office, 1908.

———. *U.S. Census, Third, 1810: New York*. Washington, D.C.: U.S. Government Printing Office, 1811.

———. *U.S. Census, Fourth, 1820: New York*. Washington, D.C.: U.S. Government Printing Office, n.d.

———. *U.S. Census, Fifth, 1830: New York*. Washington, D.C.: U.S. Government Printing Office, 1832.

———. *U.S. Census, Eighteenth, 1970: New York*. Washington, D.C.: U.S. Government Printing Office, 1971.

Van Laer, A. J. F., ed. and trans., *Early Records of the City and County of Albany and Colony of Rensselaerwyck,* 4 vols. Albany, N.Y.: University of the State of New York, 1918.

Van Laer, A. J. F., trans., *Minutes of the Court of Fort Orange and Beverwyck,* 1652–1656. 2 vols. Albany, N.Y.: University of the State of New York, 1920–1923.

"Will Book I" and "Will Book II." County Records Office, Albany, N.Y.

Albany Newspapers and Periodicals

Argus, 1813–1840.
Centinel, 1797–1806.
Christian Advocate and Journal, 1830, 1859.
Christian Visitant, 1814–1816.
Common School Assistant, 1836.
Evening Journal, 1830–1840.
Farmers', Mechanics', and Workingman's Advocate, 1830–1831.
Gazette, 1771, 1786–1840.
Guardian, 1830.
Microscope, 1821–1840.
Register, 1788–1822.
Telegraph and Christian Register, 1827–1831.
Temperance Recorder, 1832.

Addresses, Sermons, Travelers Accounts, Pamphlets and Proceedings

Acts and Proceedings of the General Synod of the Reformed Dutch Church in the United States of America in the Year 1800. New York: Forman, 1800.

"Albany Mechanics' Society." In Joel Munsell, ed., *Annals of Albany* 10 vols. Albany, N.Y.: Munsell, 1850–1859. 7:240–244.

"Albany Mechanics' Society Membership List," 1803. American Antiquarian Society, Worcester, Mass.

Albany Society for the Suppression of Vice and Immorality. *Constitution and Proceedings of the Albany Society for the Suppression of Vice and Immorality.* Albany, N.Y.: Churchill and McGlashan, 1815.

Albany Sunday School Society. "Constitution of the Albany Sunday School Society," 1817. American Antiquarian Society, Worcester, Mass.

Albany Temperance Society. "Address and Constitution of the Albany Temperance Society" n.d. American Antiquarian Society. Worcester, Mass.

Albany Young Men's Society. "A Circular to the Young Men of the State of New York from the Young Men's Society in Albany" n.d. Albany Institute of History and Art. Albany, N.Y.

A Brief Account of the Society Established in the City of Albany for the Relief of Indigent Women and Children. Albany, N.Y.: Charles R. and George Webster, 1805.

"Celebration of the Adoption of the Federal Constitution," 1788. In Joel Munsell, ed. *Collections on the History of Albany.* 4 vols. Albany, N.Y.: Munsell, 1850–1859. 3:228–235.

Charter of the Young Men's Society for Mutal Improvement in the City of Albany. Albany: n.p., 1835.

Chester, John. *Knowledge and Holiness, The Sources of Morality.* Albany, N.Y.: E. and E. Hosford, 1821.

Citizen of Albany. *Tribute to the Memory of DeWitt Clinton.* Albany, N.Y.: Webster and Wood, 1828.

Conkling, Alfred. *A Discourse Commemorative of the Talents, Virtues, and Services of the Late DeWitt Clinton.* Albany, N.Y.: Websters and Skinners, 1828.

"Constitution of the Sons of Liberty of America and Names of the Signers." *The American Historian and Quarterly Genealogical Record,* 1(1875):145–147.

Corwin, E. T., ed. *A Digest of Synodical Legislation.* New York: Reformed Church, 1906.

Davis, Robert "A View of the Albany General Market of the City of Albany, in the Summer of 1819." Albany Institute of History and Art. Albany, N.Y.

Dorr, Benjamin. *A Sermon After the Death of His Excellency DeWitt Clinton.* Lansinburgh, N.Y.: n.p., 1828.

Dwight, Timothy. "Albany As Seen by Dr. Dwight." In Munsell, *Annals,* 8:181–190.

Ferris, Isaac. *A Sermon Preached at the Request of the Board of Managers of the American Sunday School Union.* Philadelphia: American Sunday School Union, 1834.

Grant, Anne. *Memoirs of an American Lady.* London: Longman, Hurst, Ries and Orme, 1808.

Hamilton, Alexander. *Gentlemen's Progress: The Itinerarium of Dr. Alexander Hamilton, 1744.* Carl Bridenbaugh, ed. Chapel Hill, N.C.: University of North Carolina Press, 1948.

Hughes, Thomas P. *The City of Albany* In *American Ancestry,* 9 vols. Albany, N.Y.: Munsell, 1887. Vol. 1.

Jameson, J. Franklin, ed. *Narratives of New Netherland 1609–1664.* New York: Charles Scribner's Sons, 1909.

James, William, ed. *The Literary Remains of the Late Henry James.* Boston: Houghton and Mifflin, 1884.

Johnson, John Barent. *The Dealings of God with Israel and America.* Albany, N.Y.: Charles R. and George Webster, 1798.

Kalm, Peter. *Peter Kalm's Travels in North America,* Adolph B. Benson, ed. New York: Dover, 1964.

Kirk, Edward Norris. *The Greatness of the Human Soul.* Boston: T. R. Marvin, 1844.

————. *Oration.* Albany, N.Y.: L. G. Hoffman, 1836.

————. *Sermons on Different Subjects Delivered in England and America.* New York: J. F. Trow, 1840.

Manley, James R. *An Eulogium on DeWitt Clinton.* New York: Gould and Jacobus, 1828.

McDonald, John. *The Duty of America Enforced.* Cooperstown, N.Y.: Phinney, 1799.

————. *The Faithful Steward: A Sermon Preached at the Ordination of Mr. Aaron Condict.* Albany, N.Y.: Charles R. and George Webster, 1793.

Mechanics Moral Society of the City of Albany Associated for the Suppression of Vice and Immorality and the Promotion of Good Morals. Broadside. Albany, N.Y.: n.p., 1816.

"Memoir of Charles R. Webster, the Father of Printing in Albany." In Munsell, *Annals,* 5:230–240.

Morse, Dr. "Dr. Morse's Descriptions of Albany in 1789." In Munsell, *Annals,* 1:281–283.

Munsell, Joel, ed. *Annals of Albany.* 10 vols. Albany, N.Y.: Munsell, 1850–1859.

————. *Collections on the History of Albany.* 4 vols. Albany, N.Y.: Munsell, 1865–1872.

————. *Typographical Miscellany.* Albany, N.Y.: Munsell, 1850.

New York State Society for the Promotion of Temperance. *Second Annual Report of the New York State Society for the Promotion of Temperance.* Albany, N.Y., 1831.

————. *Fourth Annual Report of the New York State Society for the Promotion of Temperance.* Albany, N.Y.: Packard and Van Benthuysen, 1831.

Nott, Eliphalet. *An Address Delivered to the Candidate for the Baccalaureate in Union College, at the Anniversary Commencement, May 18, 1805.* Albany, N.Y.: Charles R. and George Webster, 1805.

————. *A Discourse Delivered at the Presbyterian Church in the City of Albany: Before the Ladies Society for the Relief of Distressed Women and Children.* Albany, N.Y.: Charles R. and George Webster, 1804.

————. *How Are the Mighty Fallen: A Discourse Delivered in the North Dutch Church in the City of Albany, Occasioned by the ever to Be Lamented Death of General Alexander Hamilton, July 29, 1804.* Albany, N.Y.: Websters and Skinner, 1806.

————. *The Providence of God Towards Isreal: A Discourse Delivered in the Presbyterian Church in Albany, the Fourth of July A.D. 1801 at the Celebration of the Twenty-Fifth Anniversary of American Independence.* Albany, N.Y.: Charles R. and George Webster, 1801.

———. *The Resurrection of Christ.* New York: Charles Scribner's Sons, 1872.

"Origin of Sunday Schools in Albany." In Munsell, *Annals,* 7:178–193.

Phelps, Henry. *The Story of the Albany Orphan Asylum.* Albany, N.Y.: Albany Engraving Company, 1893.

Proceedings of the Infant School in the City of Albany. Albany, N.Y.: Christian Register Office, 1829.

The Psalms of David with Hymns and Spiritual Songs also the Catechism, Compendium, Confession of Faith and Liturgy of the Reformed Church of the Netherlands. Albany, N.Y.: Webster, 1791.

Rochefoucault-Liancourt, Duke. "Voyage dans les Etats-Unis." In Munsell, *Annals* 4:219–239.

Rogers, E. P. *Historical Discourse on the Reformed Protestant Dutch Church of Albany.* New York: Board of Publication of the Reformed Protestant Dutch Church, 1858.

Royall, Anne. *Sketches of History, Life, and Manners in the United States.* New Haven, Conn.: By the author, 1826.

Southwick, Solomon. *An Address Delivered at the Opening of the Apprentice's Library.* Albany, N.Y.: John O. Cole. 1821.

Spafford, Horatio Gates. *A Gazetteer of the State of New York.* Albany, N.Y.: H. C. Southwick, 1813.

Spicer, Tobias. *Camp Meetings Defended, or a Brief Review of a Pamphlet Lately Published entitled "Camp Meetings Described and Exposed, and Strange Things Stated."* New Haven, Conn.: T. G. Woodward, 1828.

Sprague, William B. *A Sermon Addressed to the Second Presbyterian Congregation.* Albany, N.Y.: Packard and Benthuysen, 1830.

———. *A Sermon Addressed to the Second Presbyterian Congregation in Albany . . . on the Completion of a Quarter Century from the Commencement of the Author's Ministry among them.* Albany, N.Y.: Packard and Benthuysen, 1854.

———. *A Sermon Delivered on Sabbath Morning January 4, 1846 Containing Sketches of the History of the Second Presbyterian Church and Congregation, Albany, During Thirty Years from the Period of Their Organization.* Albany, N.Y.: Pease, 1846.

Stansbury, Arthur Joseph. *God Pleading with America.* Goshen, N.Y.: Crosswell, 1817.

Tenney, Jonathan. *New England in Albany.* Boston, Mass.: Long Island Historical Society, 1883.

Watson, Elkanah. *Men and Times of the Revolution.* 2nd ed., New York: Dana and Company, 1857.

Worth, Gorham A. "Random Recollections of Albany." In Munsell, *Annals* 10:189–218.

Young Men's Society for Mutual Improvement. *Charter of the Young Men's Society for Mutual Improvement in the City of Albany.* Albany, N.Y.: Skinner, 1835.

Secondary Sources

Alexander, Robert S. *Albany's First Church and Its Role in the Growth of the City*. Albany, N.Y.: First Church, 1988.

Armour, David A. "The Merchants of Albany, New York, 1683–1781." Ph.D. dissertation, Northwestern University, 1965.

Bailyn, Bernard. *The Ideological Origins of the American Revolution*. Cambridge, Mass.: Harvard University Press, 1967.

———. *The New England Merchants in the Seventeenth Century*. Cambridge, Mass.: Harvard University Press, 1955.

———. *The Origins of American Politics*. New York: Alfred A. Knopf, 1968.

Balmer, Randall H. *A Perfect Babel of Confusion: Dutch Religion and English Culture in the Middle Colonies*. New York: Oxford University Press, 1989.

———. "The Social Roots of Dutch Pietism in the Middle Colonies." *Church History,* 53(1981):187–199.

Barron, Hal S. *Those Who Stayed Behind: Rural Society in Nineteenth Century England*. New York: Cambridge University Press, 1984.

Bates, Ralph E. *Captain Thomas Webb*. London: Pinhorns, 1975.

Beeman, Richard R. "The New Social History and the Search for 'Community' in Colonial America." *American Quarterly,* 29(1977):422–443.

Bellah, Robert N. *The Broken Covenant: American Civil Religion in Time of Trial*. New York: Seabury Press, 1975.

———. "Civil Religion in America." *Daedalus,* 96(1967):1–21.

Berthoff, Rowland and John Murrin. "Feudalism, Communalism, and the Yeoman Freeholder." In Stephen G. Kurtz and James H. Hutson, eds., *Essays on the American Revolution*, 256–88. Chapel Hill, N.C.: University of North Carolina Press, 1973.

Bielinski, Stefan. *Abraham Yates, Jr. and the New Political order in Revolutionary America*. Albany, N.Y.: New York State American Revolution Bicentennial Commission, 1975.

———. "The Anglicization of a Dutch Village: Population Evolution in Colonial Albany, 1686–1756." Seminar paper, State University of New York at Albany, 1979.

———. "The People of Colonial Albany, 1650–1800: The Profile of a Community." In William Pencak and Conrad Edick Wright, eds., *Authority and Resistance in Early New York*, 1–26. New York: New York Historical Society, 1988.

Biemer, Linda Briggs. *Women and Property in Colonial New York: The Transition from Dutch to English Law, 1643–1727*. Ann Arbor, Mich.: UMI Research Press, 1983.

Blayney, Reverand G. McClusky. *History of the First Presbyterian Church of Albany, New York*. Albany, N.Y.: Jenkins and Johnston, 1877.

Bonomi, Patricia U. *A Factious People: Politics and Society in Colonial New York*. New York: Columbia University Press, 1971.

———. *Under the Cope of Heaven: Religion, Society, and Politics in Colonial America.* New York: Oxford University Press, 1986.

Botch, Judith. "A Comparative Analysis of 19th Century Industrialists in Albany, N.Y." Seminar paper, Albany Institute of History and Art, 1979.

Bouwsma, William J. "Intellectual History in the 1980s: From History of Ideas to History of Meaning." *Journal of Interdisciplinary History,* 12(1981):279–291.

Breen, Timothy. "Persistent Localism: English Social Change and the Shaping of New England Institutions." *William and Mary Quarterly,* 3d ser., 32(1975):3–28.

Bushman, Richard L. *From Puritan to Yankee: Character and Social Order in Connecticut, 1690–1765.* Cambridge, Mass.: Harvard University Press, 1967.

Butler, Jon. "The Future of American Religious History: Prospectus, Agenda, Transatlantic Problematique." *William and Mary Quarterly,* 3d. ser., 42(1985):167–183.

Calvin, John. *Commentaries on the Last Four Books of Moses,* 4 vols. Reverand Charles Bingham. ed. and trans. Grand Rapids, Mich.: Eerdmans, 1950.

———. *Commentary on I Corinthians,* 2 vols. John T. McNeil, trans. and ed. Grand Rapids, Mich.: Eerdmans, 1950.

———. *A Compend of the Institutes of the Christian Religion.* Philadelphia: Westminster, 1939.

Champagne, Roger James. "The Sons of Liberty and the Aristocracy in New York Politics 1765–1790." Ph.D. dissertation, University of Wisconsin, 1960.

Cott, Nancy. *The Bonds of Womanhood: "Woman's Sphere" in New England, 1780–1835.* New Haven, Conn.: Yale University Press, 1977.

Cross, Whitney R. *The Burned-Over District: A Social and Economic History of Enthusiastic Religion in Western New York, 1800–1850.* Ithaca, N.Y.: Cornell University Press, 1950.

DeJong, Gerald F. *The Dutch Reformed Church in the American Colonies.* Grand Rapids, Mich.: Eerdmans, 1978.

Douglas, Ann. *The Feminization of American Culture.* New York: Alfred A. Knopf, 1977.

Dumont, Louis. *From Mandeville to Marx: The Genesis and Triumph of Economic Ideology.* Chicago: University of Chicago Press, 1977.

Edelstein, David S. *Joel Munsell: Printer and Antiquarian.* New York: Columbia University Press, 1950.

Ellis, David. "Yankee-Dutch Confrontation in the Albany Area." *New England Quarterly,* 40(1972):262–270.

Faler, Paul. "Cultural Aspects of the Industrial Revolution, Lynn, Massachusetts, Shoemakers and Industrial Morality, 1826–1860." *Labor History,* 15(1974):367–394.

———. *Mechanics and Manufacturers in the Early Industrial Revolution.* Albany, N.Y.: State University of New York Press, 1983.

———. and Alan Dawley, "Working-Class Culture and Politics in the Industrial Revolution: Sources of Loyalism and Rebellion." *Journal of Social History,* 9(1976):466–480.

Feinstein, Howard M. *Becoming William James*. Ithaca, N.Y.: Cornell University Press, 1984.

Foner, Eric. *Tom Paine and Revolutionary America*. New York: Oxford University Press, 1976.

Fox, Dixon Ryan. *Yankees and Yorkers*. New York: New York University Press, 1940.

Geertz, Clifford. *The Interpretation of Cultures*. New York: Basic Books, 1973.

———. *Islam Observed*. Chicago: University of Chicago Press, 1968.

Gerlach, Don R. *Phillip Schuyler and the American Revolution in New York 1733–1777*. Lincoln, Neb.: University of Nebraska Press, 1964.

Gotsch, Charles Edward. "The Albany Workingman's Party and the Rise of Popular Politics." Ph.D. dissertation, State University of New York at Albany, 1976.

Greenburg, Brian. *Worker and Community: Response to Industrialization in a Nineteenth Century American City, Albany, New York 1850–1884*. Albany, N.Y.: State University of New York Press, 1985.

Gross, Robert. *The Minutemen and Their World*. New York: Hill and Wang, 1976.

Gunn, L. Ray. *The Decline of Authority: Public Economic Policy and Political Development in New York State, 1800–1860*. Ithaca, N.Y.: Cornell University Press, 1988.

Hackett, David G. "Culture and Social Order in American History." In David Bromley, ed., *Religion and Social Order: New Directions in Theory and Research*. Greenwich, Conn.: J.A.I. Press, 1991.

———. "The Social Origins of Nationalism: Albany, New York 1754–1835." *Journal of Social History*, 21(1988):660–682.

———. "Sociology of Religion and American Religious History: Retrospect and Prospect." *Journal for the Scientific Study of Religion*, 27(1988):461–474.

Hall, David, "Religion and Society: Problems and Reconsiderations." In Jack P. Greene and J. R. Pole, eds., *Colonial British America: Essays in the New History of the Early Modern Era*, 317–344. Baltimore: Johns Hopkins University Press, 1984.

Hamilton, Milton W. *St. Paul's Church: 150th Anniversary Pamphlet*. Albany, N.Y.: St. Paul's Episcopal Church, 1977.

Hammond, Jabez D. *The History of Political Parties in the State of New York*. 2 vols. Syracuse, N.Y.: Hall, Mills, and Co., 1852.

Hatch, Nathan O. *The Democratization of American Christianity*. New Haven, Conn.: Yale University Press, 1989.

———. *The Sacred Cause of Liberty*. New Haven, Conn.: Yale University Press, 1977.

Henretta, James. "Economic Development and Social Structure in Colonial Boston," *William and Mary Quarterly*, 3d ser., 22(1965):75–92.

Hewitt, Nancy. *Women's Activism and Social Change: Rochester, New York 1822–1872*. Ithaca. N.Y.: Cornell University Press, 1984.

Hislop, Codman. *Albany: Dutch, English, and American*. Albany, N.Y.: Argus Press, 1936.

————. *Eliphalet Nott.* Middletown, Conn.: Wesleyan University Press, 1980.

Hobsbawm, Eric J. "From Social History to the History of Society." *Daedalus,* 100(1971):20–45.

Hoerder, Dirk. *Crowd Action in Revolutionary Massachusetts, 1765–1780.* New York: Academic Press, 1977.

Hooper, Reverand Joseph. *A History of Saint Peter's Church in the City of Albany.* Albany, N.Y.: Fort Orange Press, 1900.

Howell, George R. and Jonathan Tenney, eds. *Bicentennial History of Albany from 1609 to 1886.* New York: Munsell, 1886.

Hutson, James H. "Country, Court, and Constitution: Antifederalism and the Historians." *William and Mary Quarterly,* 3d ser., 38(1981):337–68.

Johnson, Paul E. *A Shopkeeper's Millennium: Society and Revivals in Rochester, New York, 1815–1837.* New York: Hill and Wang, 1976.

Kass, Alvin. *Politics in New York State.* Syracuse, N.Y.: Syracuse University Press, 1964.

Kenney, Alice P. "The Albany Dutch: Loyalists and Patriots." *New York History,* 42(1962):331–350.

————. "The Dutch Patricians of Colonial Albany." *New York History,* 49(1968):249–283.

————. *The Gansevoorts of Albany.* Syracuse, N.Y.: Syracuse University Press, 1969.

————. "Private Worlds in the Middle Colonies: An Introduction to Human Tradition in American History." *New York History,* 51(1970):5–31.

————. *Stubborn for Liberty.* Syracuse, N.Y.: Syracuse University Press, 1975.

Kim, Sung Bok. *Landlord and Tenant in Colonial New York: Manorial Society, 1664–1775.* Chapel Hill, N.C.: University Of North Carolina Press, 1978.

Kitchin, William C. *Centennial History of First Methodist Episcopal Church, Schenectady.* Schenectady, N.Y.: Official Board of the Church, 1907.

Kulikoff, Allan. "The Progress of Inequality in Revolutionary Boston." *William and Mary Quarterly,* 3d ser., 28(1971):375–412.

Leder, Lawrence H. *Robert Livingston and the Politics of Colonial New York.* Chapel Hill, N.C.: University of North Carolina Press, 1961.

Lockridge, Kenneth A. *A New England Town: The First Hundred Years.* Enlarged ed. New York: W. W. Norton and Company, 1985.

————. "Land, Population, and the Evolution of New England Society." *Past and Present,* 39(1968):62–80.

————. "Social Change and the Meaning of the American Revolution." *Journal of Social History,* 6(1973):415–432.

Lynd, Staughton. "Abraham Yates' History of the Movement for the United States Constitution." *William and Mary Quarterly,* 3d ser., 20(1963):223–245.

Maier, Pauline. *From Resistance to Revolution: Colonial Radicals and the Development of American Opposition to Great Britain, 1765–1776.* New York: Alfred A. Knopf, 1972.

————. *The Old Revolutionaries: Political Lives in the Age of Samuel Adams*. New York: Alfred A. Knopf, 1980.

Mann, Bruce H. *Neighbors and Strangers: Law and Community in Early Connecticut*. Chapel Hill, N.C.: University of North Carolina Press, 1987.

Marsden, George M. *The Evangelical Mind and the New School Presbyterian Experience*. New Haven, Conn.: Yale University Press, 1970.

Marty, Martin. *Righteous Empire: The Protestant Experience in America*. New York: Harper and Row, 1970.

Matthews, Donald G. "The Second Great Awakening as an Organizing Process, 1780–1830: An Hypothesis." *American Quarterly*, 21(1969):23–43.

McAnear, Beverly. "The Albany Stamp Act Riots." *William and Mary Quarterly*, 3d ser., 4(1947):486–498.

McClintock, John T. "Albany and Its Early Nineteenth Century Schools." M.A. thesis, Harvard University, 1976.

McKinley, Arthur E. "English and Dutch Towns of New Netherland." *American History Review*, 6(1900–1901):1–18.

Meany, Joseph F., Jr. "Merchant and Redcoat: The Papers of John Gordon Macomb, April 1757–1960." Ph.D. dissertation, Forham University, 1990.

Mears, David O. *Life of Edward Norris Kirk*. Boston: Lockwood, Brooks, and Company, 1878.

Mencken, H. L. *The American Language*. New York: Alfred A. Knopf, 1960.

Merwick, Donna. "Becoming English: Anglo-Dutch Conflict in the 1670s in Albany, New York." *New York History*, 62(1981):389–414.

————. "Dutch Townsmen and Land Use: A Spatial Perspective on Seventeenth Century Albany, New York." *William and Mary Quarterly*, 3rd ser., 37(1980):53–78.

Morgan, Edmund S. "Conflict and Consensus in the American Revolution." In Stephen G. Kurtz and James H. Hutson, eds., *Essays on the American Revolution*, 289–310. Chapel Hill, N.C.: University of North Carolina Press, 1973.

Mundy, John H. and Pieter Riesenberg. *Medieval Town*. Princeton, N.J.: Princeton University Press, 1958.

Murrin, John M. "Anglicizing an American Colony: The Transformation of Provincial Massachusetts." Ph.D. dissertation, Yale University, 1966.

————. "Review Essay." *History and Theory*, 11(1972):226–275.

Narrett, David. "Patterns of Inheritance in Colonial New York City 1664–1775: A Study in the History of the Family." Ph.D. dissertation, Cornell University, 1981.

————. "Preparation for Death and Provision for the Living: Notes on New York Wills (1665–1760)." *New York History*, 57(1976):417–437.

Nash, Gary B. "Social Development." In Jack P. Greene and J. R. Pole, eds., *Colonial British America: Essays in the New History of the Modern Era*, 233–261. Baltimore: Johns Hopkins University Press, 1984.

————. *The Urban Crucible: Social Change, Political Consciousness, and the Origins of*

228   References

the American Revolution. Cambridge, Mass: Harvard University Press, 1979.

———. "Urban Wealth and Poverty in Pre-Revolutionary America." *Journal of Interdisciplinary History*, 6(1975–1976):545–584.

Nissenson, Samuel G. *The Patroon's Domain*. New York: Columbia University Press, 1937.

Norton, Thomas E. *The Fur Trade in Colonial New York, 1686–1776*. Madison, Wisc.: University of Wisconsin Press, 1974.

Pointer, Richard W. *Protestant Pluralism and the New York Experience*. Bloomington, Ind.: Indiana University Press, 1988.

———. "Religious Life in New York During the Revolutionary War." *New York History*, 66(1985):358–373.

Polanyi, Karl. *The Great Transformation*. New York: Farrar and Rinehart, 1944.

Redfield, Robert. *Peasant Society and Culture*. Chicago: University of Chicago Press, 1956.

Reynolds, Cuyler. *Albany Chronicles: A History of the City Arranged Chronologically, from the Earliest Settlement to the Present Time*. Albany, N.Y.: James B. Lyon, 1907.

Reynolds, David S. "The Feminization Controversy: Sexual Stereotypes and the Paradoxes of Piety in Nineteenth-Century America." *New England Quarterly*, 53(1980):96–106.

Richey, Russell E. and Donald G. Jones, eds. *American Civil Religion*. New York: Harper and Row, 1974.

Rink, Oliver A. *Holland on the Hudson: An Economic and Social History of Dutch New York*. Ithaca, N.Y.: Cornell University Press, 1986.

———. "The People of New Netherlands: Notes on Non-English Immigration to New York in the Seventeenth Century." *New York History*, 62(1981):4–42.

Roth, Randolph A. *The Democratic Dilemma: Religion, Reform, and the Social Order in the Connecticut River Valley of Vermont, 1791–1850*. New York: Cambridge University Press, 1987.

Rowe, Kenneth E. *Captain Thomas Webb: Albany Apprentice, It All Started in Albany*. Albany, N.Y.: Public Relations Committee of Trinity United Methodist Church, 1976.

Rowley, William Esmond. "Albany: A Tale of Two Cities 1820–1880." Ph.D. dissertation, Harvard University, 1967.

Rutman, Anita H. "Still Planting the Seeds of Hope." *The Virginia Magazine of History and Biography*, 95(1987):3–24.

Rutman, Darrett B. "Assessing the Little Communities of Early America." *William and Mary Quarterly*, 3d ser., 43 (1986):163–178.

———. "Encounter with Ethnography: A Review of Isaac's Transformation of Virginia." *Historical Methods Newsletter*, 16(1983):82–86.

———. "New England as Idea and Society Revisited." *William and Mary Quarterly*, 3d ser., 41(1984):56–61.

———. "The Social Web: A Prospectus for the Study of the Early American Community." In William L. O'Neill, ed., *Insights and Parallels: Problems and Issues of American Social History,* 57–88. Minneapolis, Minn.: Burgess Publishing Company, 1973.

———. *Winthrop's Boston: Portrait of a Puritan Town, 1630–1649.* Chapel Hill, N.C.: University of North Carolina Press, 1965.

Ryan, Mary P. *Cradle of the Middle Class: The Family in Oneida County, New York 1790–1865.* New York: Cambridge University Press, 1981.

———. "A Woman's Awakening: Evangelical Religion and the Families of Utica, New York, 1800–1840." *American Quarterly,* 30(1978):602–623.

Ryerson, Richard Alan. *The Revolution Is Now Begun: The Radical Committees of Philadelphia, 1765–1776.* Philadelphia: University of Pennsylvania Press, 1978.

Schuyler, David. "Inventing a Feminine Past." *The New England Quarterly,* 51(1978):291–308.

Schuyler, George W. *Colonial New York: Philip Schuyler and His Family* 2 vols. New York: Charles Scribner's Sons, 1885.

Schwartz, Charles D. and Oida Davis Schwartz. *A Flame of Fire: The Story of Troy Annual Conference.* Rutland, Vt.: Academic Books, 1982.

Semmel, Bernard. *The Methodist Revolution.* New York: Basic Books, 1977.

Shalhope, Robert E. "Toward a Republican Synthesis: The Emergence of an Understanding of Republicanism in American Historiography." *William and Mary Quarterly,* 3d ser., 29(1972):49–80.

Skocpol, Theda. "Cultural Idioms and Political Ideologies in the Revolutionary Reconstruction of State Power: A Rejoinder to Sewell." *Journal of Modern History,* 57(1985):86–96.

———. "Sociology's Historical Imagination" and "Emerging Agendas and Recurrent Strategies in Historical Sociology." In Theda Skocpol, ed., *Vision and Method in Historical Sociology.* New York: Cambridge University Press, 1984. 1–21, 356–391.

Smith, George L. *Religion and Trade in New Netherland.* Ithaca, N.Y.: Cornell University Press, 1973.

Stearns, Peter N. "Modernization and Social History, Some Suggestions, and a Muted Cheer." *Journal of Social History,* 14(1980):189–210.

Stein, Jess, ed., *A New English Dictionary on Historical Principles.* Oxford: Oxford University Press, 1897.

Stout, Harry S. *The New England Soul: Preaching and Religious Culture in colonial New England.* New York: Oxford University Press, 1986.

Swidler, Ann. "Culture in Action: Symbols and Strategies." *American Sociological Review,* 51(1986):273–286.

Tipps, Dean C. "Modernization Theory and the Comparative Study of Societies: A Critical Perspective." *Comparative Studies of Society and History,* 15(1973):199–222.

Trelease, Allen W. *Indian Affairs in Colonial New York: The Seventeenth Century* Ithaca, N.Y.: Cornell University Press, 1960.

Turner, James. *Without God, Without Creed: The Origins of Unbelief in America.* Baltimore: Johns Hopkins University Press, 1985.

Viner, Jacob. *The Role of Providence in the Social Order*. Philadelphia: American Philosophical Society, 1972.

Walters, Ronald G. "Signs of the Times: Clifford Geertz and Historians." *Social Research*, 47(1980):537–556.

Warren, Roland L. *The Community in America*. Chicago: University of Chicago Press, 1963.

———. "Toward a Reformulation of Community Theory." *Human Organization*, 15(1956):8–11.

Weber, Max. *The Protestant Ethic and the Spirit of Capitalism*. New York: Charles Scribner's Sons, 1958.

Weisse, Arthur James. *The History of the City of Albany, New York*. Albany, N.Y.: E. H. Bender, 1884.

Wilcoxen, Charlotte. *Seventeenth Century Albany: A Dutch Profile*. Albany, N.Y.: Albany Institute of History and Art, 1981.

Wilentz, Sean. *Chants Democratic: New York City and the Rise of the American Working Class, 1788–1850*. New York: Oxford University Press, 1984.

Williams, Raymond. *Key Words*. New York: Oxford University Press, 1983.

Wilson, John F. *Public Religion in American Culture*. Philadelphia: Temple University Press, 1979.

Wood, Gordon S. *The Creation of the American Republic, 1776–1787*. Chapel Hill, N.C.: University of North Carolina Press, 1969.

Zaret, David. *The Heavenly Contract: Ideology and Organization in Pre-Revolutionary Puritanism*. Chicago: University of Chicago Press, 1985.

Zuckerman, Michael. *Peaceable Kingdoms: New England Towns in the Eighteenth Century*. New York: Alfred A. Knopf, 1970.

Index

Page numbers in italics refer to tables.

"Act for Suppressing Immortality," 89–90
Adams, John Quincy, 46
Advocate. See Farmers', Mechanics', and Workingman's Advocate
Age of Reason, The (Paine), 148
Albany. *See also* Beverwyck; New Netherland
 compared to New England towns, 9, 10
 description, 17th-century, 13
 founding of, 4, 9
 state capitol in, 73, 81
Albany Academy, 61, 96, 106, 114
 curriculum of, 83, 97, 200n.29
Albany Bible Society, 91–92
Albany Chamber of Commerce for Public Improvement, 84
Albany Coach Manufactory, 141
Albany Congress of 1754, 185n.108
Albany *Microscope*, 98, 115
 criticism of clergy, 148–49
 criticism of evangelism, 147–50
 criticism of Kirk, 149, 151
 views on economic growth of, 150–51
 views on knowledge of, 150
 views on temperance of, 151
"Albany Society for the Suppression of Vice and Immorality," 89
Albany Sunday School Union, 84
American Board for Foreign Missions, 127

American Revolution, 4, 6, 46, 189n.35, 190n.36
Albany Dutch and, 10, 48–52, 190n.49, 191n.52
 ideology of, 37–38, 155, 160, 186n.1, 187nn.7, 13. *See also* Nationalism
 immigrants and, 55, 153
 influence on wealthy Albanians, 70
 nationalism and. *See* Nationalism
 religion and, 48
Anglican church, 31, 45
 Committee of Correspondence membership and, 52, 191n.58, 191n.61
 during Revolution, 48
Anglo-Dutch relations, 9, 10–11, 22–27, 183n.64, 185n.95
Anglomania, 34. *See also* British, culture of
Anne, Queen of England, 31
Anti-Federalist Party, 46, 58, 71, 189n.35, 190n.36
Anti-Masonic Party, 118–19
 church membership in, *145, 146*
 occupations of. *See* Occupations, Anti-Masonic Party
 supporters of, 165, 166–67, 174, 213nn.4, 5
Apprentices' Library, 96, 97
Apprentices' Society, 121
Apprenticeship, 16, 58, 71, 81, 181n.32. *See also* Parental government
Architecture
 Dutch, 3, 13, 32, 70

Architecture (*continued*)
  English, 44, 70
Argus, 116
Artisans, 16, 23, 78, 80
  differentiation of trades of, 40, 188nn.17,
    18
  families of, 16
Associate Reformed Presbyterian Church,
  196n.65

Bailyn, Bernard, 10, 37
Balmer, Randall, 30
Baptist Church, 99, 106
  admission requirements of, 130
  evangelists in, 124
  leaders of, 141
  occupations of leaders, 137, *139, 140*
  occupations of members. *See*
    Occupations, Baptist
  political activists. *See* Church
    membership, of political activists
Battle of Lexington, 52
Beeman, Richard, 160–61
Beman, Nathan S. S., 124, 131–32
Berthoff, Rowland, 38
Bethel Church, 139, 209n.55
Beverwyck, 27, 178n.9
  British conquest of, 22
  early people of, 12
  origin of name, 12, 178n.11
  renamed Albany, 22
Bible, 17, 182n.41
Bleecker family, 16
Bloodgood, Francis, 118
Bocking, Susan, 92
Bonomi, Patricia, 38
Boston, 10, 13–14
Bouwsma, William J., 160
British
  absorbed into Dutch society, 10–11,
    23–24, 177n.6. *See also* Anglo-Dutch
    relations
  control of New Netherland, 9, 13, 22
  culture of, 5, 6, 10–11, 48, 70. *See also*
    Anglomania; Language, English
  diet of, 32
  legal system of, 24–27
  poverty and, 43, 180n.27
  resisted by Dutch, 10, 23, 25–27, 29–30,
    31, 33–35, 48–52, 59, 153, 190n.48
  Sons of Liberty membership, 50, 51
  in work force, 40
British Army, 188n.18
  French and Indian attack and, 29

invasion by, 11, 39
occupation of Albany by, 32-35, 45,
  48–49
Buel, Jesse, 81
Building trades, 103
Burgoyne, General, 190n.49
Burr, Aaron, 73
Butler, Benjamin F., 207n.1

Calvin, John, 19, 20–21, 59, 181–82n.38. *See
  also* Calvinism
Calvinism, 4, 6, 95. *See also* Calvin, John
  capitalism and, 61–69, 193–94n.22
  church-state relations and, 20–21, 25, 26,
    54, 77–78, 90–91, 98, 181–82n.38
  decline of, 78, 121, 126–27, 144, 152, 154,
    208n.15
  human depravity and, 47, 73, 74, 75, 99,
    156
  membership requirements of, 93
  moral society. *See* Moral reform,
    Calvinists
  predestination, 93, 157
  temperance and, 120, 121, 153
  women and, 75, 82, 85–88, 200n.25
  world view of, 54, 163
Camp, Reverend, 68
Canada, 26, 27, 45
Canal Bank, 140
Capitalism
  in Dedham, Mass., 177–78n.7
  growth of, 6–7
  religious and social conditions and,
    61–69, 193–94n.22
  seaboard cities, 38
Catholic church, 60, 82, 106, 152
Catskill, 184n.79
Chester, John, 90–91, 127
Children, 78, 196n.3
  church seating and, 19–20
  colonial Dutch, 15
  colonial religious instruction of, 17,
    182nn.40, 42
  generational groupings of, 19, 183n.53
Church membership, 160, 209n.52
  of Calvinists, 75, 82, 199n.23
  of Common Council members, 49, 52
  of the Dutch, 10, 16–17, 39, 49, 58, 78,
    83, 87, 181n.34, 181–82n.38, 191n.58
  during 1828–1836, 124, *125,* 207n.6
  of evangelicals, 124, *125,* 144–45, 168,
    207n.6
  in Fourth Presbyterian Church, 130, 134,
    135, 142–43, *142*

Methodist, 47, 78, 82, 93–94, 99
  occupation and, 88. *See also*
    Occupations, church membership
  of political activists, 88, 144–45, *145, 146*
  Presbyterian, 58, 61, 65, 66, 78, 83, 193n.7
  of women, 75, 78, 85, 141–42, *142,*
    210n.69
  of Workingman's Party members,
    144–45
Church of England, 60
City Hall, 53, 118
Clinton, De Witt, 121, 130
  Albanian reverence for, 110, 205n.38
  Second Presbyterian Church, 126–27
Classis of Amsterdam, 30, 181–82n.38,
  185n.99
Collins, John, 25
"Colonial Albany Social History Project,"
  178–79n.21
Colonie, 128
Committee of Correspondence, 39, 52, 113,
  191n.58
Committee of the Provincial Convention,
  190n.36
Common Council, 3, 25, 44, 53, 184n.79
  British and, 24, 31, 33-35, 59
  Catholic church and, 60, 106
  church membership of, 10, 49, 52
  church seating and, 19
  Committee of Correspondence
    membership, 52-53, 191n.61
  common schools and, 114
  economic growth and, 72–73, 108–10,
    140, 195n.61
  establishment of Dutch church, 55, 60
  establishment of Methodist church, 55,
    60
  fur trade. *See* Fur trade
  Ladies Society and, 87
  members of, 10, 16, 20, 26, 31, 42, 44, 55,
    101, 106–7, 118, 189n.29, 205n.20
  objections to Anglican church of, 31
  poverty and, 55, 108–9
  Presbyterian church and, 55, 60, 65
  residence requirements of, 189n.35
  resistance of British by, 11
  Sabbath observation and, 108–10
  taxes and, 21, 33
Communal ideal, 10, 38, 177n.6
Community life
  colonial, 9–10, 177–78n.7, 186nn.1, 2
  at eve of Revolution, 38
  generational grouping in, 19, 183n.53
Congregational Church, 196n.66

Connecticut, 69, 78, 184n.76
Constitution, 46, 71, 77
Continental Congress, 52
Convention, 29
Cooper, James Fennimore, 60
Corey, William, 33
Coxsackie, 184n.79
Culture
  defined, 5, 162
  influence on social order, 4, 5, 161,
    162–63, 176n.7
Culture, Albany Dutch, 3, 5, 10–11, 13, 32.
  See also Community life
  colonial, 4
  Revolution, 191n.52
  post-Revolution, 57–58
Culture, medieval Dutch, 26, 181–82n.38,
  190n.48
Cuyler, Johannes, 28

Davis, Robert, 82
Declaration of Independence, 53, 115–16
Dedham, Mass., 177–78n.7
Dellius, Dominie, 30
Dongan Charter, 24–25, 26, 28, 30
Dongan, Thomas, 24, 26, 28, 184n.79
Douglas, Ann, 87–88
Dutch Calvinist Reformed Church. *See also*
  Calvinism
  American-trained clergy and, 186n.113
  church-state relations of, 20, 90–91
  colonial social order and, 16–17, 153–54
  Committee of Correspondence
    membership of, 52, 191nn.58, 61
  Common Council support of, 55, 60
  during Revolution, 48
  English theology and, 185n.99
  evangelism sympathy in, 146–47
  Heidelberg Catechism. *See* Heidelberg
    Catechism
  influence of Yankee invasion on, 71
  leadership of, 10, 16, 18, 20–21, 43,
    180n.29
  location of, 3, 31, 82
  membership. *See* Church membership
  political activists in. *See* Church
    membership, of political activists
  Presbyterian minister of, 59
  resistance of British by, 11, 33–35
  seating in, 18–20, 83, 182n.49
  ties to Netherlands, 59
  use of English language in, 59
Dutch law. *See* Roman-Dutch law

Dutch people
  characteristics of, 32
  diet of, 32
  resistance of British by, 11, 23, 25–27, 30,
    31, 33–35, 48–52, 59, 153, 190n.48
  views on foreign churches, 55, 181–82n.38
  views on revolution and revolt, 49,
    50–51
Dutch pietist movement, 30
Dutch West India Company, 11, 12,
    181–82n.38
  settlement of New Netherland and,
    178n.8
  slaves and, 180–81n.30
Dwight, Timothy, 70

Economy. *See also* Capitalism; Fur trade;
    Industrialization
  government intervention and, 6, 176n.10
  household, 80–81, 119–20
  imperial British, 26–27
  labor theory of value, 115, 116–17
  19th-century productivity, 106, 108–10
  panic of 1837, 6
  post-French and Indian War, 40-44
  1790's, 63–65
  views of the *Microscope* on, 176
  Yankee invasion and, 71–72
Education, 60
  academy movement, 83
  colonial, 178–79n.21, 182n.42
  Dutch charity school, 59, 132–33
  evangelists and, 126, 143–44, 211n.109
  freethinkers' views on, 150, 151
  individual ability and, 74–75
  mechanics and, 97–98
  moral reform and, 92
  Workingmen and, 114, 116, 118, 121
Ellison, Thomas, Reverend, 60
English. *See* British
Enlightenment, 46, 74, 124, 148, 207n.7
Episcopal church, 59–60, 87. *See also* St.
    Peter's Episcopal Church
Erie Canal
  completion of, 101
  De Witt Clinton and, 110
  economic activity generated by, 102, 104,
    141, 156, 195n.61
Established Church of Scotland, 66
Evangelical Christianity, 6, 164, 207n.7
  criticism by the *Microscope*, 147–50
  education and, 126, 132–33, 143–44,
    211n.109

Fourth Presbyterian Church. *See* Fourth
    Presbyterian Church
  in established churches, 146–47
  Methodist. *See* Methodist Church
  moral reform of, 121, 124, 126, 143–44,
    156–57
  new economic values and, 121, 144,
    150–51, 153, 157
  occupations of leaders, 137, *139*
  occupations of members. *See*
    Occupations, evangelical
  political activists in. *See* Church
    membership, of political activists
  temperance and, 124, 141

Faler, Paul, 95
Families
  of Dutch merchants, 15–16, 78
  size of, colonial Dutch, 15, 179n.22
Family networks, 4, 9, 15–16, 183n.55
*Farmers' Mechanics', and Workingman's
    Advocate,* 114–15, 116, 118, 167
Federalist Party, 189n.35
  Anti-Federalists and, 190n.36
  Common Council membership of, 101
  Constitution of, 46, 71, 77
  decline of, 107
  supporters of, 106
Ferris, Reverend Isaac, 146
Finney, Charles G., 124, 132
First Baptist Church. *See* Baptist Church
First Dutch Church, 146
First Great Awakening, 10
First Methodist Society, 94
First Presbyterian Church, 77, 193n.7
  membership of, 59, 88
  Sabbath observation in, 108
Foner, Eric, 37
Fort Orange, 11–12, 178n.11
Fourth of July, 39, 53–54
Fourth Presbyterian Church. *See also*
    Evangelical Christianity; Kirk,
    Edward Norris
  admission requirements in, 130
  doctrine of, 129
  education reform of, 132–33
  leaders of, 135, 139–41
  maternal association of, 143–44
  membership of, 130, 134, 135, 142–43, *142*
  membership of poor people, 128
  membership of women in, 124, 142–44,
    142
  Missionary Society of, 132

occupations of leaders, 139, *139, 140*
occupations of members, 131, 137, *138*
Old School–New School division of, 123–24
political activists. *See* Church membership, of political activists
services in, 130
Sunday school in, 129, 133
total abstinence and, 133–34
Franklin, Benjamin, 46, 83, 185n.108
Freethinkers. *See also* Albany *Microscope;* Munsell, Joel
criticism of evangelists, 148, 149–50, 211n.88
economic values, 150–51
societies of mutual improvement, 150, 152
temperance and, 151
views on education of, 148, 149–50, 151
Frelinghuysen, Dominie Theodorus, 182n.40
Frelinghuysen, Theodorus, Jr., 34, 186n.113
French, 27, 32. *See also* French and Indian War
French and Indian War (1754–1760), 23, 35, 39
memoirs of Anne Grant, 182n.42
Friends, 135
Fryer, John, 189n.29
Fur trade, 9, 10, 184n.82
with Canada, 26, 27, 45
Dutch monopoly of, 4, 10, 14, 26, 27, 34, 42, 71, 184n.79. *see also* Dongan Charter
Dutch West India Company and, 11–12, 178n.8

Gage, General, 47
Gansevoort, Leendert, 42, 189n.35
Geertz, Clifford, 160–62, 163
George III, King of England, 51
Gotsch, Charles, 119, 165
Gould, James P., 141
Grant, Anne, 34–35, 182n.42, 183n.53

Hamilton, Alexander, 32, 73
Hatch, Nathan, 37, 206n.7
Hawthorne, Nathaniel, 97
Heidelberg Catechism, 21, 49, 65, 181n.31, 182n.39, 191–92n.63
teachings of, 17–18, 21
Hewitt, Dr., 133–34
Hudson, Henry, 9

Hudson River, 11, 13, 15, 78, 102, 184n.79
Humphrey, Friend, 141

Ideologies
defined, 6, 176n.8
development of cultural meaning and, 6, 162
post-canal, 157
post-Revolutionary, 6, 176n.9
Immigrants and immigration
British, 43, 44
Catholic, 6
Dutch, 12–13
European, 11, 12, 39, 40, 187–88n.16
New England, 6, 55, 57, 69, 78, 79, 197n.9. *see also* Yankee invasion
Scotch-Irish, 44, 58, 63–65, 66, 67
Indians, 12. *See also* French and Indian War
attacks by, 10, 23, 29, 31
Fort Orange and, 11
Iroquois, 185n.108
Mohawk, 31, 33
relations with, 178n.10
sale of rum to, 33
trade, 9, 15, 27, 40
Industrialization, 6, 78, 102–3, 203n.2. *See also* Economy; Manufacturing
Inheritance practices, Dutch, 15, 26, 179–80n.24
Iroquois Indians, 185n.108

Jackson, Andrew, 115
James, Henry, 68–69
James II, King of England, 22, 28, 29
James, William, 63, 64, 65, 68, 69
Jamestown, Virginia, 9
Jogues, Isaac, 11
Johnson, John Barent, 53
Johnson, William, 33
Journeymen, 111–13, 205n.43. *See also* Workingman's Party
Journeyman Carpenters' Association, 111, 113
Journeyman Painters' Society, 111
Judicial Act, 25

Kalm, Peter, 32, 188n.23
Kinderhook, 184n.79
King William's War (1690–1698), 23
Kirk, Edward Norris
concerns of common people and, 127–28
criticism by *Microscope,* 149, 151

Kirk, Edward Norris (*continued*)
    division of Presbyterian congregation,
        123–24, 126, 127, 131, 132–33, 134–45
    education, 133, 211n.109
    Fourth Presbyterian Church, 128, 129–
        30, 133
    maternal association created by, 143–44
    total abstinence campaign of, 133–34

Labor theory of value, 115, 116–17
Ladies Society for the Relief of Distressed
    Women and Children, 86–87, 90, 92
Lancaster School, 96, 97, 114, 116
Language
    Dutch, 13, 22, 28, 48
    English, 11, 22, 25, 28, 39, 48, 59, 154
Leisler, Jacob, 28–30, 31, 49, 185n.89
Livingston family, 45, 182n.49
Livingston, Robert, 25, 28
Livingston, William, 45
Locke, John, 74, 97, 114
Long Island, 45
Lutheran Church, 82, 152, 181–82n.38

McCabe, Francis, 64
McDonald, Reverend John, 65, 66
Macomb, John, 33
Magna Carta, 25
Manufacturing, 64, 197n.10, 199n.20
Marine Bible Society, 139
Marriage
    British to Dutch, 10, 24, 30, 31, 154,
        183n.67
    church seating and, 19
    colonial Dutch, 15, 178–79n.21
    within "companies," 183n.53
Marsden, George, 127, 146
Marvin, Uriah, 139, 140
Mary, Queen of England, 28, 29
Massachusetts, 69, 78, 185n.93, 187n.13
Mayor's Court, 20, 25
Mechanics, 12, 145, 147
    conflicting with Calvinism, 95, 98, 207n.7
    curriculum of, 97–98
    ideology of, 6, 96, 97, 98–99, 156, 164
    temperance and, 153
Mechanics' Society, 80, 96, 111
"Mechanics Society for the Suppression
    of Vice and Immorality and the
    Promotion of Good Morals," 90
Megapolensis, Dominie, 182n.40
Melanchthon, Philipp, 19
Merchants, British, 15, 30, 33

departure of, during Revolution, 49,
    190–91n.51
Merchants, Dutch
    British rule and, 16, 25, 26–27, 213n.4
    business practices of, 64–65
    church leadership of, 10, 16, 18, 20–21,
        49, 180n.29, 181n.31
    church seating of, 19
    families of, 15–16, 78
    general merchants. *See* Merchants,
        general
    inheritance practices of, 15, 26,
        179–80n.24
    as mediators, 11, 27–28, 39, 52, 154
    political leadership, 4, 10, 16, 21, 25–26,
        39, 44, 71, 106. *See also* Common
        Council
    Sons of Liberty membership, 50, 51
    trade with Canada, 26, 27, 45
    wealth of, 15, 24, 43, 83–84
Merchants, general
    differentiation of, 40, 64, 171, 188nn.17,
        18
    replacing fur traders, 42, 43
Merchants, Yankee, 77, 79, 83–85
Merwick, Donna, 13, 23
Methodist Church
    admission requirements of, 148
    camp meetings of, 93, 94
    class prejudice against, 59, 60–61, 92–93
    Common Council and, 55, 60, 106
    leaders of, 94, 141
    members of, 47, 78, 82, 93–94
    moral reform, 90–93
    occupations of leaders, 139, *139, 140*
    occupations of members. *See*
        Occupations, Methodist
    political activists in. *See* Church
        membership, of political activists
    Sunday schools of, 91
    theology of, 46, 47–48, 93–94, 98–99,
        156
Methodist Tract Society, 91–92
Microscope. See Albany *Microscope*
Milbourne, Jacob, 29, 30
Modernization, 4–5, 159-60, 175n.4, 176n.7,
    177–78n.7
Mohawk Indians, 31, 33
Mohawk River Valley, 15, 78
Montesquieu, Charles, 46
Moral reform
    Calvinists and, 77–78, 88–91, 99, 196n.2,
        203n.88

evangelists and, 124, 126
  Methodists and, 90–93
  Puritans and, 77–78
Moral society, 90, 92
Morgan, Edmund, 37
Munsell, Joel, 150, 151–52, 211n.90. *See also*
    Albany *Microscope;* Freethinkers
  apprenticeship of, 96–97, 147
  criticisms of Christianity, 98, 148
  Microscope and, 147–48, 151
Murrin, John, 38

Nash, Gary, 38
National Republican Party
  church membership in, *145, 146*
  occupations of members. *See*
    Occupations, National Republican
    Party
  supporters of, 118–19, 165, 166–67, 174,
    213nn.4, 5
Nationalism
  economic productivity and, 101–2, 106,
    110, 156–57
  political unity and, 37–38, 39, 52–55, 58,
    96, 101, 155–56
Navigation Acts, 27. *See also* Canada
Neighborhood development, 81–82, 103,
    104–6, 204n.13, 205n.14
Netherlands, 12–13
  Calvinism, 181–82n.38
  church seating in, 19
  medieval society in, 26, 181–82n.38,
    190n.48
New Amsterdam, 24
New England, 10, 45, 177–78n.7
New Netherland
  British control of, 9, 22
  church, 181–82n.38
  Dutch rule in, 11, 178n.9
  slaves in, 180–81n.30
New York Assembly, 26, 45. *See also* New
    York State General Assembly;
    Provincial Assembly
New York City, 11, 28, 29, 45, 47
  Dutch merchants and, 27, 64
  sermons published in, 191–92n.63
New York State, 47, 178–79n.21
  relief of poor and, 17
  religion in, during Revolution, 48
  revolutionary constitution, 190n.36
New York State General Assembly, 49.
    See also New York Assembly;
    Provincial Assembly

Newton, Isaac, 74
Nott, Eliphalet, 73–75, 87, 196n.65

Occupations. *See also* Artisans; Merchants
  Anti-Masonic Party, 169–71, *169, 170, 173,*
    174
  Baptist, 136–37, *136, 138, 139, 140*
  of British (1756), 40, 42, *41–42*
  church membership and, 88
  of Dutch (1756), 40, *41–42*
  in Dutch church, 136
  Episcopal, 136
  of established church members, *136*
  evangelical, 136–37, *136, 137, 138, 139,*
    144–45, 152, 157, 168, 178
  Fourth Presbyterian, 135, 137, 139, *138, 139,*
    140
  freeholders, 188n.17
  growth of largest (1817–1830), 171, *170*
  inventory of, *41–42*
  Methodist, 98, 136–37, *136, 138, 139, 139,*
    140, 156, 210n.65
  National Republican Party, 167, 169–71,
    169, 170, 174, *174,* 203, 213n.4
  nineteenth-century, 79–80, 104, 197–
    98n.12, 198–99n.13, 199nn.15, 16
  political parties, 165–66, *166,* 171, 172, *172,*
    174. *See also individual parties*
  Regency Party, 145–46, *146,* 166–67, *167,*
    169–71, *169, 170, 173,* 174
  specialization of, 10, 40, 187–88n.16
  wealth and, 167–71, *168, 169,* 174
  Workingman's Party, 144–45, *146,* 147,
    152, 166–67, 169–71, *169, 170,* 172, *173,*
    174
Oneida County, 201n.45
Orphan Asylum, 109, 143–44
Overseers of the Poor, 55, 86, 108–9

Paine, Thomas, 37–38, 148, 151
Parental government, 103, 121, 129, 133
  alcohol consumption and, 119–20
  economic motives of, 120–21
  erosion of, 81, 90
People's Party, 107–8
Perry, Eli, 141
Philadelphia, 37, 187n.13
Pilgrims, 9
Pointer, Richard, 48, 58–59
Population
  during British occupation, 32–33
  of colonial Albany, 12, 15, 178n.20,
    178–79n.21, 179n.22

Population (*continued*)
  18th century, 40, 42, 44, 57, 187n.15,
    195n.50, 196–97n.4, 210n.67
  19th century, 69, 78, 103–4, 107, 165–66,
    166, 195n.50, 196–97n.4
  Yankee invasion and, 69, 195n.50,
    196–97n.4
Poverty, 10
  Albany Bible Society and, 91
  of British immigrants, 43, 44, 180n.27
  Common Council and, 55, 108–10
  distribution of (eighteenth century), 43,
    43, 44
  Dutch responsibility and, 16, 55, 59, 86
  Fourth Presbyterian Church and, 128,
    143
  Methodists and, 91–93
  political conflict and, 189n.28
Presbyterian church
  Associate Reformed, 196n.65
  capitalism and, 61–69
  Committee of Correspondence
    membership and, 52, 191nn.58, 61
  Common Council and, 55, 60, 65
  communion in, 66–67
  Congregational Church, 196n.66
  division of, 123–24, 127, 131. *See also*
    Fourth Presbyterian Church; Second
    Presbyterian Church
  evangelical. *See* Fourth Presbyterian
    Church
  First Presbyterian Church. *See* First
    Presbyterian Church
  individual ability, 73
  leaders of, 65, 66, 67, 68
  membership of, 58, 59, 61, 63, 65, 66, 87,
    106, 193n.7
  newspaper of, 120
  political activists in. *See* Church
    membership, of political activists
  during Revolution, 48, 65
  Scotch-Irish immigrants of, 58, 63,
    65–66, 67, 68
  Second Presbyterian Church. *See*
    Second Presbyterian Church
  Yankee merchants and, 84
  seating in, 83
  Session of, 66, 67–68
  Westminster catechism, 65
Printing business, 103
Professionalism, 10, 42, 197–98n.12
Provincial Assembly, 31. *See also* New York

Assembly; New York State General
  Assembly
Puritans, 10, 13, 77–78, 177–78n.7, 192n.64

Queen Anne's War (1702–1712), 23, 31

Reformed Church of the Netherlands, 17,
  19
Regency Party, 102, 107–8, 115, 118–19, 121
  church membership in, 145, *145, 146*
  occupations of. *See* Occupations,
    Regency Party
  supporters, 165, 166–67, 213nn.4, 5
Reid, Thomas, 111
Religion
  as cultural system, 4, 5, 153, 163,
    175–76n.6
  civil, 37, 159, 160, 186n.2
  "Colonial Albany Social History
    Project," 178–79n.21
  in Dedham, Mass., 177–78n.7
  definition of, 5
  18th-century New England, 10, 177–78n.7
  instruction of, 17, 182nn.40, 42
  maintenance of faith, 161
  social order and, 7, 16–17, 153–54, 157,
    159–62, 163
  wealth and, 82, 199–200n.24
Religious life
  colonial, 181–82n.38, 187n.12
  during Revolution, 38, 48–49, 190n.49
  post-Revolution, 58
  1790's, 58–61
Rensselaerwyck, 27, 178n.9
Republicans, 107
  ideology of, 6, 164
  leadership of, 106, 110
Revolution. *See* American Revolution
Rink, Oliver, 12
Roman-Dutch law, 25, 184n.81
Rotterdam, 28
Royall, Anne, 204n.14
Rutman, Darrett, 10

Sabbath observation, 108–10
St. Paul's Episcopal Church, 147
St. Peter's Episcopal Church, 82, 191n.57.
  See also Episcopal church
Saratoga, 184n.79
Schagitoke, 184n.79
Schenectady, 23, 24, 29, 184n.79
Schuyler, Abraham, 26

Schuyler clan, 16, 182nn.42, 49
Schuyler, Johannes, 31
Schuyler, Peter, 27–29, 30–31
Schuyler, Philip, 27
Second Dutch Reformed Church, 85
Second Great Awakening, 196n.73
Second Presbyterian Church
    division of, 123–24, 131, 132–35, 139,
        146–47
    doctrine of, 129
    Sunday schools in, 90, 129
    temperance and, 120
    women in, 85, 141, *142*
Sermons, 182n.39
    Fourth of July, 53–54, 191–92n.63
    as historical documents, 6, 160
    political unit, 53–54
    publication, 191–92n.63
Shakers, 99
Silversmiths, 188n.19
Skidmore, Thomas, 115–16
Slaves
    Beverwyck, 12
    church seating and, 19
    in 18th-century Albany, 58, 180–81n.30
    Methodist conversion of, 47
    Yankee invasion and, 71
Smith, Israel, 140
Social differentiation, 38, 39, 44
"Society for the Suppression of Vice and
    Immorality," 120
Sons of Liberty, 50–51
Southwick, Solomon, 96, 97–98, 115
Sprague, William, 129
Staats, Jochim, 28, 29
Stamp Act, 49-50, 51
Stansbury, Arthur, 77–78, 88
Stewart, Dugald, 97
Stout, Harry, 160
Sunday schools
    Albany Sunday School Union, 84
    Fourth Presbyterian, 129, 133
    Methodist, 91, 92
    moral society and, 90, 92
    Second Presbyterian Church, 162–64
Swidler, Ann, 188–89, 190–91
Synod of Dordrecht, 181–82n.38

Taxes, 21, 33, 180n.27
    Presbyterians and, 68
    Stamp Act, 49–50, 51

Temperance, 119–20
    Calvinist churches and, 120–21
    evangelists and, 124
    freethinkers and, 151
    mechanics and, 153
    total abstinence campaign, 133–34
    Workingmen and, 121
Temperance Society, 120, 139, 206n.79
Ten Eyck, Jacob C., 42, 189n.35
Third Dutch Church, 146
Ticonderoga, 32
Tories, 52
Townsend, John and Isaiah, 84
Trade. *See* Economy; Fur trade
Turner, James, 207n.7

Union College, 60–61, 73
Universalists, 135, 147, 211n.90
Upfold, Mrs. George, 92
Upward mobility, 20, 24, 84. *See also*
    Wealth

Van Buren, Martin, 107–8, 126, 207n.1
Van Rensselaer, Kiliaen, 11–12
Van Rensselaer, Philip, 79, 106
Van Schaick, Henry, 50
Van Schaick, Sybrant, 42
Van Slichtenhorst, Brant, 27
Vermont, 175n.5
Virginia, 9, 13, 15

Washington, George, 110
Watson, Elkanah, 195n.61
Wayland, Francis, 73–74
Wealth. *See also* Upward mobility
    in colonial Albany, 178–79n.21
    distribution of, 10, 43, *43*, 44, 46
    labor theory of value and, 115, 116–17
    occupations and, 167–71, *168, 169,* 174
    of political activists, 165, *169,* 174
    political conflict and, 189n.28
    religion and, 82, 199–200n.24
    taxes and, 180n.27
Webb, Thomas, Captain, 46–48, 154
Weber, Max, 58, 61, 63, 68, 193–94n.22
Webster, George, 80
Wendell, Elizabeth Staats, 31
Wendell, Johannes, 28
Wendell's Tavern, 53
Wesley, John, 47, 93
Westerlo, Eilardus ("Pope"), 48, 59
Westminster Catechism, 65–66

Whig Party, 37, 45, 118, 119
  origins, 134, 135
Wilentz, Sean, 115
William, King of England, 28, 29
Winne, Peter, 24
Women
  church membership of. *See* Church
    membership, of women
  colonial Dutch. *See* Women, colonial
    Dutch
  as merchants, 85–86
  moral reform and, 126, 141–44, 147,
    210n.69
  19th-century social position of, 85–88,
    201n.45
  voluntary societies for, 143–44, 210n.80
Women, colonial Dutch, 15, 85
  church seating and, 19, 20
  rights and status of, 184n.81
Wood, Gordon, 37
Workingman's Party. *See also* Journeymen
  accomplishments of, 118
  church membership in, 144–45, *145, 146*
  Common Council membership and, 118
  creation of, 112–13
  criticism by *Microscope,* 148
  dissolution of, 118
  evangelists in, 144–45
  lien law and, 113
  New York City Workingman's Party,
    102, 115–17
  newspaper of, 113, 114–15

occupations of members. *See*
  Occupations, Workingman's Party
platform of, 102, 113–16, 120–21, 126,
  132–33, 171
supporters of, 102, 112–13, 117-19, 165,
  166–67, *167,* 207n.88, 213nn.4, 5
temperance and, 120–21
Wright, Fanny, 115–16

Yale College, 45, 70, 127
Yankee, derivation of term, 195n.54
Yankee invasion, 197n.5. *See also*
  Immigrants and immigration, New
  England; New England
  changes caused by, 3, 57–58, 69–70, 75
  economy and, 71–73, 79–80, 169
  political agitation and, 71–72
  Yankee–Dutch relations and, 3, 195n.50
Yates, Abraham, 115, 179n.22, 189nn.29, 30
  Anti-Federalist Party and, 46, 71, 154,
    189n.35, 190n.36
  Committee of Correspondence and, 52
  opposition to British by, 46, 189n.32
  political rise of, 44–46, 189n.35, 190n.36
  Revolution and, 51, 155
Yates, Joseph, 24
York, Duke of, 22, 24. *See also* James II,
  King of England
Young Men's Society for Mutual
  Improvement, 138, 121, 150, 151

Zwingli, Ulrich, 19